GET BY in Spanish in One to Three Weeks

The Language Heretic's Super Crash Course in Spanish Conversation & Culture

by

L. Adams

authorHOUSE™

1663 LIBERTY DRIVE, SUITE 200
BLOOMINGTON, INDIANA 47403
(800) 839-8640
WWW.AUTHORHOUSE.COM

First published by AuthorHouse 04/01/05

ISBN: 1-4208-0665-3 (sc)

Library of Congress Control Number: 2004098204

Printed in the United States of America
Bloomington, Indiana

This book is printed on acid-free paper.

Table of Contents

Preface

This book is the result of my missing my friends in Spain while I was out of the country for an extended period of time.

As I mused on those friends one evening, I realized that many of them had had their difficulties in learning to speak Spanish, some even after attending traditional language schools for several years. Many never attended a language school for more than just an introductory course or a "do it yourself in three months" course, and others were just too lazy too take a "real" course in Spanish conversation, hoping to get it through osmosis.

What struck me as I was thinking about them was the fact that each one was frustrated. They were frustrated by the results obtained from traditional language schools and traditional language school methods of teaching a foreign language.

Some also were frustrated by the results obtained from trying to learn enough Spanish to "get by" on their own. And, a few others were even frustrated just from not being able to find a workable solution to their own personal needs to speak Spanish.

Except for my wife, none of my English speaking friends was really pleased with his/her language skills in Spanish.

I had heard it all repeated a million times:

"I just want to be able to "get by" in Spanish."

"I don't want to know all about all of the grammar."

"I don't want to know how to conjugate every single tense for every single verb."

"I don't want to learn class room vocabulary. I just want to know the nuts and bolts and some useful words."

On the evening of April 1st, 2004, in the throes of a fit of temporary insanity, I set out to write a book which would help my friends and anyone else who just wanted to learn enough Spanish to "get by," for now, while laying a good foundation for further learning later.

Whatever made me think that I could write a language book, I'll never know. Clearly, it must have been the insanity. What began as an idea, then developed into a fun project for my free time, growing into a healthy mental problem solving exercise, until, finally, it took over my life and ended as both a work of the heart and food for the soul (mine).

I do hope you appreciate my efforts and that you will receive some lasting benefit from your use of it. If you like my book, do tell a friend. I need the money. On the other hand, if you don't… then, please send me an e-mail to elherejedeidiomas@yahoo.es or write my publisher. I'd love to hear from you with any comments or suggestions, critiques, reviews, and the like.

L. Adams
August 2004

Acknowledgements

Behind every man who achieves any modicum of success there is always a woman. In my case, that would be my wife, Daniela. For her patience with my working at all hours of the day and night on this book and for her suffering far fewer restaurant opportunities than she would have preferred as a result of my writing of this book, I thank her with all my heart. In large part, it was her own experiences in learning to speak Spanish that were an inspiration for much of this book, and it is she who is the source of inspiration for all that I do in my life.

Also, I want to thank my dear friend and fellow traveler from another planet (Melmac), Mary Jane Trokel, for her insights into her long-term, mixed-results struggle with language school, for her continual interest in this project, for her encouragement, brainstorms and bright ideas, and suggestions, and most especially for her services as proof reader and copy editor. Friends like you are more rare than four leaf clovers.

I'd like to thank our very good friend (and adopted family member) Ana Maria Lagoa for our many discussions and disputes over the Spanish language, about how it is *supposed* to be spoken and the "made up" words as are so often found in Andalucia, as well as for her insights into (Spanish) time. If not for arguing with you in Spanish about Spanish, I might never have known how well I actually do know this language.

To my friends, Juan Bel and Antonio Aranda, and because of those times when they have allowed me to help them with their English, I owe tremendous thanks for the Pronunciation Guide, which is found throughout this book. If it weren't for you two and my attempts to figure out how to teach you the phonetic pronunciations in English using the Spanish sounds, the Pronunciation Guide would never have made it into this book. I believe that time will prove this to be one of the most helpful and most used features in this book.

Thanks ever so much, too, to a friend from yesteryear, Debby F. who introduced me to the University of Chicago Spanish/English Dictionary so many years ago and who has for so long served as my hidden mentor/role model in language study and skills, even though you're now just a memory tucked safely away in my heart. Gone, but not forgotten. Simultaneous translations I cannot do nor would I would I even attempt to do so. You're still the best. If not for you, I might never have noticed the linguistic differences from one Spanish speaking country to the next.

And, thanks to all of my Spanish speaking friends everywhere from whom I have learned so much.

Last, but not least, I would like to thank John Butt and Carmen Benjamin for writing the finest Spanish language grammar book* I've ever seen or used which has been so helpful to me over the past years. Every day I learn something new from you and your marvelous book. It's not a textbook; it's a tool kit for Spanish.

---

* A New Reference Grammar of Modern Spanish, 2nd Edition by John Butt and Carmen Benjamin, 1994, ISBN 0340-58390-8.

Dedication

I dedicate this book to the memory of all those who *wanted* to learn *to speak* Spanish *but never did* because they found it too difficult. If only I had known. But, then again, I used to be one of you.

L. Adams

Introduction

This course has been written primarily for five categories of individuals:

1.   Those *now planning to live* in a Spanish-speaking environment who need to get up to speed in Spanish *as quickly and painlessly as possible* in the language;

2.   Those *now planning a holiday* within the immediate future who do wish to learn to speak enough to get by in Spanish *as quickly and painlessly as possible*;

3.   Those *already residing in* an English speaking community with a substantial Hispanic population who want to communicate with their Spanish-speaking neighbors *as quickly and painlessly as possible*;

4.   Those *already having taken a "traditional" Spanish language course who want* to be able to use their knowledge of the language in order to master conversation *as quickly and painlessly as possible*;

5.   Those *now taking a "traditional" Spanish language course* who are having some difficulties and who just need some help getting the kinks out of the more difficult aspects of conversation *as quickly and painlessly as possible*.

It is *not* written for those who strive for perfect grammar.
It *is* written for those who want to be able to communicate effectively.

It is *not* written for those who wish to take an academic approach to the language with a focus on reading & writing skills.

It *is* written for those who want to CONVERSE with people in the world's Spanish speaking community.

It is *not* written for people who take themselves too seriously.
It *is* written for those who approach life with a sense of adventure and joy at experiencing new things.

No matter what your purpose, if you want to learn to *speak* Spanish enough to GET BY, *quickly and painlessly*, this book will help.

If you say to yourself before you begin this course that "I'll never really be able to speak Spanish", then we can guarantee that you won't.

On the other hand, if you approach this course as an adventure in learning and as an opportunity to communicate in a language spoken by more than 500 million other earthlings, then you will enjoy and appreciate the radically different approach we take to assisting you in reaching your goal.

Author's Note to Readers

There is a fair amount of narrative in this book, especially at the beginning. In fact, there is much more narrative than you would ordinarily find in the average language book or self-instructional text.

Please bear with me and understand that there is truly a 'method to my madness' and the manner in which I expose you to my 'heresy'.

Much of the narrative deals with Hispanic culture.

As well, a great deal of it addresses your mental preparation for speaking Spanish, so that you are mentally prepared to speak Spanish much sooner than would ordinarily be the case.

The farther into the course you get, the less narrative you will find. It does pick up speed, much like the snowball rolling downhill.

For now, you need to understand how and why this course is structured the way that it is, so read on.

Chapter I.
Success in Spanish Conversation: The Basics.

I am a *linguistic heretic.**

   If professional language teachers were given a choice as to the one person in the world they would most like to burn at the stake for *linguistic heresies*, I would be their choice.

WHY, you ask, would they want to do that?

Because I am going to expose you to my beliefs and opinions on language learning, something they must see as 'heretical'. They know it's the truth, but they don't want to hear it and they don't want YOU to hear about it.

The source of my heresy is that I believe:

   • *Traditional language courses are far too academic.*

   • *They are entirely too focused on grammar, verb endings, parts of speech and translation.*

   • *They don't teach the student to carry on everyday conversation in the language, nor do they endeavor to develop in the student the* **confidence** *necessary to do so.*

If you are like most people who take a language course:

---

* noun: a person who holds unorthodox opinions in any field (not merely religion)

You really only want to learn to speak well enough to carry on a conversation, to GET BY. You want to be able to talk, *to converse -* with real people who speak Spanish - in a minimum period of time.

Reading and writing skills are secondary. You don't want to spend years learning grammar; you don't have the time anyway.

Traditional language courses don't accomplish these objectives.

Our objectives in this course are:

   • *To teach you to do that very thing that traditional courses don't: to Converse, to TALK, to Carry on a Conversation, about real things with real people who speak Spanish.*

   • *To help YOU to <u>build</u> the <u>confidence you need</u> so you can apply what you learn in order to converse with real Spanish speakers in Spanish.*

   • *Finally, to get you <u>speaking</u> comfortably and with confidence <u>within days and weeks</u>,* not months or years.

<u>My Heretical Rule No. 1.</u>

In your own native English, most of you who read this, language teachers included, make grammatical mistakes every day in speaking and writing, even after years of study.

So, it's logical that even attempting to achieve grammatical perfection in any foreign language is a fantasy. It's just NOT going to happen.

So don't even THINK of trying to be perfect.

Just concentrate on trying to communicate <u>as well as you can</u>, and you will achieve your goal of speaking Spanish in one to three weeks.

Why Most Language Students Give Up.

Verb conjugations in most foreign languages are so complicated, when compared to English, that the struggle to learn them is *the single greatest reason for giving up on learning a foreign language.*

In a language with 16 tenses (at least some of which don't even exist in English), this can be a nightmare for most students.

Almost all language courses teach at least 10 tenses, some of which are almost non-existent in modern English and therefore that much more difficult to comprehend.

Logically, if we can eliminate most of the frustration of memorizing 8 to 10 *or more* tenses for endless numbers of verbs, it has to make it easier to learn and a lot less frustrating.

Well, that's exactly what we're going to do. We are going to eliminate 90% of this frustration by focusing ONLY on what you absolutely *need* to know.

Most foreign language courses are really courses in foreign grammar with endless grammar rules. We eliminate more than 90% of the rules and simplify the rest, so you can focus on conversation NOW.

• This is NOT a course in foreign grammar and verb conjugations.

Most language courses are translation courses. Translations are nice if we're studying Caesar's Commentaries on the Gallic Wars in Latin, but when one is conversing, translating always causes problems in communication. We spend 90% of our time helping you to understand, to comprehend and to express yourself.

• This is NOT a course in development of foreign language translation skills.

In this course, you are expected to spend 90% of your study time SPEAKING (and listening to) this foreign language called Spanish.

• <u>It IS a foreign language speaking course.</u>

The preceding statements are SO important, I'm going to repeat:

<u>YOU are EXPECTED to spend 90% of your time SPEAKING Spanish, not learning verb conjugations and grammar!</u>

This IS a foreign language speaking course!

In conversation, the *interpretation* of the spoken word is far more important to your *understanding* and to your *communicating* than is making a perfect translation.

We want you to be able to interpret and understand as much as possible of what you hear and to know how to express what you need to express in such a way that a native speaker of Spanish can interpret exactly the meaning of what you say -- even if you don't express yourself "perfectly" or "translate" precisely.

If you've previously taken a language course, you will find this course to be radically different from any other approach to language instruction that you may have experienced.

Most language courses stress perfection in both grammar and verbs.

We stress *imperfection*, nominal grammar, and *only* a Dynamic Dozen verbs.

We focus 90% of our efforts on giving you <u>only</u> the *tools* you need to help you get started and to get by *speaking* Spanish.

Reducing the Learning Curve.

We are going to give you the tools and show you how to use them so that YOU can *communicate* effectively in Spanish in from 1 to 3 weeks, depending on the time YOU are willing to devote to this text and to the exercises it contains.

And from today, you will be able to feel confident that you are on the road to success with a few, easy tips (and demonstrations) to get you on your way... IMMEDIATELY!!!!!

By using shortcuts I have learned over many years of studying Spanish myself, *we **will** reduce your overall learning curve by as much as 90%.* *

It is NOT our intention to make you a grammatically perfect, fluent speaker of academic Spanish.

It IS our intention to get you quickly to the point of being articulate enough in Spanish to communicate in that language, *in spite of* the grammar. Nothing more, nothing less.

From that point on, like children, the more you converse, the better your language skills will become.

---

* Where practical, concepts and rules of grammar are simplified. Where not practical for the purposes of this course, they may actually be ignored. Also, verb conjugations other than the present tense will be ignored completely. If this is of concern, then this may not be the right course for you.

My Heretical Rule No. 2.

Four things you must accept now in order to be successful <u>quickly</u> in learning to speak and converse in Spanish are:

*A.) Your <u>grammatical mistakes and errors are</u> <u>**un**important</u> so long as you are understood. Remember, most of the people you are going to be talking with are NOT SCHOLARS… they're just folks like you, and they make mistakes in grammar, too.*

*B.) Vocabulary <u>is **the** single most important part</u> of communicating in any language. You can and must build vocabulary while driving, shaving, putting on your make-up, having your morning coffee, watching television, all the time. Yes, you can!*

*C.) Knowing how to do <u>verb conjugations</u> is **not** <u>critical</u> to learning to communicate. Learning and using verbs in their simplest forms is just another part of vocabulary building.*

*D.) Your <u>accent is **un**important,</u> so long as words are <u>properly</u> pronounced. You must practice your pronunciation continuously.*

Why is this My Heretical Rule No. 2?

Because, with an adequate vocabulary and reasonably good pronunciation, *you will be understood*, in spite of that dreadful academic disease known as *"grammatical insufficiency"*.

As One Student to Another.

Now, let me tell you a little of how this course came to be and how and why I believe it will work for you.

For more than 40 years, I have been a *student* of the Spanish language and of Spanish and Latin American culture.

After three years of studying Latin in secondary school, I began my study of the Spanish language in 1961 as a first year university student. My language professor was from Mexico and the text was the typical Spanish grammar book.

During my third year of university level Spanish language studies, I had a Cuban language professor tell me that it would take an English speaker at least 20 years to master the conditional and subjunctive moods in Spanish and to not even waste my time trying to learn them.

Never having been an individual who appreciates being told that he *can't* do something, I was determined that, at some time in my life, I would prove him wrong. It was many years before the opportunity and *the need* to do that finally came together.

By 1990, I had mastered most of the grammar, the verb conjugations, and even the accent, but I still had not *learned* the language. Then, again, I wasn't really motivated to master the language. Where I lived, I could more easily speak "*Espanglish*".

The important point of all this is that, with 3 years of secondary school Latin studies and 3 years of university level Spanish language studies behind me, not to mention a $10,000, 3 week, intensive, full-immersion, language course from one of the better known commercial "schools" of language, I still could not carry on a "real" conversation in Spanish, even after 30 years.

I could read and write, but I always had to have a dictionary handy. I knew the rules of grammar, knew all of the verb conjugations, had the pronunciation down pat, had a really good accent, (even knew the subjunctive but not how to use it consistently well) but I still didn't *know* the language and certainly couldn't carry on an extended, in-depth conversation in it.

Although my opportunity to really and truly become fluent in the Spanish language, including the mastering of the conditional and subjunctive moods, didn't come for another 25 years after that Cuban language professor's comments, I eventually did prove him wrong. Well, half-wrong.

Reading the Dictionary.

During the past 11+ years, I have built a substantial vocabulary (living in Spain helps), but it was not until I began the process of seriously and intensively *building a vocabulary* that I began to really <u>learn</u> the language and to develop the fluency that I wanted to achieve.

After more than 10 years of *"reading" the dictionary* (and speaking, of course), I am now often accepted as a native speaker. This is especially true in Latin America, thanks in no small measure to my accent (Thank you, Fidel, for all those refugees)-

> -- *But, without the ability to communicate my ideas through a really substantial vocabulary, that would NOT be the case.*

After more than 40 years, I still study.

Now, after more than 40 years of studying (but not necessarily *learning*) the language, I STILL spend time with my dictionary every day, adding at least 5 to 10 new words per day. And, I study some aspect of grammar every day.

Eventually, you may do that, too, if you really want to 'master' Spanish –

> -- *but <u>only after you've learned to speak and communicate effectively</u>.*

Spanish is Actually EASY to Learn.

Although this may sound contradictory to my immediately preceding comments, it is my opinion that <u>Spanish is probably the easiest of all foreign languages for an English speaker to learn</u>.

Traditional teaching technique does nothing to make it as easy as it really is; rather, it just makes it more difficult than it ought to be.

Most Spanish language instructional courses, whether organized and in a classroom environment or self-study with tapes and whether academic or commercial, <u>do not</u> focus on conversation. They may SAY they do, but they really just direct the student toward mastery of reading and writing and THEN speaking the language being studied.

Except for the more expensive and labor-intensive, full-immersion language courses (e.g. Berlitz Schools of Language* or International Inlingua Schools of Language*) which do focus on speaking, every language course I have ever seen takes essentially the same approach.

- Nominal emphasis on vocabulary.
- Lots of rules of grammar.
- Lots of verb conjugations.
- Moderate emphasis on perfecting pronunciation.
- Lots of translations but little or no interpretation.
- Little discussion of cultural differences.

The emphasis always seems to be on translating simple sentences which demonstrate the RULES for the use of pronouns, verbs and verb conjugations, other RULES of grammar and only enough "*specified*" vocabulary to carry through the simple "conversation" of the lesson for

---

* The names of Berlitz Schools of Language and International Inlingua Schools of Language are trademarks of those schools. They offer results-oriented, intensive conversation only instruction with native speakers of the languages offered in a "learning language only" environment, i.e., that is, no English is spoken during any of the instruction. One is immersed in the language from the beginning. These courses are stressful but effective.

the purpose of demonstrating the RULES which are the object of that lesson.

Even where conversation is emphasized, because of the heavy emphasis on Rules of Grammar and verb conjugations (and not enough time learning the sounds of Spanish), the average student is so intimidated by the experience that the classroom experience of forced (or enforced) conversation becomes counter-productive. It actually serves to impede one's progress toward the goal which is the reason for the taking of the language course in the first place.

Well Meaning Failure to Educate.

I do not mean to imply that there is a vast conspiracy on the part of academia to deprive the masses of the ability to easily speak a foreign language. Rather, I think most academics are well intentioned.

I also believe that the field of education has strangled its ability to educate students effectively with:

- too much emphasis on structure,

- too much emphasis on duplicable lesson plans, and

- too much emphasis on being able to "scientifically" measure even the tiniest statistical deviation in learning on its way to becoming a "profession" *comparable* to law and medicine.

In large part, I fear that the professional field of pedagogy has finally lent credence to that old adage that "those who can do, and those who can't teach" and *they* teach others how (not) to do it.

I Don't Care About Rules and Structure.

For our purposes, I DON'T really care all that much about structure, even less about rules.

I DO care about <u>communicating</u> in Spanish comfortably, without embarrassment, and with good clarity and relatively good accuracy. I haven't always felt that way.

From Zero to Fluent Without a Course.

After watching my wife go from an absolute non-speaker of Spanish to relatively fluent speaker in less than 2 years and to achieving almost native speaker skills within 5 years—

-- with only her husband for a dictionary, and without benefit of grammar book, text books, language course or any other kind of study -- I realized that she had achieved a mastery over the language that few foreigners ever have and that she got there the same way children learn a language -- one word at a time.

Now, she is mistress of the double *entendre* in Spanish.

She occasionally drove me nuts along the way with her absolute and total disregard for grammar (she still does so), but, by the same token, she sometimes has to "interpret" for me these days what the less-than-well-educated *Andaluz*[*] in the street has to say in his *Andalusian* dialect and with his/her locally-coined words.

At times, my Spanish is just TOO educated to get the job done, and, frankly, my wife has a better ear for the less-well-educated dialects of Andalusia than do I. Even *Madrileños*[**] often have a difficult time understanding the local *Andaluzes*, so I don't feel too badly.

I can discuss politics, philosophy and religion with educated native speakers of Spanish all day long. My wife is quite comfortable with the community gossip (and in the local dialect). Come to think of it, I haven't mastered that ability even in English. And, of course, as she has

---

[*] A Spaniard resident in the province of Andalusia. Also, the dialect spoken in Andalucia is referred to as 'El Andaluz'.

[**] Citizen or resident of Madrid, Spain.

pointed out to me after having read the preceding sentence, her skills are not just applicable to gossip; they can be applied (and are) in many other areas of conversation.

I can only say to you that YOU CAN learn, too, the same way she did -- or as closely as we can do it in a written course.

The advantage you will have with *this* course is that you will have at your fingertips all of the tricks, techniques and short cuts that BOTH of us have learned over our years of studying this language, as well as the borrowed expertise of others.

Heretic's Confession

Let me also tell you that my Spanish isn't PERFECT. Anyone who looks hard enough can and undoubtedly will find something to fault.

I am NOT a Professor of Language in Spanish.

I'm just a guy who has had a lifelong love affair with the Spanish language and culture and who knows how difficult it is for most people to bridge the gap between the desire to speak Spanish and actually speaking Spanish.

THE Most Important Secret to Learning Spanish.

What most of us never realize (and it is too seldom pointed out to us by language teachers) is that we ALREADY HAVE a significant *Spanish vocabulary* of perhaps as many as 5,000 to 10,000 words, and many of us could be blessed with an even greater vocabulary of which we are not even aware.

The problem is, because most of us as adult students of Spanish don't know we ALREADY HAVE so many words at our command in the Spanish language, we never use them.

Spanish is sometimes known as the Vulgar Latin. What is today modern Spanish is 85% the same as it was 2,000 years ago. It is living Latin.

Much of English, like Spanish, French, Italian, Portuguese and Romanian, comes to us from Latin. Because so many words share common Latin roots among these languages, there is a tremendous overlap. This overlap manifests itself in what are known as cognates -- that is, words that look and sound almost the same and have the same meanings in both languages.

Heretic's Commitment

In this Spanish language course, <u>we will stress discovering and learning to utilize your already existing and substantial Spanish vocabulary of cognates,</u> as well as building and using additional "foreign" (Spanish) vocabulary not otherwise based on Latin. You WILL learn to speak Spanish in one to three weeks.

With the vocabulary we will give you in this book, you will know all the words you need to know to be able to converse intelligently on just about any subject.

You already know quite a few words in Spanish just because you speak English. For instance, how many of you don't recognize the 'English' words which follow and which happen to be borrowed from Spanish?

<u>English</u>   <u>Spanish</u>   <u>Pronunciation Guide</u>
(Underlined syllables in the Pronunciation Guide are accented or stressed syllables)

English	Spanish	Pronunciation Guide
Banana	Banana	*Bah-<u>nah</u>-nah*
Bravado	Bravata	*Brah-<u>vah</u>-tah*
Burro	Burro	*<u>Boo</u>-rroh (Roll the "rr")*
Cafeteria	Cafetería	*Kah-fay-tay-<u>ree</u>-ya*
Cocoa	Cacao	*Kah-<u>ka</u>-oh*
Fiesta	Fiesta	*Fee-<u>es</u>-tah*

Gringo	Gringo	_Greeng-go_
Lasso	Lazo	_Lah-so_
Mosquito	Mosquito	_Moh-skee-toh_
Mulatto	Mulato	_Moo-lah-toh_
Patio	Pátio	_Pah-tee-oh_
Pimienta	Pimiento	_Pee-mee-en-toh_
Pinto	Pinto	_Peen-toh_
Poncho	Poncho	_Pone-choh_
Potato	Patata	_Pah-tah-tah_
Rodeo	Rodeo	_Roh-day-oh_
Siesta	Siesta	_See-es-tah_
Taco	Taco	_Tah-koh_
Tobacco	Tabaco	_Tah-bah-koh_
Tomato	Tomate	_Toh-mah-tay_
Tornado	Tornado	_Tore-nah-dough_

Gosh! I'll bet you've never seen those words before, have you? And, even though we use them in English every day, they ARE Spanish words.

You've now just added 21 "new" words to your Spanish vocabulary, most of which you probably didn't know were Spanish words, but all of which you ALREADY knew.

Is the whole course this easy? No. But, it's <u>almost</u> this easy.

Accent the Important Things...

In these pages, we will stress the issue of practicing your pronunciation more than in some other courses but in a manner we trust will be a little easier to use and more useful to YOU, the beginning Spanish speaker. Much of the help on pronunciation skills through the Pronunciation Guides was actually developed as a consequence of our trying to teach Spanish speakers to properly pronounce English.

Pronunciation Guides.

For every new word, word group or idiomatic expression, we provide a word Pronunciation Guide, which is based on phonetically pronouncing letters using the *English sounds* to arrive at a reasonably accurate approximation of the Spanish pronunciation.

Having the Pronunciation Guide available at the first and every subsequent point of use of a word means that you don't have to constantly refer back to a pronunciation key in the front of your text or in the front of a dictionary in order to remember how to produce certain sounds in Spanish.

Because you are *constantly* reminded of how the letters sound, by the end of this course, your correct pronunciation of Spanish words should have become almost second nature. Correct pronunciation will have been demonstrated and reinforced for you literally thousands of times.

Two points to keep in mind are that the vowels always have the same sounds and that every single letter in a Spanish word (except for the written letter "*h*") is sounded in the pronunciation of a word. So, once you have mastered the pronunciation, you'll never have much difficulty with the written word, either in spelling or in reading.

So long as you will open your mouth and PRACTICE PRONOUNCING the words and continue to practice pronouncing the words OUT LOUD, you will have little difficulty in mastering the sounds of Spanish.

Pronounce the syllables in the Pronunciation Guides as you would pronounce them in English in order to arrive at an approximation of the sound of the word in Spanish. Accent or emphasize the underlined syllables. That's all there is to it.

Your Accent is Unimportant.

You will always have an accent, and there's nothing you can do about that. Who do you know who *doesn't* have an accent of some sort?

Then, again, a little 'foreign' accent can be really sexy or attractive. Think of how often you've seen someone in the movies with an accent who, if they spoke English like you do you probably wouldn't even have noticed, but, with their nice 'foreign' accent in English, you thought they were really special.

Where would James Bond be without the "Bond girls" with their sexy accents?

You CAN and you MUST *pronounce* the words reasonably accurately.

But, who knows? Maybe some Spanish speaker will think *your* accent is sexy.

Throw in Some Colour.

We'll also give you quite a few idiomatic expressions to add colour to the language. We don't want your conversation to sound dull and lackluster, after all.

Idiomatic expressions often set the tone of conversation, serve to make certain points more clear and understandable.

Understanding the "colour" can also help you to avoid embarrassing mistakes in the *use* of language. We don't want you embarrassing yourself by putting your foot in your mouth, not even when you're wearing your chocolate shoes.

Speaking of colour, all those not-so-nice words and expressions that everyone always seems to want to know are contained in Appendix IV in the back of this book.

Knowing the Language Means Knowing the Culture.

Then, we are going to try to acquaint you with essential differences, in general, between English speaking cultures and Spanish speaking cultures. You cannot learn a language without learning and understanding something about the culture that uses it.

Understanding cultural differences will also help you to be accepted as a visiting foreigner instead of just a "*gringo*" ("<u>green</u>_g-go") or "*extranjero*" ("ex-trahn_g-<u>hair</u>-oh") or "*giri*" ("<u>hee</u>-ree"). It will also help you to get the most out of your experience in whatever Spanish speaking country you find yourself.

Besides, all of us need a little culture in our lives, don't we?

You Are the Interpreter.

In my opinion, *interpretation* is key, not translation. Translation always leads to problems. Interpreting what you hear and interpreting for others what you want to say is the most important thing.

As my friend, Mary Jane (an ex-pat American living in Spain), said to me only recently on this point:

"For the English speaker, Spanish is spoken from the inside out… so you must listen and get the whole picture… don't try to dissect and analyze what the speaker is saying… YOU AIN'T GOT TIME… You'll miss the boat!"

Hear, hear!

The easiest way to see this fact demonstrated in action is to take a look at the Council of Ministers of the European Union.

Half of the problem they have in the Council is the fact that everything said by any minister is TRANSLATED into more than a dozen languages. The translators do no interpretation; it's not allowed and it's not their job. The only 'interpretation' that is done is by politicos who then try to 'interpret' the translation, rather than the original comments in the language of the speaker. It's no wonder they never get anything done.

For example, how does one translate "Bob's your uncle" or "That dog won't hunt"? One has to get behind the literal translation and interpret what actually is meant by what is being said. Having translated it (if it can even be translated), who *can* convey what is meant without some interpretation?

So, we don't what you to translate; we want you to interpret and to understand.

What to Expect From This Course.

What you're going to be receiving in this *The Heretic's Crash Course in Spanish Conversation & Culture* is a compilation of all of the shortcuts I have discovered to language learning during my more than 40 years as a STUDENT of Spanish. These are ideas and concepts and techniques (some of which were just "light bulbs" that went on over my head) that make getting up to "conversational speed" easier and faster.

Then, there are more shortcuts and simplifications discovered in the process of helping my wife go from ground zero to fluent, and even more shortcuts discovered by teaching English to Spanish speakers.

If you decide never to go beyond the purchase of this course and the purchase of a good Spanish-English/English-Spanish dictionary,* you will still be able to communicate *effectively* and to *GET BY* in Spanish.

---

* A good dictionary is an absolute MUST. We recommend the University of Chicago Spanish-English/English-Spanish Dictionary in paperback. You may also want to have a small pocket dictionary for when you're away from home. See also the list of recommended books and publications in Chapter XXV.

Please notice that I am not saying that you will be *fluent* in the language in the sense that you will not only know the right words but that your verb usage will be spot on and your speech will be always grammatically correct.

If that's what you're expecting, this is not the course for you.

Let's be serious... you want to have enough time to enjoy *conversing* in your new language... *not sitting alone in front of grammar books and missing the fun* and personal satisfaction of speaking Spanish. Right?

So, if you consider fluency in a language to be the ability to communicate effectively with native speakers of that language, then you can be fluent in Spanish by applying what we will teach you in these few pages.

Observation.

Women seem to have an easier time learning language than do men, mainly because women are more right-brained than men. So, if only one member of your family is going to learn Spanish over the next three weeks for that upcoming holiday trip, better it should be Mom than Dad. Sorry, Chaps. That's not to say that you shouldn't try. It just may take you a little longer than Mom.

What Not to Expect From This Course.

If you're expecting that you buy and read this book and that we then pour in the information, shake it up a bit and you're instantly a Spanish speaker, you will be disappointed.

You must commit to applying yourself to the task, knowing that you are accomplishing something you really want to do... to converse with new Spanish speaking friends... to share their hopes, their dreams, their opinions and their jokes... to experience their culture... to enjoy the wine and the tapas and the very different cuisine... and to do it all in a relatively short period of time.

Experiencing life. Isn't that what it's all about?

My Heretical Rule No. 3.

Do have fun with this course. Taking yourself too seriously will impair your ability to learn. Strangely enough, the more fun you have and the more relaxed you are, the easier it is for you to learn.

Part of experiencing Spain or Latin America is the fun of sharing in the culture and all of the exciting things the locals do.

One of the most fun things associated with experiencing life, and one of life's most satisfying experiences, is learning a second language.

Make it fun. Make it fun. Make it fun. Don't be afraid to laugh at yourself either.

And, on that note, let's start having some fun. Go to **Chapter II**, and we can begin learning some of that "we already know it" vocabulary.

Chapter II.
Introduction to Cognates and
The Dynamic Dozen.

Vocabulary is THE single most important aspect of learning a language and being able to communicate in it.

Heretic's Axiom

Words are to thinking as coat hangers are to clothes.

If you don't have a hangar, you can't hang your clothes.

If you don't have the words, you can't 'hang' your thoughts.

In fact, without an adequate vocabulary, there will be thoughts you will be incapable even of having, let alone expressing.

Therefore, WORDS empower thought <u>and</u> communication.

Without an adequate vocabulary with which to express both the concrete and the abstract, you will lack the basic necessities required for either forming or communicating ideas, concepts and/or facts.

Hence, a robust vocabulary is a necessity for anyone who wishes to be an intelligent thinker and/or an effective communicator.

Why do we want to focus on building vocabulary first in this course?

Children and Functional Illiterates.

Well, that's the way <u>children learn</u> a language. They first build vocabulary. One word at a time.

<u>Really Important Fact:</u>
Children <u>don't even begin</u> to study grammar until they <u>already speak</u> their native language fairly well and are <u>then finally ready</u> to begin to learn the <u>written</u> language.

Many people who are considered <u>functionally illiterate</u> (i.e., can neither read nor write) are still quite articulate with the spoken language. Why? Because they have a good vocabulary. It's surely not because they understand the rules of grammar and verb conjugations, except intuitively.

As you well know, even very small children can communicate what they want with the use of even single word sentences, completely lacking in verbs.

"Biscuit me" (or, *"cookie"*), *"milk"*, *"ball"*, *"doggie bow wow"*, *"car"*, *"Mikey go"* (Whoops, a verb!), *"me eat"* (Oops, another verb!) are all effective communications by toddlers -- perhaps not as articulate as we would like, but communicative nonetheless.

Worst Case Scenario.

If you *never* use this **_The Heretic's Crash Course in Spanish Conversation & Culture_** for anything other than as a means of building vocabulary through discovery, you will *still* be able to communicate many of your needs and wants in Spanish speaking countries and, with some careful thought, understand *much* of what is spoken to you.

Foreigners Speaking English.

Think about it. How many times have you met a foreigner who says, *"I no speak very good the English"* but who nonetheless manages to communicate with you quite effectively, IF you're willing to listen to him/her?

For example, *"I go bank, ask money. They not give, say must sign paper, need passport"* would be typical of things that I have heard foreigners express in English. Yet, we would say that this foreigner speaks English, if we were asked, wouldn't we?

Not unsurprisingly, I have also heard the same kinds of things in Spanish. As I have understood it in English, I also have understood it in Spanish.

And *there is no reason that a Spanish speaker won't understand you* if that's as good as your Spanish EVER gets (unless he/she just doesn't want to understand).

As English speakers, we sometimes take it for granted that everyone speaks English. Yet, frankly, we're not very good listeners, especially when it comes to listening to someone who doesn't speak English well.

English speakers seem to think that the most effective way to communicate with a foreigner is to do so in a very loud voice, as though they were deaf as opposed to having a problem in understanding our language. Thank goodness, people in *most* non-English speaking countries don't suffer from this affliction.

Even though it isn't a fact, we somehow have come to expect that foreigners in our territory ought to "automatically" know English. When they do, we tend to pay more attention to them than when they don't.

In fact, when a non-English speaker is in our English speaking country, we too often ignore him/her or we tend to think negatively about that person. Furthermore, we don't really show our appreciation the way we should to the person who has gone to the trouble to try to communicate with us in English.

Yet, in other countries, *local people are overjoyed that you have taken the trouble to learn even just a few words in their language,* and they will go out of their way to be helpful to you, even if you can only say "*please*" and "*thank you*" and "*good morning*" in their language.

I speak two languages fluently, but I speak seven more at least to the extent of being able to be polite simply because I understand how much native speakers of those languages appreciate it.

If you will apply what we will teach you in this course, you will surely know enough to be polite, and your conversational Spanish will be FAR better than the example given in English above within a very reasonable period of time.

My Heretical Rule No. 4.

Build vocabulary religiously. Every day. For the rest of your life.

In Spanish. Even in English. You can never know too many words in any language.

Throw the Rule Book Out the Window.

We are not going to spend a great deal of time on Rules in this course, except for "*My Heretical Rules*". And, even of those, there aren't many.

Those rules of grammar that are absolutely essential we will tell you about and explain, but we don't intend to burden you with rule upon rule which you probably aren't going to remember anyway.

The most complicated aspects of Spanish grammar are in the categories of verbs and uses of pronouns, and they are often the reasons that many a student of language (and not just Spanish) has given it up for a lost cause.

Most Spanish language courses spend a tremendous amount of time teaching about verb conjugations, regular and irregular verbs, orthographically changing verbs, defective verbs, tenses of verbs, ad infinitum.

You only have to recognize that there are 16 different verb tenses in Spanish, of which 14 are in common use, and that there are 6 different verb endings for each tense to realize that learning verbs can be very complicated.

It's even more obvious when you realize that there are 9 possible "persons" for the 6 different verb endings for each tense (that's only 126 possible persons using 96 different endings for every verb) to really cause the student to get really tense.

<u>If you're tense, you can't learn.</u>
I don't want you to be tense.

My Heretical Rule No. 5.

Don't get tense over verb tenses.

In this course, <u>you will have to master only one verb tense</u>. If the truth were told, <u>you don't even have to master that,</u> <u>but we want you to</u>, and you'll be glad you did.

<u>Mastery</u> of only this one verb tense <u>will enable you</u> <u>to effectively form the 4 most commonly used tenses</u> in Spanish, and you will only have to master this tense for 12 verbs and five "persons", not nine. That means 5 choices of ending for every verb instead of 126.

Already we will have reduced your learning curve for verbs by more than 95% for each of the 12 verbs. For all other verbs, we're going to show you how to cut your effort by 99.99%, if you want.

Introducing The Dynamic Dozen.

Mastering the present tense of this Dynamic Dozen:

<u>Dynamic Dozen</u>		<u>Pronounced</u>
ESTAR	("to be"),	*Es-<u>tahr</u>*
SER	("to be"),	*Sair*
IR	("to go"),	*Eer*
TENER	("to have"),	*Teh-<u>nair</u>*
PODER	("to be able")	*Poh-<u>dair</u>*
HABER	("to have"), an auxiliary verb	*Ah-<u>bair</u>*
SOLER	("to usually do..."),	*So-<u>lair</u>*
SABER	("to know"),	*Sah-<u>bair</u>*
HACER	("to do" or "to make"),	*Ah-<u>sair</u>*
ACABAR	("to finish"),	*Ah-kah-<u>bar</u>*
DECIR	("to say" or "to speak"),	*Day-<u>seer</u>*
DAR	("to give")	*Dahr*

...will enable you to express just about *anything* that you will ever need for effective communications, past, present and future.

The simplest way to understand verbs and use them is the way that we are going to teach you.

These are the ONLY verbs we're going to teach you in conjugated form. Guaranteed!   Other verbs you learn about can be learned in infinitive* form only.

My Heretical Rule No 6.

If you know how to conjugate TENER, ACABAR and DECIR in the present tense, you will still be able to conjugate more than 90% of all other Spanish verbs in the present tense without even thinking about it.

In total, we're going to want you to learn the present tense conjugations for a maximum of 12 verbs, the Dynamic Dozen. You don't absolutely HAVE TO do that, but you'll be far more fluent if you do. That's just 60 words.

Of course, you'll learn lots of other verbs, but you won't have to conjugate them (unless you want to).

Believe it or not, eventually, you'll want to conjugate other verbs (even in other tenses), and you may even begin doing it without quite realizing that it's happening. Because of that possibility, we include one short chapter on the formation of the present tense, which is applicable to all verbs in Spanish.

Verbs add action to language. Without verbs, your speech lacks vitality and life, so the more verbs you use, the more vibrant, lively, colorful and effective your speech will be.

---

* Infinitive: In English, usually consists of the word "to" followed by the verb, e.g. "to go."

You just don't have to know how to conjugate every verb that you use.

You don't!

The Wonderful World of Cognates.

Study of cognates will demonstrate that *you ALREADY have an effective vocabulary in Spanish of more than 5,000 words* (People with vocabularies in excess of 50,000 English words may already have a cognate vocabulary as large as 10,000 to 15,000 words in Spanish).

You have probably never heard of a language course that starts out acknowledging that you already have such an effectively large vocabulary in your chosen language of study.

There are between 600,000 and 1,000,000 words in English. English has by far the richest vocabulary of any language (Spanish and French have only about 100,000 words each, by contrast).

But, if the average English speaking person has a total vocabulary of only 10,000 to 15,000 words in his/her own language, it still shouldn't come as any great surprise that a large percentage of that vocabulary could be transferable to another language, like Spanish.

As evidence of what I say, how many of you cannot distinguish the similarity between *"education"* and *"educación"* ("Pronounced "eh-doo-kah-see-<u>own</u>")? Same word, same meaning, sound almost the same, spelled almost the same. Or, how about between *"fantasy"* and *"fantasía"* (Pronounced "fahn-tah-<u>see</u>-ya") or *"distinguished"* and *"distinguido"* ("Pronounced "dees-teen-<u>ghee</u>-dough")?

Cognates. Wow!

You may already have a vocabulary equal to 50 to 60% of that of your typical native speaker of Spanish.

If the truth be told, with the lack of higher education (or even completion of secondary school) in much of the Spanish speaking world, including Spain, your vocabulary actually could be equal to or greater than that of the "average" Spanish speaker's and a far richer one, in terms of the kinds of words you know, to boot.

The average native speaker of Spanish may typically have a total useful vocabulary of between 5,000 and 15,000 words; however, he probably only uses 1,000 to 1,500 of those words on a regular basis.

Familiarity with cognates, together with some additional basic non-cognate vocabulary, means that you may only have to learn a *total* of 1,000 to perhaps 2,000 words in Spanish to carry on a conversation (based on the average number of words used by the average native speaker).

If you learn 500 new (*non-cognate*) Spanish words, *in addition to* all the cognate words you already know, then you can become a highly effective and articulate conversationalist in Spanish, able to converse with anyone, and you can reach this point in as little as one to three weeks.

If you were to commit to learning 50 new (*non-cognates*) words a day, you could accomplish this (500 words) in as little as ten days.

Our expectation is that you may go a little more slowly and that you probably won't exceed 25 new NON-COGNATE words per day. The long-term memory portions of your brain function better when data input is in small bits and bytes, rather than kilobytes and megabytes.

The *cognate* words you DO already know (yes, you do, even if you don't yet fully believe it), but it will take a good one to two weeks for you to realize this and for us to help you "remember" the vast majority of them, especially the more useful ones.

<u>My Heretical Rule No. 7.</u>

It is important for you to understand that you don't have to wait, in fact cannot wait, one to six weeks to begin speaking. You must begin speaking TODAY.

Finally, we will teach you some of the most commonly used idiomatic expressions, so that you can add some additional colour to your speech, as well as assuring that you will recognize these idioms when they come up in conversations.

It's one thing to say, "You are correct" and quite another to say, "you're damned right". So, we want to be sure you have some added flavour from idiomatic expressions.

EXERCISE 1:

Think of ten words that you know in English, which end in "-ION" and write them down below:

1.
2.
3.
4.
5.
6.
7.
8.
9.
10.

Now, go to your dictionary and look up those ten words in the SPANISH to English part of your dictionary.

How many of the words did you find, albeit with a slight spelling change?

Didn't expect to find English words in the Spanish dictionary, did you?

Go ahead. Pick another 10, and try it again.

EXERCISE 2:

Now, here's my list of Spanish cognates.

Without referring to your dictionary, how many of them do you recognize?

How many of them can you define?

Write down what you think the words mean. THEN, when you have completed this part of the exercise, go to your Spanish-English dictionary and look them up.

Don't just take my word for it. Prove it! You <u>DO</u> know these words.

<u>Spanish</u>   Pronounced

Note: All Pronunciation Guides will show the accented syllable either underlined (as herein below) or italicized. Pronounce the syllables phonetically as you would in English, for now. You'll be close, if not perfect.

1. Anécdota   *ah-<u>neck</u>-doh-tah*
2. Balance   *bah-<u>lahn</u>-say*
3. Calificación   *kahl-ee-fee-kah-see-<u>own</u>*
4. Departamento   *day-pahr-tah-<u>men</u>-toh*
5. Entusiasmo   *En-too-see-<u>azz</u>-moh*
6. Flexible   *Flex-e<u>e</u>-blay*
7. Gasolina   *Gah-soh-<u>lee</u>-nah*

8. Hipotético   *Ee-poh-teh-tee-koh*
9. Indisposición   *Een-dees-poh-see-see-own*
10. Judicial   *Hoo-dee-see-ahl*

Guess what? You just learned 10 new useful words in Spanish, and they're all ENGLISH words you already know.

Your new Spanish vocabulary in the first two chapters is now up to nearly 50 "new" words, all of which you already knew. So, how hard can it be? The hard part comes next: Pronunciation.

Think about this:

It took me 35 years to figure out the whole story about cognates, because no one had ever told me about them. What I know now is that, by studying cognates, one can build 10 years' worth of vocabulary in about ten months.

Chapter III.
The Sounds of Spanish.

We're not going to bore you here with funny little symbols that you don't understand anyway, or use terms like *alveolar* or *bilabial* or *fricative* to explain how and where to put your tongue or your lips or your teeth in order to be able to pronounce words in Spanish. There's no need, and it's unnecessarily complicated for your purposes.

We're just going to teach you how to pronounce the words phonetically, using more or less the same technique you learned in grammar school for pronouncing and learning to spell in English.

The one thing I must re-emphasize to you right now is the fact that <u>this is a crash course in *conversational* Spanish.</u>

My Heretical Rule No. 8.

*You have to **talk**, you must **talk** and you will **talk**.*

***Talk** to yourself.*

***Talk** to a study partner.*

***Talk** to someone else who knows some Spanish and knows how words are pronounced correctly.*

*Or, better yet, **talk** to a native speaker.*

*But, no matter how, and no matter with whom, **TALK**, **TALK, TALK**. Even if it's just to yourself.*

Until you can construct complete sentences, just practice pronouncing the words, again and again. I know. BORING! Trust me, you'll get past boring pretty quickly.

What I Know About YOU.

I stress this to you now, because I know two things about YOU and your efforts in learning to *speak* a language:

1.) You don't want open your mouth to speak a foreign language unless *you* can speak it "perfectly", and
2.) All students of language, including *You,* are self conscious about speaking.

I know more than just a few Brits who have lived in Spain for 30 years or more, who understand nearly every word in Spanish they hear, but who can't (or won't) speak because <u>they are afraid</u> that their spoken Spanish won't be perfect and/or they're embarrassed about *HOW THEY MIGHT SOUND!*

What a pity!

Get that mindset out of your head right now! We're operating under a new and improved paradigm here.

You can't converse if you don't talk. So, open your mouth and let those Spanish sounds flow forth. Don't be bashful or shy.

So what if your accent isn't that of a native speaker? You're <u>not</u> a native speaker of Spanish and you never will be, but you can still communicate in Spanish quite effectively -- IF you allow yourself to do so.

One more thing that I know about <u>you</u> is this:

Because of the position of your tongue and your lips and your jaw in forming the vowel sounds of Spanish and pronouncing the words, the muscles in your face, which you use to speak, are going to be repositioned ever so slightly. Because of this and especially in the beginning, your jaw muscles are going to hurt. The more you talk, the more they'll hurt, but also the sooner you'll get past the physical pain of speaking Spanish.

Hey! No pain, no gain! Right?

<u>Vowels.</u>

Spanish is the easiest of all languages in the world to pronounce. The VOWELS <u>always</u> sound the same, and the consonants vary little.

Every letter in every syllable (except the written Spanish "h") is pronounced, and they always sound the same (the written "h" in the <u>pronunciation guide</u> IS pronounced).

In English, we say that the vowels are the letters "a", "e", "i", "o", "u", and sometimes the letters "w" and "y".

In Spanish, the "*vocales*" are the letters "a", "e", "i", "o", "u" and sometimes the letters "ll" and "y".

To help you master the pronunciation of the vowels, at the end of this next little section, I'm going to teach you a rhyme that I learned from a Cuban kindergarten teacher when I was mastering pronunciation many years ago. The more you practice this little rhyme, the better will be your mastery of the "*vocales*" of Spanish.

Now, let's explore "*las vocales*" in Spanish. Then, we'll tackle "*las consonantes*".

Las Vocales.

"A"   Pronounced just as when the doctor puts the tongue depressor in your mouth and says: "Say 'Ah' ", but clipped short.

Think of the "a" sound you hear in the "art". It's a short "ah", not a long "ah". Clip it short with no drawl. In the pronunciation guide, it's shown as "ah".

"E"   Pronounced like the letter "a" in the word "hay" or "hey" or **the word "egg"**, but clipped short.

NOTE: I have chosen in the pronunciation guides to use "HEY" in lieu of "HAY" because of a peculiarity of certain British dialects to turn words like "day" and "hay" and "say" into "daeiy", haeiy" and saeiy" (Think of "Professor 'enry ' iggins" and "My Fair *Laieydee*", and you'll know what to avoid here).

Canadians, it's just like the "ey" you put on the ends of sentences. Yanks, all it is "hay" like in "hayride". **Think of the "e" in "café".**

Nonetheless, <u>for purposes of our phonics</u>, it (the letter "e") will be reflected here in the phonics guides as "*ey*". If you see the words "say" or "bay" in the pronunciation guides, just remember "hey". They ("hay" and "hey") sound the same.

"I" Pronounced like the letter "e" in the word "be" or the word "seen", but clipped short. Shown herein as "ee". It's an "eeee" sound but only "i" long. Clip it short. **Think of the "i" in the word "siesta", or in the word "machine".**

NOTE: *The sounds in the word "siesta" (or, "fiesta") capture the exact sounds of the three most difficult vowels for most English speakers to master, that is, the "a", the "e" and the "i".*
How does it sound? Like: "See-<u>ehs</u>-tah". Siesta.

"O" Pronounced very roundly, like it's shape and sounds like the "o" sound of the word "dough", clipped short. We're talking here a "dough" sound with a "doe" length. Got it? **Think of the "o" in "Note", i.e., short and round.** The pronunciation guide will show "oh" or "dough"

"U" Does NOT have a "Y" sound in front, as in English, but is pronounced like "oo" in the word "boot" or "soon" or as "ooh", but clipped short. That's an "ooooooooh" sound but only "u" long. Clip here. **Think of "oo" in the word "scoot".**

So, now we have the essentials of our rhyme:

"a, e, i, o, u"
(pronounced as "ah", "ey", ""ee", "oh", "oo")

"El burro sabe más que tú".
(pronounced as *"L <u>booh</u>-rroh <u>sah</u>-bay mahs kay too"*)

If you haven't figured it out already, this means:

"a, e, i, o, u,
the donkey knows more than you (do)."

Vowel sounds in Spanish are always clipped short, and they are never <u>drawled</u>. You also have to use your lips and open your mouth a bit more for the vowels in Spanish than you do in English.

Las Consonantes.

As for the consonants, they are *b, c, ch, d, f, g, h, j, k, l, ll, m, n, q, r, rr, s, t, v, w, x, y, z,* and they are pronounced as follows:

"B" & "V"   Pronounced as almost the same letter in Spanish, but they are pronounced more softly and without closing the lips completely, as we do in English.

If you have to pick one, pick "*b*" without closing your lips or try to pronounce a "*Bv*" sound. For example, the word "*uva*" ("oo-Bvah") means "*grape*", but I have seen less educated Spanish speakers write "*uba*". They don't hear the difference. If you simply must, you *can* pronounce them as in English.

"C" & "S" & "Z"   Pronounced as "*S*" in English. Lisping the "Z" or the "C" (making them sound like a "*th*") only makes you sound like the "*gringo*" who went to language school and "*thinks*" he/she talks like a native. Don't do it.

"C"   Can also be pronounced with a hard "*k*" sound before "*a*", "*o*", "*u*", "*l*" or "*r*".

"CH"   Pronounced always as "*ch*" in "chuck wagon" or "*cuchara*" ("koo-<u>char</u>-ah", "spoon").

"D"   Pronounced like "*d*" in English, but not as hard; rather, it's almost a "*dh*" sound, especially in the middle of a word.

"F"   Pronounced as in English.

"G"   This one's tricky, and it depends on the word. In words beginning with "*ga*", "*go*", "*gu*", and "*gui*" or "*gue*", the "*g*" is pronounced hard as in English.

BUT

In words beginning with "*ge*", "*gi*", the "*g*" sounds like a hard "*h*" in English.

"GUI" Represent the sounds "*ghee*" and "*gay*" (or "*geh*"), respectively.
"GUE"

"H" The LETTER "*H*" is never pronounced, even though it is written. It sounds like, well... nothing.

"J" Pronounced like "*h*" in English, but harder.

"K" Pronounced like the "*k*" in the "Tell Yo Mama t' Pahk da <u>*Kah*</u>." of Ebonics; that is, "*k*" followed by "*ah*", or "*kah*".

"L" Pronounced like "*L*" in English, i.e., "*el*".

"LL" Pronounced like the letter "*y*" in English. "*Yoyo*" from English comes out "*Llollo*" or "*yoyo*" in Spanish. They sound the same. I used to live in a community that had its own dog. His name was, I thought, "*Yogi*". That's what I always called him, until the day I saw where one of the security guards had written his name as "*Llogi*".

Thereafter, I called him "*Llogi*", but he didn't seem to notice the difference (there wasn't one). He was a really good dog, too.

"M" Pronounced as in English.

"N" Pronounced as in English, although in certain words (especially "*n*" final letter) it almost sounds like "n_g". For example, the word "*pan*" (meaning "bread") sounds more like "$pahn_g$".

"Ñ" Pronounced as "*ni*" in onion or the "*ny*" in "canyon". The word "canyon" in English comes from "*cañon*" in Spanish. Looks different, sounds the same. Cognate, eh?

"P"   Pronounced always the same as the "*p*" in "*spot*"; that is, it's harder than the normal English "*p*".

"Q"   Pronounced as a "*k*", always written in combination with a "*u*"; words like "*queso*" ("cheese" and pronounced "kay-so").

"QUI"   Represent the sounds "*key*" and "*kay*" (or, "*keh*"), respectively.
"QUE"

"R"   Pronounced much more firmly than in English. Especially for Brits and Americans from the south, this letter is pronounced like the "*r*" in "royal", not "ahhr" or "ah", ("pahk the kah") as in British or southern American English usage. Sometimes almost has a "*d*" sound.

"RR"   The letter "r" at the beginning of a word or the double "rr" written in the middle of the word mandates that the letter be rolled or, as they say in language school, trilled. Softer than a rolled Scottish "*r*" or German "*r*", but rolled nonetheless. This is difficult for most English speakers.

        Pretend you're Scottish, and it'll come out fine. Practice this one by repeating "*I took the ferrocarril to the aeropuerto de puerto rico*" and rolling all of the "r's" as if they were all doubled. You know you've got it when you can say this one without getting your '*tang tonguelled*'.

        IF you find you just can't wrap your tongue around this one, don't worry. Just make your best effort. You'll still be understood.

"T"   Pronounced as in English.

"W"   Pronounced as in English; the letter "*W*" ONLY occurs in <u>foreign</u> words and/or words of foreign origin.

        There is, however, a "gw" sound in Spanish. It is created by the letter "*ü*" used in combination with the letter "g" to form the syllables "*güe*" and "*güi*", as in "*lingüistico*".

A simple "w" sound is also formed by the combination of "h" and "u", as in "*hueso*", pronounced "wheso".

A "kw" sound is created in Spanish with the letter combination of "cu", as in "*cuestion*".

"X" Pronounced as "*x*" or "*s*" in English (except in the personal name, "*Xavier*", in which case, it sounds like "*h*"). Historically, the letter "*x*" has been pronounced as "*sh*" and "*h*" and "*s*".

Today, you will hear it as "*S*" (which is correct) at least as often as you will hear the "*x*" sound of English (which is also correct). Example: "*extranjero*" ("foreigner" and pronounced as either "es-trahn-<u>hair</u>-oh" or as "eks-trahn-<u>hair</u>-oh").

"Y" Pronounced as in the Spanish letter "i", that is, as "ee" or as a "ll" sound, i.e., "y" as in yellow.

Note:

An additional word about vowel sounds:

With the letter combinations of "*ui*", "*ue*", and "*ua*", used in such words as "*buitre*" (buzzard), "*cuenta*" (account, bill), and "*cuándo*" (when), the result is a "w" sound in conjunction with the preceding consonant, so that these words come out sounding like "<u>bwee</u>-tray", "<u>kwen</u>-tah", and "<u>kwan</u>-dough", respectively.

Also, "*ua*" in conjunction with "*j*" gives a "*wh*" sound, so that a name like "*Juan*" is pronounced "<u>whahn</u>" (rhymes with "swan") but never "wan", as so many English speakers like to do.

"ai" "ay" sounds like "i" in English "side". "au" sounds like "ow" or "ou" in "sound". "ei" or "ey" sounds like "ey" in "they". "ey" sounds like the vowel sounds of "hey you" without the "y" sound.

"oi" or "oy" sounds like "oy" in English boy. "ü" in "güi" and güe" creates a dipthong sound as is heard in English "Guinevere."

Vowel sounds in Spanish also require that you to open your mouth more than they do in English, and, often, the consonants, such as "*b*", "*v*" and "*d*" require you not to close your mouth as much as you do in English, but the differences are so subtle that, even if you use the English sound, you won't be too terribly wrong.

My Heretical Rule No. 9.

"b" and "v" sound the same. "c" and "s" and "z" sound the same. "ll" and "y" sound the same. Got it?

Note to Brits: None of the foregoing means BRITISH English pronunciation. A British *accent* is one thing. British *pronunciation* is quite another.

A proper British accent WITH proper British *pronunciation* will overpower the Spanish that you speak, so stifle the urge.

You won't go wrong if you try to practice speaking English more like a Canadian or an American, because you will achieve the Spanish pronunciation much more closely.

Better yet, try to imitate English as it is spoken by those fine actors Antonio Banderas or Ricardo Montalban or the delightful actress Salma Hayek. This will give you a clue, too, to how they pronounce the letters in Spanish.

I simply die when I hear a Brit order a "*Kaaaah-faaaaaaay Kooorr-taaaaaah-doooughooo*", instead of "*Cafe Cortado*" ("kah-<u>fay</u> cohr-<u>tah</u>-dough"). That is NOT Spanish. Don't forget to CLIP those vowels, Brits.

Note to Yanks: Please, leave the Scarlett O'Hara accent in "Gone With The Wind" where it belongs. Spanish is not a drawled language. Yes, I know that Vivian Leigh was English. That's beside the point.

Likewise, Americans, it is "*muchas gracias*", pronounced as "moo-<u>chahs</u> grah-seeyahs", not as "muuchh-assss graasssy-assss". Please!

Note to Aussies: The sound you hear in "G'day" down under does NOT exist in Spanish. You got that?

Note to Yanitos*: The word is "*no-chay*", NOT "*noh*-shay" and "*Fo Co Na*" is not Spanish.

Imitation Is NOT Just A Great Form of Flattery.

One of the things that you can do which will help you constantly to practice your Spanish pronunciation is to try to pronounce English words with the Spanish sounds.

Again, imitation of Antonio Banderas or Ricardo Montalban will help you a great deal. If you can speak ENGLISH with a Spanish speaker's accent, then your Spanish will sound pretty good, too.

I used to pass for Cuban by doing that very thing (plus, just a sprinkle of Spanish with a Cuban accent). What a hoot!

I remember one time many years ago being in a famous Cuban restaurant in Tampa, USA, and having the waiter say, "*Perdóneme, señor. ¿Usted es cubano?*" ("Excuse me, sir, are you Cuban?").

I was stunned (and flattered), but all I could say was "*No, lo siento.*" ("No, I'm sorry."). I had the accent. I just couldn't talk enough to pull it off, and the waiter didn't ask me for a written answer which I couldn't have given anyway for lack of a dictionary.

Every morning on your daily commute, read the billboard advertising <u>AS IF</u> it were written in Spanish, pronouncing each letter with its

---

"Yanito" is a Spanish term for someone from the British territory of Gibraltar on Spain's southernmost tip.

Spanish equivalent. Keep in mind that, except for the written letter "*h*", all letters in a Spanish word are pronounced.

Then, add in your best "television" accent to your Spanish pronunciation of English words. It really and truly helps. Try it. You won't feel so self-conscious practicing this kind of verbal exercise alone in the car, and you'll get lots of practice. You don't even need a Spanish dictionary to do it.

Here's an example of exactly what it is that I want YOU to do:

In the years after the initial exodus of Cubans in 1959/60 to North America, there was a radio advertisement for a furniture store in south Florida that catered to the Cuban community. The name of that store was *Furniture Warehouse*.

Their radio jingle in Spanish was hysterically funny to those who, at the time, weren't familiar with Spanish, because they didn't sing "furniture warehouse". They sang "*foor-nee-too-ree Wah-ree-aus*", because, pronouncing them (the English words) in the Spanish way, that's how it sounded.

Or, try the American expression "garage sale" pronounced as in Spanish: "Gah-rah-hey Sah-lay".

Americans and Canadians, try to picture in your mind the little dog that advertises for Taco Bell. "*Yo quiero Taco Bell*" means "I love Taco Bell". He's got a great accent for a dog, and his pronunciation is perfect.

Brits, you have many opportunities to hear native speakers from Spain simply because of European television news. Listen to the way the English is spoken by Spanish speakers and glean the accent and pronunciation from what you hear. Imitate the sounds of someone like Javier Solana and other Spaniards you might hear on the news.

If you want to try an interesting experiment for your ears, try watching Andalucia's great actor Antonio Banderas in "*The Mask of Zorro*" and Miami's incomparable Gloria Estefan in "*Music of the Heart*" and compare their accents in English. His is Spanish, hers Cuban. See if YOU can *hear* the differences. If you can hear the differences, then you can imitate them.

Placing the emPHAsis on the Right SyLLAble.

An additional word on pronunciation. All languages place emphasis on certain syllables as opposed to others. In Spanish, there are three possibilities:

Most Spanish words are pronounced with emphasis on the penultimate (next to the last) syllable. <u>Example</u>: *Cor<u>ta</u>do* (cut)

Words ending in a consonant generally place the emphasis on the last syllable. <u>Example</u>: *Peninsu<u>lar</u>* (peninsular).

Words not meeting one of those two RULES will have an " ´ " accent mark over the vowel in the syllable requiring emphasis. <u>Example</u>: *Pro<u>pó</u>sito.*

So, when you see them written, you will know now which syllable requires emphasis. When you hear them spoken, it should be pretty obvious which syllable is accented.

Nonetheless, in the Pronunciation Guides, we will still continue always to underline or italicize the accented syllable.

Las Letras del Alfabeto.

Now that you know how all the letters *sound* when spoken in a word, it's time to learn your ABC's.

Although we take it for granted that the alphabet is the alphabet, it isn't. In Spanish, the letters of the *alfabeto* ("ahl-fah-<u>beh</u>-toh") have different names. And, there are more of them.

This won't ever seem important to you until the first time you have to spell your name for someone.

So, we are going to review the Spanish alphabet on this page, giving you the names of the letters. Please take the time to learn the names of the letters. You'll be glad you did.

El Alfabeto

A	*a*	*ah*	N	*ene*	*en-nay*
B	*be*	*bay*	Ñ	*eñe*	*en-yay*
C	*ce*	*say*	O	*o*	*oh*
CH	*che*	*chay*	P	*pe*	*pay*
D	*de*	*day*	Q	*cu*	*koo*
E	*e*	*ey (as in "hey")*	R	*ere*	*ere*
F	*efe*	*ef-fay*	RR	*erre (rolled)*	*erre*
G	*ge*	*hey (back of throat)*	S	*ese*	*es-sey*
H	*hache*	*ah-chay*	T	*te*	*tay*
I	*i*	*ee (as in "key")*	U	*u*	*ooh*
J	*jota*	*hota (as in "hotel")*	V	*uve*	*ooh-vay*
K	*ka*	*kah*	W	*uve doble*	*ooh-vay do-blay*
L	*ele*	*el-lay*	X	*equis*	*eh-keese*
LL	*elle*	*ey-yay*	Y	*I griega*	*e gree-eg-a*
M	*eme*	*em-may*	Z	*zeta*	*say-tah*

Please note that "rr" is not a letter of the alfabeto, but it does represent a separate sound from "r". Also, "ll" and "ch" are no longer actual letters of the alfabeto, but they are still treated as such for the most part by many Spanish speakers, especially older speakers.

EXERCISE 3:

Practice saying and spelling your name and your address with the SPANISH spelling and pronunciation... for the time when you'll need to do it for real. Do this six times minimum.

EXERCISE 4:

Brits: Say "*Cafe Cortado*" 10 times without elongating the vowels.

Yanks: Say "*Muchas Gracias*" 10 times without drawling.

Aussies: Say "G'day, *Señor*". Now, can you say "day" like the rest of us?

Irish: Say "Top o' the *mañana* to ya, *Padre*".

NZ folks: Say "*Bvaaa*" without closing your lips.

Gibraltarians: Say "*Yanito*" or "*Llanito*", whichever you find easier.

My Heretical Rule No. 10.

Learn the letters of the alfabeto.

ONLY when you have learned to pronounce the __names__ of the letters of the alfabeto should you proceed beyond this chapter.

We want you to spend all the time you need to get comfortable with the sounds of Spanish as reflected above in this Chapter III. Unless and until you are completely comfortable with the sounds and their differences from English, you won't be ready to go too much farther in the text.

Practice with the new vocabulary below, as well as with vocabulary previously given. Then, practice with billboards, magazine advertising (even that written in English), until you feel totally comfortable with the Spanish sounds. Then, move on to Chapter IV.

Here's Some More "New" Vocabulary You May Recognize:

English	Spanish	Pronunciation Guide
Baseball	Béisbol	*Beys-bowl*
Clip	Clip	*Cleep*
Cocktail	Cóctel	*Coke-tail*
Hamburger	Hamburguesa	*Ahm-boor-gay-sah*
Hobby	Hobby	*Hobby ("h" pronounced)*
Knockout (boxing)	Nocaut	*No-cawt*
Leader	Lider	*Lee-dair*
Meeting	Mitin	*Mee-ting*
Microchip	Microchip	*Mee-kroh-cheep*
Pancake	Panqueque	*Pahn-kay-kay*
To Park	Parquear	*Pahr-kay-ahr*
Sandwich	Sandwich	*Sahn-weech*
Sexy	Sexy	*Sex-ee*
Stop	Stop	*Eh-stop*
Ticket	Ticket	*Tee-kate*
Yuppie	Yupi	*Yoo-pee*

Well, your vocabulary is up to 80 + words now. Have you learned anything new about the Spanish vocabulary apart from the differences in pronunciation? Every one of those 80 words is in use everyday as part of the ENGLISH language. So, I would hope that you have not learned anything new.

Does it get any easier? No, but it does get more difficult. Hang in there. You'll get where you're going.

Chapter IV.
The Wonderful World of Cognates.

Cognates are words that look pretty much the same, mean the same and sound almost the same in both languages. You've already seen some 80 cognates already. You just didn't <u>realize</u> they were cognates. That's all.

Most words with roots in Latin will have cognates in other languages. That's why Spanish, French, Italian, Portuguese, and Romanian (the Romance languages) are so often studied by English speakers. English has a great deal in common with these languages.

German has a great many cognates in Italian and English, and even Swedish is not unaffected by the language of the Romans.

The simplest way to begin to demonstrate for you how to enhance your discovery of cognates is to begin with prefixes, suffixes and word endings. In the subsequent chapters, we'll go to root words, as well. For now, we'll begin with the beginnings and endings of words.

NOTE: The reason for this exercise is to help you to have that little *light bulb* go on over your head and for *you* to recognize that <u>you really do know all or most of the words that follow in English; therefore, you already know them in Spanish, too. You just didn't know it.</u>

The principal thing to keep in mind is that, more often than not (though not always), English words that begin or end with the following prefixes and suffixes will have a very similar counterpart in Spanish.

The purpose of the following non-exhaustive lists is to demonstrate the point of the preceding statement and to begin to shed some light for you on how many words you really and truly ALREADY do know in Spanish.

In this chapter alone, you will "discover" Spanish vocabulary of more than 100 of these words that you already knew but didn't know you knew.

Pay particular attention to spelling differences and to the ACCENT differences, as well as what you now recognize as differences in the sounds of the letters, especially the vowels.

Strangely, once you're comfortable with the Spanish sounds, you won't see nearly as much difference between these cognate words in English and Spanish as you will your first time through them.

In this following section, we will show you 120 cognates, 10 each for 12 different prefixes and suffixes:

"DIS-".

Almost any word that begins with "DIS-" in English will often begin with "DES-" in Spanish or with the same "DIS-", as in English. "DIS" in English means to *undo* something or to *reverse* something, and it means the same thing in Spanish.

Some examples:

English	Spanish	Pronounced
to disarm	desarmar	dez-ahr-*mahr**
to discern	descernir	dez-sair-*neer*
disastrous	desastroso	dez-sahs-*troh*-soh
to discontinue	descontinuar	dez-kohn-teen-oo-*ahr*
discreet	discreto	dees-*krey*-toh
disobedience	desobediencia	dez-oh-bey-dee-*en*-see-ya
dispassionate	desapasionado	dez-ah-pah-see-oh-*nah*-dough
discontent	descontento	dez-kohn-*ten*-toh
disgust	disgusto	dees-*goos*-toh
dispense	dispensar	dees-pen-*sahr*

---

* When you see the letter "z" in the pronunciation guide, pronounce it <u>as if</u> it were "ss", as in the English word "dress".

Almost any cognate NOUN word that ends in "-TION" in English
will end with "-CION" in Spanish. In English, we pronounce "-*tion*"
as "*shun*"; in Spanish, we pronounce "-*cion*" as "*see-own*" Notice the
accent marks.

Some examples:

English	Spanish	Pronounced
anticipation	anticipación	ahn-tee-see-pah-see-*own*
demonstration	demostración	dey-moh-strah-see-*own*
discrimination	discriminación	dees-kree-mee-nah-see-*own*
hospitalization	hospitalización	ohs-pee-tahl-ee-sah-see-*own*
equalization	igualización	ee-gwahl-ee-sah-see-*own*
limitation	limitación	lee-mee-tah-see-*own*
fermentation	fermentación	fair-meyn-tah-see-*own*
manifestation	manifestación	mahn-ee-feys-tah-see-*own*
election	elección	ey-leck-see-*own*
selection	selección	sey-leck-see-*own*

<u>*"-LY"*</u>.

Almost any cognate adverb which ends in "-LY" in English will end with "-MENTE" in Spanish.

Some examples:

English	Spanish	Pronounced
rapidly	rapidamente	*rah*-pee-dah-men-tey
immediately	inmediatamente	en-med-ee-ah-tah-*men*-tey
dishonorably	deshonorablemente	dez-own-or-ah-bley-*men*-tey
diversely	diversamente	dee-vair-sah-*men*-tey
rarely	raramente	rah-rah-*men*-tey
accordingly	por consiguiente	pour kohn-see-ghee-*en*-tey

(Hey, there have to be exceptions, and there are; awake now, are we?)

English	Spanish	Pronounced
consistently	consistamente	kohn-sees-tah-*men*-tey
effectively	efectivamente	ey-feck-tee-vah-*men*-tey
fortunately	afortunadamente	ah-four-too-nah-da-*men*-tey
lucidly	lucidamente	loo-see-dah-*men*-tey

"-ANCE" or "-ENCE".

Almost any cognate noun which ends in "-ANCE" or "-ENCE" in English will end in "-ANCIA" or "-ENCIA" in Spanish.

Some examples:

English	Spanish	Pronounced
Brilliance	brillantez	bree-yan-_tess_

(another nominal exception, but still a cognate)

English	Spanish	Pronounced
governance	gobernancia	goh-bair-_nahn_-see-ya
exuberance	exuberancia	ex-oo-bair-_ahn_-see-ya
flatulence	flatulencia	flah-too-_len_-see-ya
abundance	abundancia	ah-boon-_dahn_-see-ya
resonance	resonancia	rez-oh-_nahn_-see-ya
protuberance	protuberancia	pro-too-bair-_ahn_-see-ya
obedience	obediencia	oh-bey-dee-_en_-see-ya
occurrence	ocurriencia	oh-coo-rree-_en_-see-ya
permanence	permanencia	pair-mahn-_en_-see-ya

Almost any cognate adjective or past participle which ends in "-ATED" will end in "ADO" (masculine) or "ADA" (feminine) in Spanish.

Some examples:

English	Spanish	Pronounced
llluminated	iluminado	ee-loo-mee-_nah_-dough
laminated	laminado	lah-mee-_nah_-dough
desecrated	desecrado	dey-sey-_crah_-dough
consecrated	consagrado	kohn-sah-_grah_-dough
designated	designado	dez-eeg-_nah_-dough
pontificated	pontificado	pohn-tee-fee-_kah_-dough
dominated	dominado	dough-mee-_nah_-dough
segregated	segregado	sey-grey-_gah_-dough
abbreviated	abreviado	ah-brey-vee-_ah_-dough
accelerated	acelerado	ah-sell-air-_ah_-dough

More on this particular form of suffix in a later chapter in which we learn about past participles.

Almost all cognate nouns which end in "-ISM" in English will be found with an ending of "-ISMO" in Spanish.

Some examples:

English	Spanish	Pronounced
materialism	materialismo	mah-tey-ree-ahl-*ees*-moh
generalism	generalismo	henh_g-air-ahl-*ees*-moh
communism	comunismo	koh-moo-*nees*-moh
socialism	socialismo	so-see-ahl-*ees*-moh
facism	facismo	fah-*sees*-moh
pacifism	pacifismo	pah-see-*fees*-moh
patriotism	patriotismo	pah-tree-oh-*tees*-moh
radicalism	radicalismo	rah-dee-kahl-*ees*-moh
nepotism	nepotismo	ney-poh-*tees*-moh
feudalism	feudalismo	fey-oo-dahl-*ees*-moh

Most cognate nouns ending in "-SY", "-THY", and "-CY" will be found in Spanish ending with the suffix "-SÍA".

Some examples:

English	Spanish	Pronounced
fantasy	fantasía	fahn-tah-*see*-ya
hypocracy	hypocracía	ee-poh-krah-*see*-ya
antipathy	antipatía	ahn-tee-pah-*tee*-yah
sympathy	simpatía	seem-pah-*tee*-ya

(English "th" is generally converted to just a "t" in Spanish)

English	Spanish	Pronounced
empathy	empatía	eym-pah-*tee*-ya
monogamy	monogamía	moh-noh-gah-*mee*-ya
monarchy	monarquía	moh-nahr-*kee*-ya

(hard "ch" and "k" in English are converted to "que" and "qui" in Spanish)

English	Spanish	Pronounced
biology	biología	bee-oh-loh-*hee*-ya
psychology	sicología	see-koh-loh-*hee*-ya

(the "psy" in English generally changes to "si" in Spanish)

English	Spanish	Pronounced
genealogy	genealogía	hey-ney-ah-loh-*hee*-ya

"PRE-".

Almost all cognate nouns and verbs which begin with "-PRE" in English will be found with a corresponding word in Spanish.

Some examples:

English	Spanish	Pronounced
prenatal	prenatal	prey-nah-*tahl*
prevent	prevenir	prey-veyn-*eer*
prehensile	prehensíl	prey-en-*seel*
predict	predecir	prey-dey-*seer*
prediction	predicción	prey-deek-see-*own*

("tion" in English is converted to "cion" in Spanish)

English	Spanish	Pronounced
premium	prémio	*prey*-mee-yo
preferred	preferído	prey-fair-*ee*-dough
precedent	precedente	prey-say-*den*-tey
prejudice	prejuicio	prey-*hwee*-see-yo
preparation	preparación	prey-pahr-ah-see-*own*

"ANTI-".

Almost all cognate nouns which begin with "-ANTI" in English will be found with a corresponding word in Spanish.

Some examples:

English	Spanish	Pronounced
antipathy	antipatía	ahn-tee-pah-_tee_-ya
antibiotic	antibiótico	ahn-tee-bee-_oh_-tee-koh
anticipation	anticipación	ahn-tee-see-pah-see-_own_
to anticipate	anticipar	ahn-tee-see-_pahr_
antiseptic	antiséptico	ahn-tee-_sep_-tee-koh
antique	antiguo	ahn-_tee_-gwoh
antisocial	antisociál	ahn-tee-soh-see-_ahl_
antidote	antídoto	ahn-_tee_-dough-toh
antiquated	anticuádo	ahn-tee-_kwah_-dough

Almost all cognate nouns and verbs which begin with "IN-" in English also begin with "IN-" in Spanish.

Some examples:

English	Spanish	Pronounced
incognito	incognito	een-cohg-*nee*-toh
indigestion	indigestión	een-dee-hes-tee-*own*
inability	inhabilidad	een-ah-bee-lee-*dahd*
inaccessible	inaccesible	een-ahk-sess-*ee*-bley
inactive	inactivo	een-ahk-*tee*-voh
inadequate	inadecuado	een-ah-dey-*kwah*-dough
inconsiderate	inconsiderado	een-kohn-see-dair-*ah*-dough
incontestable	incontestable	een-kohn-tess-*tah*-bley
inanimate	inanimado	een-ahn-ee-*mah*-dough
to incapacitate	incapacitar	een-kah-pah-see-*tahr*

"-ITE".

Almost all cognate nouns which end in "-ITE" in English will be found with an ending of "-ITA" or "ITO" in Spanish.

Some examples:

English	Spanish	Pronounced
stalagmite	stalagmita	stah-lahg-*mee*-tah
anthracite	anthracita	ahn-thrah-*see*-tah
plebiscite	plebiscito	pley-bee-*see*-toh
termite	termita	tair-*mee*-tah
dynamite	dinamita	dee-nah-*mee*-tah
infinite	infiníto	een-fee-*nee*-toh
malachite	malaquita	mahl-ah-*kee*-tah
parasite	parásito	pah-*rah*-see-toh
petite	petito	pey-*tee*-toh
requisite	requisito	rey-kee-*see*-toh

Most nouns and almost all verbs which end with "-ATE" in English will end in "-ATO" (nouns) or "-AR" (verbs).

Some examples:

English	Spanish	Pronounced
bicarbonate	bicarbonato	bee-kahr-boh-*nah*-toh
to duplicate	duplicar	doo-plee-*kahr*
to pollinate	polinizar	poh-lee-nee-*sahr*
to participate	participar	pahr-tee-see-*pahr*
to radiate	radiar	rah-dee-*ahr*
to speculate	especular	es-pey-koo-*lahr*
to stimulate	estimular	es-tee-moo-*lahr*
to liberate	liberar	lee-bair-*ahr*
to graduate	graduar	grah-doo-*ahr*
deviation	desviación	dez-vee-ah-see-*own*

What you may have noticed by now is the fact that most of the cognates you have seen so far are, in American terms, "50 cent words"; i.e., they are generally representative of a more sophisticated vocabulary than is used by just the everyday working man/woman in English speaking countries.

Interestingly, most of these "50 cent words" are not considered to be particularly highbrow in Spanish.

To sum up the issue of Prefixes and Suffixes, here's a quick summary of the most consistent comparisons between English and Spanish.

PREFIXES:

English	=	Spanish (w/ exceptions)
Anti-	=	Anti-
Ante-	=	Ante-
De-	=	Des-
Dis-	=	Dis-
Pre-	=	Pre-
Re-	=	Re-

SUFFIXES:

-ed	=	-ado
-ess	=	-iz, -esa
-hood, -ity	=	-idad
-ing	=	-ando, -iendo
-ly	=	-mente

(NOTE: The suffixes in Spanish of "-AR", "-ER", "-IR" form the infinitive ending of a verb and are equivalent to putting "to" in front of the verb in English. Most words you will see ending in "AR", "ER", "IR" will generally be the infinitive of a verb. The equivalent English suffix can be found, for example, in cognate words ending in "-ate". See above "-ated" endings and drop the "d" for some examples.)

These lists of words above are hardly exhaustive. There are many many other cognates, most of which are NOT "50 cent words" and some of which you already use regularly -- there are at least 25,000 of them to choose from. Beginning to get the idea?

English Words Which Begin With "S".

One other important thing to keep in mind when seeking out cognate words is the fact that very few cognate words in Spanish begin with the letter "S". Among cognates, most English words beginning with "S" will be found in Spanish to begin with the letter "E". So, for example, "stupendous" from English becomes "estupendo" in Spanish.

Let's look at some examples:

English	Spanish	Pronunciation Guide
Stupendous	Estupendo	Es-too-*pen*-dough
Scale	Escala	Es-*kah*-lah
To Scald	Escaldar	Es-kahl-*dahr*
To Scandalize	Escandalizar	Es-kahn-dahl-ee-*sar*
Scarlet	Escarlata	Es-kahr-*lah*-tah
Scepticism	Escepticismo	Es-sep-tee-*seez*-moh
Scholastic	Escolástico	Es-koh-*lahs*-tee-koh
Scorpion	Escorpión	Es-kohr-pee-*own*

Although the lists above contain more than 100 words, you may find that no more than 25% to 30% of them are words that you would ordinarily use on an everyday basis.

Even if that percentage you recognize and use were to be as low as 10%, against a universe of some 25,000 English language cognates, and if that percentage were to remain constant, you could still count on some 2,500 cognates to be in *your* personal vocabulary. That's 1/2 of the number of words in the *average* vocabulary of more than 80% of all native speakers of Spanish. In whatever case, it's substantial.

EXERCISE 5:
All of the English words in the list below have Spanish forms (cognates).

<u>Before going to the dictionary to look up the Spanish equivalent of the English words, make the effort to try to **GUESS** what the Spanish form of the word might be.</u>

When you have completed all of your <u>guesses</u>, THEN go to your dictionary to look up the Spanish equivalent.

If you come close, give yourself one "Attaboy". Worry more about how it sounds than how it's spelled. I can't "hear" your spelling errors when you're speaking.

<u>English</u>	<u>Your Guess in Spanish</u>	<u>Dictionary Equivalent</u>
frigid		
to confirm		
fritter		
frivolous		
corporation		
inconceivable		
practice		
concentrate		
bracelet		
pervert		
rifle		
prince		
princess		
royal		
airport		

English	Your Guess in Spanish	Dictionary Equivalent

to magnify
proportion
to pay
to clarify
garden
manipulate
fanatic
chocolate
chemical
penicillin
lavatory
hygiene
relax
tranquil
stomach
fillet
diagram
map
fetish
to caress
indigestion
inflammation
antiseptic
to copulate
to urinate
toilet
to procrastinate
bureaucracy
category
to circulate
circumstance
to estimate
and on and on and on...   25,000 words worth.

Now that <u>you know that you already know</u> so many words in Spanish, you shouldn't be quite so intimidated by the prospect of learning Spanish as your second language.

At this point, your NEW Spanish cognate vocabulary, newly <u>discovered</u> that is, is in excess of 200 words, most of which you will now remember for the rest of your life.

Not only that, because they're words you already know, you won't have to rack your brain to remember them when the need arises. *They're already there, in your brain, just waiting for the time when they are needed.*

EXERCISE 6:

Your job, from here on out (and for the rest of your life) is to identify all of those 25,000 cognates, one word at a time. So take your dictionary in hand and begin to identify as many cognates as you can. Just remember to read the definitions.

Not all words that look the same or sound the same actually mean the same, although most do. Please see Appendix III on page 333 for a list of 1000 useful cognates.

False Cognates.

There are false cognates, too. That is, there are words that look and sound the same but have different meanings in Spanish.

For example, the word "*decepción*" in Spanish means "disappointment". Looks pretty much the same, sounds pretty much the same as English "deception" but with a completely different meaning.

We devote an entire chapter to false cognates later in the book. Please see Chapter XXVI on page 305 on False Friends for a list of FALSE cognates.

Still, 99% of the look-alike, sound-alike words <u>are</u> cognates with almost the same spelling, almost the same pronunciation and with pretty much the same meanings.

For this ongoing exercise, get yourself a couple of wire wound notebooks, steno notebooks or daily log books and record all meaningful cognates as you learn them in one of those notebooks (all non-cognate words will go into the other notebook).

NOTE: Please, don't just write down cognates just for the sake of writing them down. If you see a cognate, which, in English, is a word you aren't familiar with, you won't remember it. So, don't bother adding it to your personal list of cognates.

My Heretical Rule No. 11.

Your list of cognates should be one, which is meaningful to you with words that you are already familiar with in English, so that you will have no difficulties in remembering the words that are in it.

Chapter V.
The Secret to Remembering (and Learning).

<u>The Secret to Remembering.</u>

It is a proven fact that there are three types of learner:

1. The visual learner.
2. The auditory learner.
3. The active learner (who learns by doing).

There is another proven fact of learning that you probably have never heard, but it is valid nonetheless.

<u>If something is repeated SIX times, it will be indelibly imprinted on your memory forever.</u>

Let me repeat that:

If something is repeated SIX times, it will be indelibly imprinted on your memory forever.

If something is repeated SIX times, it will be indelibly imprinted on your memory forever.

If something is repeated SIX times, it will be indelibly imprinted on your memory forever.

If something is repeated SIX times, it will be indelibly imprinted on your memory forever.

Let me repeat one last time that, if something is repeated SIX times, it will be indelibly imprinted on your memory forever.

Even if you don't repeat it six times, seeing and hearing combined will give you far greater retention than either seeing or hearing alone. Seeing *and* hearing results in 3 to 4 times the retention of just hearing, and 2 to 3 times the learning and retention of only seeing the words.

So, practice talking to yourself, reading to yourself and even doing your exercises out loud.

Don't mutter under your breath. Speak up!

Write everything. Say everything. Repeat everything.

<u>Write newly learned words in a notebook regularly until the same word has been included in a list, used in conversation or both at least six times. Practice saying the words, preferably in a conversation, at least six times.</u>

No matter which type of learner you are, we've tried throughout this course to satisfy your needs for seeing, or hearing, or experiencing.

What we cannot help you with is the repetitions within your learning style. YOU must provide those repetitions.

My personal rule for myself with respect to maximizing my ability to remember and learn new words that I find otherwise difficult to remember has resulted in:

<u>My Heretical Rule No. 12.</u>

Use each newly learned, non-cognate word in conversation at least six times within the first 24 to 48 hours after learning it.

It works. You will never have to think about it again. You will know what you need to know when you need to know, even if you don't know that you know. Know what I mean?

Spend some time right now in your dictionary (Spanish language side, of course). Just slide your finger down the columns, and, every time you spot a word that looks familiar or which you feel might be useful to you, check the definition.

If, in fact, you actually knew with reasonable accuracy what the word means, highlight it with a yellow or orange highlighter pen. In no time at all, you'll have a Technicolor dictionary.

This exercise will also serve as one of the six exposures to the words that you need for recall. Next time you visit these words, you should make a list of them with their definitions and include them your notebook.

Chapter VI.
Introduction to Hispanic Culture.

As I said earlier, people in those countries where Spanish is spoken, as in most other non-English speaking countries, really appreciate any effort you make to communicate with them in their native language.

Further, you need to understand that culturally, manners, customs, and morés may be different from what you are accustomed to as a native speaker of English living in an English speaking country.

What we want to accomplish in this lesson is to introduce you to a few expressions which will demonstrate some good manners and courtesy and which will engender those feelings of empathy on the part of the native of the Spanish speaking country you are going to visit (or live in).

Then, we want to give you an example of the differences in culture that you might expect to experience.

First, the simple stuff, most of which you will have heard on television or in the movies.

Greetings By The Time of Day.

From daylight until 1:00 p.m. (in Spain, could even be 2:00 p.m.) it is "morning", and the typical greeting is:

"Buenos Dias."

This is said as:

"Bway-nos Dee-yahs"

Although the word "*día*" ends in "*a*", it is a masculine noun, so any adjective which stands *before* it is written and pronounced with a masculine ending, i.e., "*o*".

So, *"Buenos Dias."*

This greeting is common universally and should be used generously as a morning's greeting, even in the hotel with the hotel staff, shop clerks, the policeman on the street or, in short, just about everybody.

After about 1:00 or 2:00 p.m. (depends on when the shops close for siesta), it becomes afternoon, and the typical greeting is:

"Buenas Tardes."

This is said as:

"Bway-nahs Tar-deys"

In Spanish speaking cultures, it remains afternoon at least until dark, and, depending upon the season, could actually extend to well after 8:00 or 9:00 in the evening (especially in southern Spain). Again, this is a universally used expression with just about anyone for any reason during the afternoon hours.

Once it gets dark, it becomes nighttime, and the greeting is:

"Buenas Noches."

This is said as:

"Bway-nahs No-chays"

You may wish to preface any of these greetings with *"hola"* (pronounced "O-lah") when meeting someone or greeting in some setting other than just being polite. It means "hello" or "hi".

Forms of Address: Familiar or Formal.

We've already pointed out that Spanish speaking cultures have a tendency to be more formal than English speaking ones, and now might be a good time to introduce the basic form of address in both familiar and formal terms.

For example, a Spanish speaker of your acquaintance comes to your breakfast table in the hotel dining room, and you might rise and say, *"Hola, José* (pronounced "Hoh-<u>say</u>"), *buenos dias. ¿Como estás?* (Pronounced as: "<u>Coh</u>-moh Es-<u>tahs</u>" which means "how are you?")".

Which brings us to a bit of cultural trivia of great importance.

In Spanish, as in French, German, Italian and many other languages, there is a linguistic distinction between those we know well and those we don't. With those we know well, depending on the culture, we are able to apply the *familiar* forms of address, and, with those we don't know well, our elders and those in positions of authority, we must apply the *polite* or *formal* form of address.

In the preceding example, *"Hola, José, buenos días. ¿Como estas?"* implied that the person addressed (*José*) was someone known to us very well or someone much younger than ourselves or, even perhaps a child. This is the *<u>familiar</u>* form of address. You are safe using this in most parts of Spain most of the time.

In Latin America, using the familiar form of address is much more restricted and much less common among foreigners. There, you will find the use of the formal or polite form much more prevalent and much more expected, and you may expect that some people will be offended if you use the familiar form of address (occasionally happens in Spain, too) without leave to do so.

So, you need to know the *polite* form of address, as well.

The formal or polite form of "how are you" is *"¿Como está Usted?"* (Pronounced as: "<u>Coh</u>-moh Es-<u>tah</u> Ooh-<u>stead</u>")

The originally formal, now polite, form of the word "YOU" is *"USTED"*. This is a truncated version of *"vuestra merced"* ("your grace") that was originally used in the Spanish court and replaced the original Latin formal, *"VOS"*.

The familiar form of the word "YOU" is *"TÚ"*.

In the first example above, the *"TÚ"* was implied by the verb ending in "s" ("*estás*").

By dropping the "s" ("*está*"), the formal or polite form of address would have been implied.

However, in order to be safe, it is always better to use the word *"USTED"*, <u>unless</u> the person you're conversing with specifically asks you to *"Habla de tú"* ("<u>Ah</u>-blah Day Too") or to use the *"tuteo"* ("too-<u>tay</u>-oh"), in which case you can use *'tú"*.

So, to refresh this little bit of culture, we have:

"Good morning, how are you?"
"Buenos Días, ¿como está Usted?"
"Good afternoon, how are you?"
"Buenas Tardes, ¿como está Usted?"
"Good evening (or good night), how are you?"
"Buenas Noches, ¿como está Usted?"

You will find that, familiar or polite, <u>in the plural</u> you are <u>always</u> safe using the <u>polite</u> form, *"USTEDES"* (pronounced "Ooh-<u>stead</u>-eys").

In Latin America, it is quite common to hear small children and even the family pets referred to by *"Ustedes"*, instead of the more traditionally taught *"Vosotros"*.

In this course, we will not be using or teaching the *"Vosotros"* form (i.e., 2nd person, plural, familiar), even though there are some who believe that it is not possible to speak to a Spaniard without the use of the *"vosotros"* form.

In Spain, for example, the *"vosotros"* (familiar) form is gradually being replaced by the *"ustedes"* (polite) form in the plural (as has already happened in most of Latin America), AND the *"usted"* (polite) form is rapidly giving way (in Spain) to the *"tú"* (familiar) form in the singular.

By using the polite *"ustedes"* form in the plural in all cases, plural forms will always be the same and always both the formal and the familiar will use the same form in all geographical regions. That reduces the effort required to learn the verb conjugations (and the amount you have to remember) by $16^{2/3}$%.

Saying "Please" and "Thank You" and Cultural Good Manners.

On this issue, much has been written, little resolved.

It is said that, in English speaking cultures, we tend to use "please" and "thank you" a great deal, even to the point of overkill. These comments have usually been made by native speakers of Spanish, not native speakers of English.

My personal opinion is that, in English, these three words are not often enough used these days.

Comparison of Cultures: Going Out to Dinner.

In Spanish speaking cultures, however, "please" and "thank you" aren't used as much as in English (in my opinion, they probably aren't used often enough in Spanish, at least not in Spain).

Let me give you an example of some cultural differences by way of comparative scenarios:

Scenario 1:   Dinner in New York.

Let's suppose we're in a restaurant in New York. After we've been seated by the maitre'd, the waiter comes promptly to the table and asks if we would like something to eat, and we say:

"Yes, please. Would you bring us a menu?"

The waiter returns with the menu, we order our meal by saying, *"I would like..."*, etc. Often, the waiter will return to take our orders while we are still perusing the menu. This always gives *me* the feeling of being rushed.

Let's say that we have ordered a bottle of wine to accompany our dinner. The waiters ask, *"Would you like me to pour?"* We respond by saying, *"Yes, please."* He pours. We say, *"thank you"*.

If it's a really upscale restaurant, the *sommelier* will bring the bottle, have an extra glass for tasting, and expect the one who ordered the wine to give it a taste test before pouring.

A little while later, as we are about to begin on our first plate, we discover that our salad fork is dirty.

We quietly attract the waiter's attention, and, when he comes to our table, we say almost in a whisper so as not to attract the attention of other diners, *"This fork is dirty. Could I have a clean one, please?"* The waiter brings a clean fork, and we respond by saying *"thank you"* yet again.

When we have finished our salad or other first plate and the waiter sees that: a.) The plate is empty, and b.) We have stopped eating from it,

78

he will come to the table and ask if we are finished with that plate. If we indicate that we are finished, he then will retire the plate/s. Again, the waiter receives a "*thank you*" for his troubles.

Often, the entrée will arrive even before we have finished with our first plate.

When the entrée arrives, we find that our fish is not properly prepared, and we tell the waiter. He, in turn, immediately informs us that he will take it off of our bill (check) and asks if we would like a new portion of fish prepared to our liking or if we would prefer to order something else. We decide on a reorder of the fish, and everything goes smoothly, as we would expect it to go.

When we finish the entrée, the water comes almost immediately and, as he's retiring the plates, asks if we would like coffee or dessert. We, of course, say, "*Yes, thank you. I'd love a coffee, and could you bring me the cheese cake, please.*"

When we have finished the cheesecake and our coffee, the waiter passes by the table and asks if there will be anything else. Getting a "*no, thank you*" as a response, he's back in five minutes with the bill (check) discreetly tucked into a little wallet, which he places unobtrusively on the table.

We pay the check, leaving a 15% to 20% gratuity (the norm in New York), leave the folder with the gratuity for the waiter on the table and, on leaving the restaurant, we thank the waiter (and the maitre'd) for an excellent meal.

Arriving outside at the valet attendant's desk, we hand over the receipt for the car, pay the $15.00 to $25.00 parking fee, hand the car parker a $1.00 bill or two as a gratuity, along with another "thank you", and we leave.

Scenario 2:   *La Cena en España.*

Now, let's change the setting to Spain, not Madrid (too touristy), but let's say Barcelona or Sevilla or Málaga.

We go into the restaurant and the host tells us to seat ourselves wherever we would like.

After a time, one of three or four waiters who are standing around talking about last night's football game between *Barza* (the football team for Barcelona) and *Real Madrid* (the real football team in Madrid and meaning Royal Madrid - there is another football team, but we won't mention it), breaks free, comes to our table and says:

"Hola, buenas tardes. ¿Algo para beber?" ("Hi, good afternoon. Would you like something to drink?")

We say *"Si, por favor"* ("Yes, please"), and we give him our order for *"dos botellas de Evian y dos traguitos de gin tónico"* ("two bottles of Evian - *naíve* spelled backwards - and two gin tonics).

He's back shortly with two glasses that smell of fish, two small bottles of Evian and two glasses which contain our gin tonics.

Because we look "foreign", a couple of ice cubes have been placed in the glasses, along with a slice of lemon (this is a holdover from the days when the water didn't smell so fine as Evian). The glasses smell like fish, because they have been washed and rinsed in the same sinks where fishy serving dishes have also been washed. So, the lemon helps.

As we drink our water and sip our gin tonics, we wait for the waiter to return with the menus.

After some time waiting, we finally call the waiter over and ask him for menus. *"La carta, por favor"*, *"carta"* meaning an '*a la carte*' menu, as we are accustomed to in English speaking countries. *"Menu"* in Spanish means a "fixed" meal at a fixed price, as we often find in English pubs posted on the slate by the entrance.

He returns with the menus and disappears again.

After about 20 to 30 minutes, if and when he finally sees that the menus are closed and lying on the table in front of us, he will come and ask if we have decided on something to eat. *"¿Qué le apetece?"* which means translates to "what makes itself appetizing to you?" but really means, "what flips your switch?"

We give him our order, saying *"yo quisiera..."* which means "I would like... " -- that's a use of subjunctive mood in English and in Spanish, by the way -- and the waiter goes away to deliver our order to the kitchen.

Before the meal comes, the waiter is back with the wine which was part of our order, pours a taste to be tried, and, upon approval (*"bueno"* because wine, *"vino,"* is masculine), he proceeds to fill the wine glass of everyone at the table. He doesn't ask, and no one says "thank you" for this service.

As we're on our first course, we discover a dirty fork.

In a normal voice as he passes within hearing distance of us, we say *"Oiga!?"* to attract his attention.

When he comes to our table, we say, *"me hace falta un tenedor. Este está sucio"*, meaning "I need another fork. This one's dirty".

He takes the fork, looks at it as though he doesn't really believe it could be dirty, disappears to the tableware cabinet, gets a cleaner fork and returns, placing the clean fork on the table next to our plate.

When we have finished the first plate and once our knives AND forks have been placed side-by-side across the diameter of the plate, the waiter will come and collect the plates and silverware -- but not before we have performed this simple ritual.

Upon trying the entree, we discover (as before) that the fish is not properly prepared. We again call the waiter using *"¡¿Oiga!?"* and explain the problem.   The waiter does not ask if we would like something else. Instead, he says he can take it back to the kitchen and have it cooked some more. We tell him we would like a *"solomillo"* or fillet steak (filet mignon) instead of the fish.

Had we asked for the fish again, we may well have gotten the <u>same</u> fish, recooked, and, as any chef will tell you, you can't recook fish. That's not to say that a Spanish waiter won't try to convince you that it's o.k. to recook fish or that it's a different fish. So, we order the steak instead.

Again, when the silverware is placed in the proper position on the plate, the waiter will return and retire the plates and silverware. He then returns and asks if we would like a dessert, *"un postre".* AFTER dessert, he will offer coffee (*café*) but certainly not before and not WITH the dessert.

After coffee, we are offered drinks, and, even if we choose not to have anything more to eat or drink, the waiter is likely to return with a complimentary chilled liqueur (*"un traguito"*) and some homemade biscuits ("cookies"), called *"galletas",* as a *"cortesía de la casa".*

After this complimentary liqueur and any other drinks we may or may not have, we will continue to sit and wait and wait and wait.

Finally, when we are unwilling to wait any longer or when we are finally ready to depart, we will call the waiter over and ask for *"la cuenta, por favor",* meaning the "bill ("check"), please".

The waiter returns with the bill, either by handing it to us or by dropping it on the table and walking away. On reviewing the bill, we discover that the fish is STILL on the tab, in addition to the fillet.

At this point, we have the option of spoiling an otherwise good meal by arguing about the issue of the fish on the bill or paying for it. It's even possible that, if we comment on it, the waiter would tell us that

HE tried our fish and thought that it was fine. I have seen it happen and in a 1st class restaurant, too.

Whether the fish is deducted from the bill or not, we will place cash in the little wallet sufficient to cover the cost of the meal plus a 3% to 5% gratuity or *"propina"*.

If in Barcelona, leaving a 5% gratuity is likely to cause the Catalán couple at the next table over to pick up half or more of the gratuity you leave for the waiter, handing it back to you and saying that "we don't want to spoil them". I've actually had this happen to me at an upscale Mexican restaurant in Barcelona.

As we rise to leave the restaurant, we finally offer a *"gracias por todo. Buenas noches"* ("thank you for everything" and "good night") to all of the staff for an excellent meal, well prepared and well served.

We find our car on the street and, perhaps, tip the old retiree who kept an eye on it for us € 2.00, thank him with an *"estupendo"* ("es-too-pen-dough") when he tells us our car is still as we left it, and we leave.

What's the Difference?

There are some substantial differences in these two scenarios, reflective of both customs and table manners and of the use of "please" and "thank you".

The Spanish version of the dinner is not atypical.

In Latin America, you will find it less structured than the Spanish version and closer to the American version of things. America's influence is obviously stronger in Latin America than in Europe.

In North America, good service is an art form; in Europe, one prays for good service.

Suffice it to say that the Spanish version is equally as formal as the New York version, but with more emphasis on ritual courtesies and the way of doing things than on saying "please" and "thank you".

The placing of the silverware diagonally across each plate as it's finished (even if you didn't use the knife) is an indication of good breeding and not to do it this way indicates that you are a bit of a barbarian.

Likewise, although it more often than not comes as a shock to Americans, the sequence is first the meal, then the dessert, THEN the coffee. Anyone who would have coffee with the dessert is, again, truly a barbarian.

Also, more Americanized establishments don't "give anything away". In Spain, the "*traguito*" and the "*galleta*" are customary and seen as a cost of doing business, and a small one at that.

Again, in those more Americanized environments, you'll find that the need to "turn over" the table is stronger, whereas in Spain you've actually rented your table for the evening and are free to enjoy it until closing time and beyond, if you wish.

As an Americana friend of mine recently remarked, "it can be a real culture shock to go to dinner at 9:00 p.m., begin eating at 10:00 p.m., and still be seated at the same table at 3:00 a.m. without anyone ever asking you to leave".

In more Americanized locales, gratuities are expected to be more generous, because the waiters "work for tips".

In Spain, and in most of Europe, waiters are paid a salary and share the tips equally. So, a good waiter makes the same tips as a bad waiter. Consequently, we see some reduction in the quality of service, except in the finest establishments. In fact, downright surly waiters in both France and Spain are not exceptional.

However, in addition to being able to call *"Oiga!?"* (which translates literally as "hear" in this imperative form and <u>should be interpreted as a polite *"hey, you"*</u>) in order to attract the waiter's attention, you do need to be able to say *"por favor"*, as well as *"gracias"* or *"muchas gracias"* or *"gracias por todo"*.

A tremendously good word to learn which will stand you in very good stead at any time and is valuable and meaningful to a person who "works for tips" is the word *"estupendo"*. A parking attendant is as likely to accept *"estupendo"* as a tip as a €2.00 coin and to do so almost as happily. With or without a tip, *"estupendo"* is very high praise and is like a breath of spring to people in the service business.

EXERCISE 7:

So, in this lesson, you learned the Spanish words and phrases listed below. What do they mean in English?

<u>Spanish</u>	<u>Pronunciation Guide</u>	<u>Meaning?</u>
Hola.	*Oh*-lah	
Buenos días.	*Bway*-nohs *Dee*-yahs	
Buenas tardes.	*Bway*-nahs *Tahr*-deys	
Buenas noches.	*Bway*-nahs *Noh*-chays	
Como estás?	*Koh*-moh Es-*tas*	
Como está Usted?	*Koh*-moh Es-*tah Oos*-ted	
Tú.	TooH	
Ustedes.	Oos-*teh*-dehs	
Algo para beber?	*Ahl*-goh *Pah*-rah Bey-*bare*	
Por favor	Pour Fah-*vohr*	
Dos botellas de...	Dohs Boh-*tay*-yahs Dey	
Evián	Eh-bvee-*ahn*	
La carta.	Lah *Kar*-tah	
Qué le apetece?	Kay Lay Ah-pey-*tey*-say	

Yo quisiera...	Yo Kee-see-*ehr*-ah	
Bueno	*Bway*-noh	
Vino	*Vee*-noh	
Oíga!?	*Oy*-gah	
Me hace falta...	May *Ah*-say *Fahl*-tah	
Un tenedor	Oon Ten-ey-*dohr*	
Éste está súcio.	*Es*-tey es-*tah soo*-see-oh	
Solomillo	Soh-loh-*mee*-yo	
El postre	El *Pohs*-tray	
Café	Kah-*fay*	
Traguito	Trah-*ghee*-toh	*Highball or Shooter*
Galleta	Gah-*yet*-ah	
La cuenta	Lah *Kwen*-tah	
Propina	Pro-*pee*-nah	
Gracias por todo	*Grah*-see-yahs Pour *Toh*-dough	
Muchas gracias	*Moo*-chahs *Grah*-see-yahs	
Estupendo	Es-too-*pen*-dough	
Euro	*Ey*-oo-roh	
La Cena	Lah *Say*-nah	
Cortesía de la casa	Kor-teh-*see*-ya De La *Cah*-sah.	

Are we having fun yet?

EXERCISE 8:

Write the vocabulary above in one of your notebooks. Pay attention to any accent marks. If it helps, write down the pronunciation, as well.

EXERCISE 9:

Read the words out loud several times. Practice the pronunciation. You must get comfortable with the sounds. Your jaw muscles will hurt for a while, especially if you get into an extended conversation with someone, because the muscles you need to form the sounds aren't the same ones you use in English – or at least they're not used in the same way.

EXERCISE 10.

Now, for your cultural exercise, list as many cultural differences as you can between the two scenarios. To what would *you* attribute those differences?

EXERCISE 11:

Here are more high frequency cognates for you to add to your word lists:

English	Spanish	Pronunciation	Meaning?
To Accept	aceptar	ah-sep-<u>tahr</u>	
Air	aire	<u>aye</u>-ray	
Basic	básico	<u>bah</u>-see-koh	
Center	centro	<u>sane</u>-troh	
Clear	claro	<u>klah</u>-roh	
Control	control	cone-<u>troll</u>	
Detail	detalle	day-<u>tah</u>-yey	
Double	doble	<u>dough</u>-blay	
Equal	igual	ee-<u>gwall</u>	
Error	error	air-<u>rroar</u>	
Family	familia	fah-<u>mee</u>-lee-yah	
Favor	favor	fah-<u>voar</u>	
To Dispute	disputar	dees-poo-<u>tahr</u>	
Dislexic	disléxico	dees-<u>lex</u>-ee-koh	
To Educate	educar	ed-oo-<u>kahr</u>	
Divine	divino	dee-<u>vee</u>-noh	
To Domesticate	domesticar	doh-mess-tee-<u>kahr</u>	
To Elevate	elevar	ell-ey-<u>vahr</u>	
To Establish	establecer	ess-tah-bley-<u>sair</u>	
To Divert	divertir	dee-vair-<u>teer</u>	

Habitual	habitual	ah-bee-too-<u>awl</u>
To Formulate	formular	for-moo-<u>lahr</u>
Fabulous	fabuloso	fah-boo-<u>loh</u>-sew
Floral	floral	flow-<u>rahl</u>
Inclusion	inclusion	een-kloo-see-<u>own</u>
To Insist	insistir	een-sees-<u>teer</u>
Hedonism	hedonismo	ey-dough-<u>nees</u>-moh
To Imitate	imitar	ee-mee-<u>tahr</u>

English	Spanish	Pronunciation	Meaning?
Immensity	inmensidad	een-men-see-<u>dahd</u>	
Infested	infestado	een-fehs-<u>tah</u>-dough	
Inspection	inspección	een-speck-see-<u>own</u>	
To Interpret	interpretar	een-tare-prey-<u>tahr</u>	
To Laminate	laminar	lah-mee-<u>nahr</u>	
Legality	legalidad	ley-gahl-ee-<u>dahd</u>	
Machiavellian	maquiavélico	mah-kee-ah-<u>vehl</u>-ee-koh	
Magic	mágico	<u>mah</u>-hee-koh	
To Obstruct	obstruir	obe-stroo-<u>eer</u>	
Nontoxic	atóxico	ah-<u>toax</u>-ee-koh	
Navigable	navegable	nah-vey-<u>gah</u>-bley	
Menstrual	menstrual	mens-troo-<u>ahl</u>	
Morals *(n, pl)*	moral *(sing, fem)*	mow-<u>rahl</u>	
Offend	offender	oh-fen-<u>dair</u>	
Overabundant	superabundante	soo-pair-ah-boon-<u>dahn</u>-tey	
Overestimate	sobreestimar	sew-brey-es-tee-<u>mahr</u>	
Panoramic	panorámico	pahn-oh-<u>rahm</u>-ee-koh	
Pirate	pirata	pee-<u>rah</u>-tah	
Pronounceable	pronunciable	pro-noon-see-<u>ah</u>-bley	
To Provoke	provocar	pro-voh-<u>kahr</u>	
Racial	racial	rah-see-<u>ahl</u>	
Rechargeable	recargable	rey-kahr-<u>gah</u>-bley	
Senile	senil	say-<u>neel</u>	
Skeptical	escéptico	ess-<u>kep</u>-tee-koh	
Toxic	tóxico	<u>toax</u>-ee-koh	
To zigzag	zigzaguear	zeeg-zah-gay-<u>ahr</u>	

Chapter VII.
Introduction to the Dynamic Dozen.
The Verbs "Ser" and "Estar"

At the beginning of this book, I told you that you would only absolutely have to learn TWELVE verbs in only one tense. In this chapter, we'll look exclusively at the first two of those verbs:

Ser (this is the infinitive form) means "to be" in a permanent sense.

Estar (this is the infinitive form) means "to be" in a temporary or transitory sense.

We are going to learn to <u>conjugate</u> these two verbs in this lesson. Perhaps it would help to define "conjugate".

"Conjugation" simply means that a different form of the verb is used depending upon whom or what is the subject of the sentence in each tense (i.e., present, past or future).

For example, in English, one says "I go", "you go", "he goes", "she goes", "we go", "you go", and "they go". In this present tense conjugation of the verb "to go" ("to go" is the infinitive of the verb) in English, we have two forms of the verb in use, i.e., "go" and "goes".

The important thing that we want to accomplish now is to clearly distinguish between "*Ser*" and "*Estar*" and how they are used (since they both mean "to be"), and this chapter will be devoted exclusively to that issue.

For your purposes, _"Ser"_ pertains to _characteristics, features and descriptions_ of people and things that are _permanent_ in nature. It has other uses, but we aren't concerned with those here. You use "_Ser_" as your "to be" verb to describe things that are permanent and/or intrinsic.

"_Ser_" as used in the sense of the PRESENT is conjugated as follows:

Spanish	_Pronounced_	_Means_
Soy	_soy (as in beans)_	_I am_
Eres	_air-eys_	_You are (familiar)_
_Es_	_Es_	_You are (formal)/ He/She/It is_
Somos	_soh-mos_	_We are_
Son	_sown_	_You are (all forms)/They are_

The endings of verbs are what make them function. Without the proper ending, the verb doesn't truly reflect the person to whom it applies. Unlike English, where our verb form has to agree WITH the noun or pronoun as to person and number, in Spanish, the verb alone determines the person and number. Nouns and pronouns do not exclusively control the verb ending.

My Heretical Rule No 13.

To make it as simple as possible, when remembering verb endings, there are ONLY these possibilities:

"I"

"YOU" (singular familiar)

"HE"/"SHE"/"IT"/"YOU" (singular polite)

"WE"

"THEM"/"YOU" (plural, familiar/polite)

Now, also please take note of the fact that *the verb itself stands alone.* That is, <u>there is no subject pronoun in front of it,</u> as in English. That is to say that "*soy*" means "I am", and it stands alone, i.e., does not require the pronoun "*yo*" which is understood from the form of the verb.

Generally, Spanish verbs <u>don't require subject pronouns</u>, because the person referred to is <u>denoted by the form of the verb itself</u>, as we saw above.

However, there are subject pronouns in Spanish. They are:

Person	Spanish	Sounds like	Means
1st Singular	*Yo*	*Yo (as in yo yo)*	*I*
2nd Singular	*Tú*	*Too*	*You (familiar)*
3rd Singular	*Él*	*Ell*	*He*
3rd Singular	*Ella*	*Ey-yah*	*She*
3rd Singular	*Usted ("Ud.")*	*Ooh-stead*	*You (formal)*
1st Plural	*Nosotros*	*No-sew-trosse*	*We*
2nd Plural	*Ustedes ("Uds.")*	*Ooh-stead-ace*	*You (plural)*
3rd Plural	*Ellos*	*Ey-yose*	*They (masculine)*
3rd Plural	*Ellas*	*Ey-yas*	*They (feminine)*

These have been grouped together to show their relationship to the verb endings.

You will see that all three 3rd person singular forms use the same verb ending, and the 2nd and 3rd person plural use the same verb endings. Therefore, there really are ONLY 5 verb endings you ever even need to learn.

There is no *subject* pronoun for "IT".

My Heretical Rule No. 14.

In Spanish, these pronouns are not generally used with the verb. But, for clarity, you can either use them all the time or only when in doubt or only when it will make what you're saying more clear. More on this subject later. For now, you should learn the pronouns with the verb endings.

"*Estar*" as used in the PRESENT sense of the word is conjugated as follows:

Spanish	Pronunciation Guide	Means
Estoy	Es-_toy_	I am
Estás	Es-_tahs_	You are (familiar)
Está	Es-_tah_	You are (formal)
Está	Es-_tah_	He/She/It is
Estamos	Es-_tah_-mos	We are
Están	Es-_tahn_	You are (all forms)
Están	Es-_tahn_	They are

Now, you can see the two verbs compared and with their pronouns:

SER*	ESTAR*
Yo soy	Yo estoy
Tú eres	Tú estás
Él es	Él está
Ella es	Ella está
Usted es	Usted está
Nosotros somos	Nosotros estamos
Ustedes son	Ustedes están
Ellos son	Ellos están
Ellas son	Ellas están

Now that we know what they look like, sound like and mean, let's look at how these two very important verbs are used, in order to more clearly distinguish between them.

"*Ser*", as we have said, deals with things which are permanent or intrinsic. It's also used to form the passive.

** Nine people are listed, but there are still only 5 (count 'em) verb endings.

Examples:

English	Spanish
I am (That's pretty permanent)	*Yo soy*
It is quiet here. (A permanent condition in this place)	*Es tranquilo aquí.*
The earth is brown. (Brown soil is brown soil)	*La tierra es marrón.*
I am short. (Unless I'm a child, I won't get any taller)	*Soy bajito.*
I am tall. (I'm tall or I'm not. Right?)	*Soy alto.*
The car is a Toyota. (Tomorrow it's a BMW?)	*El coche (Sp) es un Toyota.*
The car is a Toyota. (It will still be a Toyota tomorrow)	*El carro (L. A.) es un Toyota.*
The horse is big. (Will the big horse get smaller?)	*Él caballo es grande.*
You are pretty. (You are naturally and physically pretty)	*Tú eres bella.*
She is good looking. (She is good looking. Period.)	*Ella es guapa.*
He is handsome. (He's a handsome. It's in the genes.)	*Él es guapo.*
He is a drunk. (He's an habitual drunkard.)	*Él es borracho.*

Anything that is temporary or has to do with motion or physical position requires the use of the verb **"*Estar*"**. It's also used to form the progressive.

Examples:

English	Spanish
I am here. (Where will I be later?)	*Estoy aquí.*
Ít is quiet here. (Later it will be noisy.)	*Está tranquilo aquí.*
It's brown now (Chameleon's DO change colors?)	*Está marrón.*
I am tired. (Later, I'll be rested.)	*Estoy cansado.*
I am confused. (I hope this is only temporary.)	*Estoy confundido.*
The car is parked. (Later, I will drive it away.)	*El coche (Sp) está aparcado.*
The car is parked. (I had to drive it to get it here.)	*El auto (Lat Am) está aparcado.*
The horse is running. (It won't run forever, will it?)	*El caballo está corriendo.*
She looks really nice. (She's dressed now. Later, swim togs.)	*Ella está (de) guapa.*
He looks handsome. (He's even wearing a necktie.)	*Está guapo hoy.*
He is drunk. (He'll have a hangover later.)	*Está borracho.*

I call your attention to the last example in each list.

<u>It is really important for you to understand this distinction between permanent and transitory.</u>

If we say that the man *"es borracho"*, we mean he **IS** a drunk, that it's part of his character, that he is, in fact, most probably an alcoholic.

On the other hand, if we say that the man *"está borracho"*, we mean he is drunk **RIGHT NOW**, but we don't imply that he is drunk all the time or that he is an alcoholic.

Let's take the distinction one step further and say *"él es borracho; no está borracho"*; that is, "he *is* a drunk, but he's not drunk *right now*".

The same could apply, for example, to the word "ugly".

A truly and permanently ugly person or thing is an ugly person or thing, no matter what, and we would use the *"Ser"* form of "to be". That is, we would say *"es feo"* or *"es fea"*, depending on whether we're referring to a masculine person or thing or a feminine person or thing.

As Sir Winston Churchill once responded to Lady Nancy Astor when she accused him of being drunk, "yes, Lady Astor, I am drunk. And, you are ugly. But, tomorrow, I shall be sober".

Translating this to Spanish, one would apply *"ser"* to Lady Astor, and, in this instance, *"estar"* to Sir Winston. That is: *"Sí, Señora Astor, (yo) estoy borracho. Y, Usted es fea. Mañana, (yo) estaré* sóbrio."*

Forming the Progressive.

<u>Another use of *"Estar"* is to form the progressive.</u>

---

* Proper use of the future tense of "estar" mandates "estaré".   However, the distinction between "ser" and "estar" is clearly made.

An example of the progressive would be "I am writing (now)" or "*estoy escribiendo*". Right now, this use of the verb isn't important to you, but it will be a little later in this course. This is a very important use of the verb *"Estar"*.

EXERCISE 12:

For now, thinking back to your list of cognates, form a sentence using as many of the cognates as you can NOW remember in a sentence with the appropriate form of "to be", depending on the characteristic of the cognate and using the appropriate pronoun, if applicable, for each person, i.e., I, you, he, she, it, we, they.

For example:

"I am incognito."   *"Estoy incognito"*.

Why *"estar"*? Because *"incognito"* implies some sort of disguise which one would infer would not be a permanent part of one's make-up. If it were permanent, it wouldn't be a disguise, would it? Instead, it would be "me".

For example:

"It's me." (Properly, "It is I".)   *"Soy yo"*.

Why *"ser"*? Because being myself (i.e., "being '*me*' ") is a pretty permanent condition, is it not?

Mark each practice sentence that you construct as to whether the condition is permanent or transitory.

Do at least 10 for practice. Be sure to use only words you already know how to pronounce.

I'll give you the first one.

1.   He is a communist. *Él es comunista.*   *Undoubtedly for life.*
2.
3.
4.
5.
6.
7.
8.
9.
10.
11.

Remember that the form of the sentence with these two verbs is the same as it is in English. That is, they take the same form as "to be", "is", "are" as in English. The difference is that there are two forms of "to be", "is", and "are", unlike in English.

When you have completed that exercise, check the examples below. Then, move on to the next lesson.

EXAMPLES:

1. She is drunk.   *Ella está borracha.*
2. The princess looks nice.   *La princesa está de guapa.*
3. Philosophy is academic.   *La Filosofía es académica.*
4. Penicillin is medicine.   *La Penicilina es medicina.*
5. Penicillin is a strong antibiotic.   *La Pencilina es un antibiótico fuerte.*
6. It's a very cold day.   *El día está muy frío.*
7. The prime minister is relaxed.   *El primer ministro está relajado.*
8. That guy is a parasite.   *Ese tipo es parásito.*
9. Today he's a fanatic about Abba.   *Hoy está fanático de Abba.*
10. Bureaucracy is not positive.   *La burocrácia no es positiva.*

Here are some more high frequency cognates for your list:

English	Spanish	Pronunciation
Action	acción	ack-see-<u>own</u>
To Affect	afectar	ah-feck-<u>tahr</u>
To Appear	aparecer	ah-pair-ey-<u>sair</u>
Basis	base	<u>bah</u>-say
Case	caso	<u>kah</u>-sew
Cause	causa	<u>kow</u>-sah
Central	central	sen-<u>trahl</u>
Character	carácter	kah-<u>rahk</u>-tair
Class	clase	<u>klah</u>-say
To Combine	combinar	kohm-bee-<u>nahr</u>
Common	común	koh-<u>moon</u>
Condition	condición	kohn-dee-see-<u>own</u>
To Contain	contener	kohn-tey-<u>nair</u>
To Contribute	contribuir	kohn-tree-boo-<u>eer</u>
To Cooperate	cooperar	koh-oh-pair-<u>ahr</u>
Copy	copia	<u>koh</u>-pee-ya
To Create	crear	kray-<u>ahr</u>
Day	día	<u>dee</u>-ya
To Decide	decidir	dey-see-<u>deer</u>
To Depend	depender	dey-pen-<u>deer</u>
To Descend	descender	dey-sen-<u>dair</u>
To Describe	describir	deys-cree-<u>beer</u>
Difference	diferencia	dee-fair-<u>ehn</u>-see-ah
Difficult	difícil	dee-<u>fee</u>-seel
Direct	directo	dee-<u>reck</u>-toh
Infection	infección	een-feck-see-<u>own</u>
Ecstasy	éxstasis	<u>ecks</u>-stah-sees
Atrocity	atrocidad	ah-troh-see-<u>dahd</u>
Sexy	sexy	<u>sex</u>-ee
Cemetery	cementario	sey-men-<u>tahr</u>-ee-oh
Origin	origen	oh-<u>ree</u>-hen
Solution	solución	sew-loo-see-<u>own</u>
Structure	estructura	ey-strook-<u>too</u>-rah
Altitude	altitud	ahl-tee-<u>tood</u>

Smog	esmog	ey-<u>smog</u>
Contact	contacto	cone-<u>tack</u>-toh
Symbol	símbolo	<u>seem</u>-boh-low
Absorbent	absorbente	ahb-sore-<u>ben</u>-tey
Celsius	Célsio	<u>sell</u>-see-oh
Duration	duración	doo-rah-see-<u>own</u>
Universal	universal	oo-nee-ver-<u>sahl</u>

Chapter VIII.
How to Form the Present Tense.

In this chapter, we're going to explore how to form the present tense.

To accomplish this, we're going to give you a template that, if you learn it, will enable you to conjugate almost any Spanish verb in the present tense, *even if you've never seen the verb before.*

My Heretical Rule No. 15.

If you learn nothing more about verbs than what we tell in this chapter, you should learn this. It will be the most important <u>verb</u> information of all. It gives you the secret to using ANY verb in Spanish with ease.

Please learn this template. You <u>will</u> be glad you did.

Even if it is your choice to learn the conjugations in present tense of only the Dynamic Dozen, it won't hurt you to be familiar with the templates.

First, it will be a help in remembering how to conjugate the Dynamic Dozen, because, in a sense, it summarizes the conjugations for all of them.

Secondly, one of the things we DO know is that, once you begin conversing comfortably, you'll start to show an interest in properly conjugating verbs, at least in the present tense.

Verb Endings.

Most verbs in Spanish are regular (or only very slightly irregular), and ALL verbs in Spanish end in either "AR", "ER", or "IR" in the infinitive.

These two letter suffixes are the equivalent of the English "to" as in "to do".

To conjugate ANY verb, you can use the templates below. It may not make you "exactly" right on irregular verbs, but <u>you'll be so close that no one will notice</u>.

All that is necessary is to drop the "-ar", "-er", or "-ir" ending and replace it with the ending for the appropriate person.

So, let's take a look at the first of the templates on the next page.

"-AR" Verbs:

The formation of the Present Tense for ALL regular verbs ending in "-AR" is as follows (pronoun attached for clarity):

Spanish Pronoun	Verb Stem	Ending		Person	English Pronoun
Infinitive	XXXXX-	AR		Infinitive (To)	(none)

Singular

Yo	XXXXX-	O		1st	(I)
Tú	XXXXX-	AS	*(Fam.)*	2nd	(YOU)
Usted	XXXXX-	A	*(Pol.)*	2nd	(YOU)
Él/Ella	XXXXX-	A		3rd	(HE/SHE)

Plural

Nosotros	XXXXX-	AMOS	1st	(WE)
Ustedes	XXXXX-	AN *(Pol/Fam)*	2nd	(YOU)
Ellos/Ellas	XXXXX-	AN	3rd	(THEY)

Go the next page to review "-er" verbs.

"-ER" Verbs:

The formation of the Present Tense of ALL regular verbs ending in "-ER" is as follows (pronoun attached for clarity):

Spanish Pronoun	Verb Stem	Ending		Person	English Pronoun
Infinitive	XXXXX-	ER		infinitive (To)	(none)

Singular

Yo	XXXXX-	O		1st	(I)
Tú	XXXXX-	ES	*(Fam.)*	2nd	(YOU)
Usted	XXXXX-	E	*(Pol.)*	2nd	(YOU)
Él/Ella	XXXXX-	E		3rd	(HE/SHE)

Plural

Nosotros	XXXXX-	EMOS		1st	(WE)
Ustedes	XXXXX-	EN	*(Pol/Fam)*	2nd	(YOU)
Ellos/Ellas	XXXXX-	EN		3rd	(THEY)

Go to the next page to review "-ir" verbs.

"-IR" Verbs:

The formation of the Present Tense of ALL regular verbs ending in "-IR" is as follows (pronoun attached for clarity):

Spanish Pronoun	Verb Stem	Ending		Person	English Pronoun
Infinitive	XXXXX-	IR		Infinitive (To)	(none)

Singular

Yo	XXXXX-	O		1st	(I)
Tú	XXXXX-	ES	*(Fam.)*	2nd	(YOU)
Usted	XXXXX-	E	*(Pol.)*	2nd	(YOU)
Él/Ella	XXXXX-	E		3rd	(HE/SHE)

Plural

Nosotros	XXXXX-	IMOS	1st	(WE)
Ustedes	XXXXX-	EN *(Pol/Fam)*	2nd	(YOU)
Ellos/Ellas	XXXXX-	EN	3rd	(THEY)

The principal difference between "-AR" verbs and "-ER"/"-IR" verbs is that:

The *letter "A"* figures in all of the endings for the "-AR" verbs, (except for first person (I) which is almost always an "-O" ending and "-AMOS" in first person plural), and

The *letter "E"* figures in almost all the endings for the "-ER"/"-IR" verbs, (except 1st first person singular which is almost always an "-O" ending and first person plural).

The principal difference between "-ER" verbs and "-IR" verbs is that:

In the first person plural, "-ER" verbs reflect "-EMOS", and

In the first person plural, *"-IR"* verbs reflect *"-IMOS"*.

Otherwise they are essentially the same.

Not all verbs are regular. Many are irregular, such as *"SER"* and *"ESTAR"* and do not follow the format laid out above. For example, the first person singular in each of those verbs ends in *"OY"*, not *"O"*.

My Heretical Rule No. 16.

If you apply this template to any unfamiliar verb, Spanish speakers are so in tune with foreigners speaking Spanish and having difficulties in mastering verb conjugations, they'll usually figure out what you're trying to say and, perhaps, even offer you the correct form, if you haven't already fallen over it.

So, if you can get your mind around the three templates and realize that "a" figures in the endings of "-ar" verbs and "e" figures in the endings of "-er" and "-ir" verbs, you will have no problem using any verb -- ever.

---

*

My Heretical Rule No. 17.

As a Last Resort and at any time when you are in doubt about the correct endings of any verb you're not familiar with, just use the infinitive form of the verb by itself and use the appropriate pronoun to clarify the "who".

---

* Note: One thing to remember when you are speaking with people. If you don't recognize the verb (and it could even be one that you know), don't be afraid to ask for the person you're speaking with to tell you the infinitive of the verb. Just ask, "Cuál es el infinitivo de ese verbo?" ("kwal ehs el een-fee-nee-*tee*-voh de *es*-sey *bvehr*-boh?"). With that information in hand, you can go to your trusty dictionary to determine the meaning. That accomplished, you should be able to conjugate the verb reasonably well, using your templates as a guide.

For example, "*YO ESTAR CANSADO*" makes very clear that YOU are the one who is <u>tired</u>, even though your use of the verb is not grammatically correct. Everyone will know what and who you mean.

This is the easiest way to use any verb with which you are unfamiliar, even though it is the most grammatically incorrect.

What's important is that *it works*, and it *takes the pressure off of you* to remember the precise conjugation of the verb.

<u>And, remember: Mistakes are allowed.</u>

I'd much rather see you trying to talk and making mistakes than not making mistakes because you're not trying to talk.

EXERCISE 13:

Although we have not yet shown you the other ten verbs that we want you to learn, they are listed below. Based on the templates above, attempt to conjugate each of these ten verbs in the present tense. Don't worry if you're wrong. You'll be close, and you'll get the correct forms shortly.

1. "Ir"   Irregular verb – it conjugates **as if** the verb infinitive were "VAR".
                    "*Ir*" Pronounced "ear"

2. "Tener"   Slightly irregular in first person, "g" before the "o".
                    "*Tener*" Pronounced "teh-nair"

3. "Soler"   Irregular verb – it conjugates **as if** the infinitive were "Sueler".
                    "*Soler*" Pronounced "sew-lair"

4. "Saber"   Irregular in first person – "*Sé*", instead of the obvious "sabo".
                    "*Saber*" Pronounced "sah-bair"

5. "Hacer"   Irregular in first person – "g" before "o".
              "*Hacer*" Pronounced "ah-sair"

6. "Acabar"   Totally regular.
              "*Acabar*" Pronounced "Ah-kah-bar

7. "Decir"   Irregular in first person - "g" before "o".
              "*Decir*" Pronounced "day-seer"

8. "Dar"   Irregular in first person – "y" after the "o"
              "*Dar*" Pronounced "dahr"

9. "Poder"   Irregular verb – conjugates **as if** infinitive were
              "Pueder".
              "*Poder*" Pronounced "poh-dair"

10. "Haber"   Irregular verb – "*he*" in 1st person, rest **as if** infinitive
              were "Her".
              "*Haber*" Pronounced "Ah-bair"

We're going to cover these ten verbs in the following chapters, so be sure to come back to check your conjugations against the actual ones.

Additional High Frequency Cognate Vocabulary for You to Add to Your Word Lists:

English	Spanish	Pronunciation
Form	forma	*for*-mah
General	general	heh-neh-*rahl*
Group	grupo	*groo*-poh
Idea	idea	ee-*dey*-ah
Important	importante	eem-pour-*tan*-tey
List	lista	*lees*-tah
To obtain	obtener	ob-ten-*nair*
To occupy	ocupar	oh-koo-*pahr*

To operate	operar	oh-pair-*ahr*
To pass	pasar	pah-*sahr*
Pause	pausa	*pow*-sa
Perfect	perfecto	pair-*feck*-toh
To permit	permitir	pair-mee-*teer*
Reason	razón	rah-*sown*
Secret	secreto	sey-*kreh*-toh
Symbol	símbolo	*seem*-boh-low
System	sistema	sees-*tey*-mah
Total	total	toh-*tall*
United	unido	oo-*nee*-dough
Use	uso	*oo*-sew
Bike	bici	*bee*-see
Fax	fax	*phahx*
Math	mates	*mah*-teyss
Stereo	estéreo	ehs-*tair*-ey-oh
Bow wow	guau guau	gwow gwow
Click	click	cleek
Ding dong	din don	ding dong
Pronunciation	pronunciación	proh-noon-see-ah-see-*own*
Equivalent	equivalente	eh-kee-vah-*lehn*-tey
Abbreviation	abreviatura	ah-brey-vee-ah-*too*-rah
Ironic	irónico	ee-*roh*-nee-koh
Privacy	privacidad	pree-vah-see-*dad*
Avant-garde	vanguardia	vahn-*gwahr*-dee-yah
Unity	unidad	oo-nee-*dahd*
Pleasure	placer	plah-*sair*
Mascarade	mascarada	mahs-kah-*rah*-dah
District	distrito	dis-*tree*-toh
Urban	urbano	oor-*bah*-noh
Crime	crimen	*kree*-men
Restaurant	restaurante	rehs-tow-*rahn*-tey
Delicious	delicioso	dey-lee-see-*oh*-sew
Bottle	botella	boh-*tey*-yah
Protection	protección	proh-teck-see-*own*

Chapter IX.
More Dynamic Dozen: The Verb "Ir"

The verb "*ir*" means "to go", as in "I go", "he goes", "she goes", etc.

As in English, it is also used to say, "*I am going to...*", as in "*I am going to take a bath*". That's what makes it a critical verb, because it can also create a *sense* of the future without your needing to know the future tense, as in English, and it is also useful in its basic sense of "to go".

So, let's see how "*ir*" is conjugated:

Pronoun	Spanish	Sounds Like	Means
(Yo)	voy	bvoy	I go, I am going
(Tú)	vas	bvahs	you go, (familiar), you are going (sing)
(Él)	va	bvah	he goes, he is going
(Ella)	va	bvah	she goes, she is going
(Usted)	va	bvah	you (polite) go, you are going
(Nosotros)	vamos	bvah-mos	we go, we are going
(Ustedes)	van	bvahn	you (formal) go, you are going (plural)
(Ellos)	van	bvahn	they (masculine) go, they are going
(Ellas)	van	bvahn	they (feminine) go, they are going

If you are going to use this verb in the traditional sense of "going" somewhere or to do something, i.e., before a following verb, then <u>you must use the preposition "*a*"</u> (pronounced "ah") after the verb form of "*ir*", i.e., "*ir a...*". This is equivalent to placing the "to" before the following verb in English.

Notice that the verb, "*IR*", is irregular only in 1st person singular, i.e., "*voy*" instead of the expected "*vo*", and it conjugates as if it were an "ar" verb.

<u>See the examples below and on the following page:</u>

English	Spanish	Sounds like
I am going to the store.	Voy *a* la tienda.	Voy ah lah tee-enda
I am going to take a bath.	Voy *a* banarme.	Voy ah ban-yar-may
I am going shopping.	Voy *a* compras.	Voy ah comb-prahs
I am going next year.	Voy el año que viene.	Voy el an-yo kay vee-enny
(Lit. the year that comes)		
I (am) go(ing) fast.	Voy rápido.	Voy rah-pi-do
I am going to the bathroom.	Voy *al* baño.	Voy ahl bahn-yoh

And, that, as they say, is all there is to it. Now, write these short sentences in your notebooks together with their translations. Then, read them aloud several times to help seat them in your memory.

One of the prime examples of this "swallowing" of letters that makes me laugh every time I hear it is the expression *"no es nada"* ("it's nothing" and is pronounced as "no es nah-dah") erupting from the lips of a not-too-well educated Andalusian Spanish speaker as *"no e' na'"* (but, pronounced as one word, "no-ey-nah"). *That* is a well-eaten phrase.

Past & Present Participles of *"IR"*.

Note that this is not a normal verb in the sense of its past and present participles. The past participle is *"IDO"* ("gone") and the present participle is *"YENDO"* ("going"). Past and present participles will manifest their significance for you shortly.

One issue with this verb, which bears repeating, has to do with the preposition "*a*":

If the verb is not used alone, as in "*voy*" ("I'm going") or "*vamos*" ("we are going"), and is followed by a destination or an activity or destination expressed by a following verb, then this preposition must be used.

For example, "I am going to the store" is rendered "*voy a la tienda*". That preposition "*a*" means "to". Likewise, "I am going to read a book" is translated as "*voy a leer un libro*". Again, this preposition is required.

Words Often Used With "IR".

Dónde.
Dónde means "where". Pronounced "*doan*-day".

You would use it in this form to say, "Where is it?" i.e., "*¿Dónde está?*" or "Where am I?" "*¿Dónde estoy?*"

A Dónde.
Literally, these words mean "to where". Only "*a dónde*" can be used where motion is involved. Pronounced "ah *doan*-day".

If you want to say, "Where am I going?" then you are really saying, "to where am I going?" Therefore, you must put the preposition "*a*" in front of "*dónde*", and it would appear as "*¿A dónde voy?*" or "Where are you going?", "*¿A dónde vas?*"

Por Dónde.
This one means "through", "where", or "which". Used in a question, it means "through where" or, more accurately, "which way". Pronounced as "pour *doan*-day".

Asking for directions, you might say something to the effect of "which way do I go to get to Barcelona?" which would translate to "*¿por dónde voy a llegar a Barcelona?*"

Ahí, Allí, and Allá.
All of these mean: "There". They are pronounced as "ah-*ee*", "ah-*yee*", and "ah-*yah*", respectively.

"*Ahí*" implies closest distance. "It is just there", or "*está ahí*". Or, for example, in exclamation, "there it is (right there)!", "¡*ahí está!*" Or, "*por ahí*", "right over there".

"*Allí*" implies that something or someplace is farther away than "*ahí*". It can more easily be inferred through the idiom, "*Por allí*", which means "through that place". If it's out of sight, it's probably "*allí*".

"*Allá*" really means "over there (somewhere)" and implies even greater distance and/or an indefinite, vague location. This is even more clearly to be inferred from the idiom, "*más allá*", which means "farther".

Of the three, "*allí*" is the most common. You will always be safe using this one, except with respect to the idiom, "*más allá*" which can only be expressed as "*más allá*".

Aquí and *Acá.*
Both mean "here". In many parts of Latin America, "*acá*" is used instead of "*aquí*", while in Spain, "*acá*" is seldom used in favor of "*aquí*". "*Aca*" really means more "over here". They are pronounced as "Ah-<u>kee</u>" and "Ah-<u>kah</u>". When calling his dog, the Spaniard says, "*Perro, ven aquí*", (ven_g ah-<u>kee</u>). The Latin American says, "*Perro, ven acá*", (ven_g ah-<u>kah</u>).

"Acá" and "Allá".
As used in Spain, both of these indicate a vagueness not necessarily present in their use in Latin America. Also, "*allá*" is more often used for great distances in Latin America than in Spain.

The other important point with these two words is that, unlike "*ahí*", "*allí*" and "*aquí*", "*acá*" and "*allá*" can both take an intesifier, e.g., "*más allá*" for "beyond" or "*lo más allá possible*" for "as far over there as possible".

Frente, En Frente De, En Frente A, Hacer Frente.
"*(la) frente*" means "forehead". It does *not*, by itself, mean "front". Pronounced as "*fren*-tay".

"*En frente de*", however, means "in front of", in the sense that "he is (standing) in front of me".

"*En frente a*" means "facing" or "in front of (opposite)", as in the building across the street from your bank is "*en frente a*" or "facing" your bank.

"*Hacer frente*" means "to face", as in "that house faces my house" or "they faced each other in debate".

Fachada.
When you mean the front of something, such as the face of a building or the front of a house, one uses "*façade*" in English or "*fachada*" in Spanish (fah-*cha*-dah)

Delante, Delante De.
"*Delante*" means "before" or "in front". "*Delante de*" means "in front of" in the sense of "he is (in line) in front of me". It's definitely a 'position' word, not a 'presence' word. Pronounced as "day-*lahn*-tay".

Delantera.
"*(la) delantera*" means the "front" or "forepart" of something, as in "the front of the car". Pronounced as "day-lahn-*tay*-rah".

Atrás, Detrás.
"*Atrás*" means "back", "behind" or "backwards". For example, "it's on the back of the seat", "*está en la parte atrás del asiento*". Pronounced as "ah-*trass*" and "day-*trass*".

"*Detrás*" and "*detrás de*" mean "behind" something. "It's behind the sofa" would be, for example, "*está detrás del sofa*".

"*Por detrás*" means "from the rear" or "from behind", as in "the car came up from behind", i.e., "*se acercaba el coche por detrás*".

Hacía atrás.
This means backwards in the sense of "the car was moving backwards" or "in reverse", e.g., "*el carro estaba moviendo hacía atrás*". Pronounced "ah-<u>see</u>-ah ah-<u>trass</u>".

NOTE:
A good illustration of these can be found in the English terms "front seat", "back seat", "headlights" and "taillights". "Front seat" is "asiento delantero", "back seat" is "asiento trasero". "Headlights" are "faroles" and "taillights" are "faroles traseros".

Recto.
This word means "straight" or "straight ahead", as in "go straight here", i.e., "*vaya recto aquí*". Pronounced as "*reck*-toe".

A La Derecha.
"*Derecha*" means "right". "*A la derecha*" means " to the right", as in "go right here", i.e., "*vaya a la derecha aquí*". Pronounced as "ah lah day-*ray*-chah".

A La Izquierda.
"*Izquierda*" means "left". "*A la izquierda*" means "to the left", opposite to "*a la derecha*" above. Pronounced as "ah lah ees-kee-*air*-dah".

Ante and Antes.
These two are often confused. Don't confuse them. Pronounced as "*ahn*-tay" and "*ahn*-taise". "*Ante*" means "in the presence of…" which is a physical position or "faced with…" while "*antes*" means 'before' in the sense of time.

So, for example, I was before the altar, "*estaba ante del altar*". "*Antes*" would be used in the sense of "I got there before he did", "*he llegado antes que él*".

That's why.

"*Por eso*" means "therefore", but it is very commonly used to express "that's why".

Although you may be tempted to say "*por qué*" ("why"), just remember that, if you want to express "that's why", "*por qué*" cannot be used. Instead, use "*por eso*", e.g., that's why I didn't go", "*por eso no fui*". It is pronounced as "pour <u>es</u>-sew".

The Verb *"ir"* Contrasted With the Verb *"venir"*.

"*ir*" , as you already know, means "to go", while "*venir*" ("Bvay-<u>neer</u>") means "to come".

In English, one might ask someone "would you like to 'come' with me". In Spanish, this construction is not possible. "Go" ("*ir*") in Spanish implies FROM somewhere to somewhere else, the focus being on point of departure. "come" ("*venir*") in Spanish implies TO a destination, the focus being on point of arrival.

So, you can "go" FROM your house, or someone else can "come" TO your house. It is not possible in Spanish to "come with me" FROM my house TO somewhere else, as it is in English.

Other Verbs of Motion.

Llegar.	To arrive	*"no ha llegado todavía"*. "he hasn't arrived yet" Pronounced: Yay-<u>gahr</u>
Salir	To leave.	*"ha salido ya"*. "he's already left". Pronounced: Sah-<u>leer</u>
Andar	To walk. To go about.	*"anda más despácio, por favor"*. "walk more slowly, please". Pronounced: Ahn-<u>dahr</u>
Caminar	To walk.	*"caminamos en los pasos de Díos"*. To follow a path. "we walk in the footsteps of God". Pronounced: Kah-mee-<u>nahr</u>
Saltar	To jump.	*"Saltan todas las ranas"*. "All the frogs are jumping". Pronounced: Sahl-<u>tahr</u>
Conducir	To drive.	*"ya tengo el carné(t) de conducir"*. "I already have a driving permit". Pronounced: Kohn-doo-<u>seer</u>
Volar	To fly.	*"el vuelo sale a las cuatro"*. "the flight leaves at four". Pronounced: Bvoh-<u>lahr</u>
Parar	To stop.	*"estoy parado por el semáfero"*. "I am stopped for the traffic signal". Pronounced: Pah-<u>rahr</u>
Embarcar(se)	To embark.	*"nos embarcamos a las tres horas"*. "we embark at three o'clock". Pronounced: Em-bar-<u>car</u>

Desembarcar(se) To disembark   *"me he desembarcado en Barcelona"*.
"I disembarked in Barcelona".
Pronounced: Des-em-bar-<u>car</u>

Mover(se)   To move.   *"el coche se mueve hacía mí"*.
"the car moves toward me".
Pronounced: Moh-<u>vair</u> (say)

Mudar(se)   To move (house) *"nos hemos mudado a casa nueva"*.
"we've moved to a new house".
Pronounced: Moo-<u>dahr</u> (say)

Resbalar(se)   To slide, slip. *"nos resbalamos en el hielo"*.
               To skid.   "we're sliding on the ice".
Pronounced: Rais-bahl-<u>ahr</u>

Resbalón (n.) A Skid   *"la marca de resbalón"*.
"the skid mark".
Pronounced: Rais-bahl-own

Patinar   To skate   *"patinamos en invierno"*.
"we skate in winter".
Pronounced: Pah-tee-<u>nahr</u>

Nadar   To swim   *"yo sé nadar"*.
"I know how to swim".
Pronounced: Nah-<u>dahr</u>

Correr   To run   *"corre, hijo, corre"*.
"run, son, run".
Pronounced: Co-<u>rrehr</u>

Tropezar   To trip   *"he tropezado por la piedra"*.
"I tripped on the rock".
Pronounced: Tro-pay-<u>sar</u>

Despedir(se)	To take leave	*"aún no me despide"*.
	To say good-bye	"she doesn't even tell me 'good-bye'".
		Pronounced: Des-pay-<u>deer</u> (say)

<u>NOTE:</u>

Departir   To TALK: Pronounced as "day-par-<u>teer</u>".
Although it may appear to be a cognate, "departir" <u>does not mean</u> "depart".
It is a synonym for "hablar" and means "to talk".

Chapter X.
"YO-ismo" The Verb "Tener"

Now, would seem a good time take a break from verb conjugations and to tackle the topic of "*yo-ismo*".

Spanish verbs, as you have seen, are very person specific.

That is, there can only be ONE form of the verb for "**I am**", "**I go**", "**I have**", etc.

Usually that form in the present tense ends in the letter "*o*" or "*oy*". English speakers have a tendency to <u>always</u> use the pronoun "*yo*" with the verbs, because we are so accustomed to expressing "**I**" in English in connection with and to clarify every verb we use.

In Spanish, using the pronoun "*yo*" all the time *sounds very egotistical* and, to some Spanish speakers, is downright *offensive*. It just sounds like <u>"me, me, me, look at me, me, me, I'm so special, me, me, me"</u>.

That's because if you want to say, "I'm going to the store", "*voy a la tienda*" is pretty specific. No one else can be meant by that form of the verb "*ir*" ("*voy*", "I go") except "I". To put the pronoun for "I", that is, "*yo*" in front of the verb form is redundant and, it *does* sound self-centered.

<u>The real use of the subject pronouns is for **emphasis**.</u>

For example, one might be disputing who is going to go the store and who isn't, so you might hear "**I am going to the store, and, implied, "you're not**" ("***YO** voy a la tienda, [y **TÚ** no]*"). If there were no emphasis required, you would simply hear "*voy a la tienda*".

Get it? The real point here is not to overuse the pronouns, especially the pronoun "yo". Try to let the verb form itself state the subject of the verb, unless you want to stress who is meant for emphasis or clarity.

In the case of "*Usted*", you can never go wrong using this pronoun with the verb for clarification and out of respect. Even Spanish speakers don't object to you talking about "them, them, them". They're just like the rest of us.

The Verb "*Tener*".

The verb "*tener*" means "to have" in the sense of possession.

As in English, "I have a book", "I have a cold", "I have a dog", "I have a new car", or "I have an idea". It also has a form which implies obligation, the same as English, i.e., "I have to..."

"*Tener*" is conjugated as follows:

Pronoun	Spanish	Sounds Like	English
(yo)	Tengo	Teyn -go	I have
(tú)	Tienes	Tee-en-neys	You (fam.) have
(Ud.)	Tiene	Tee-en-ney	You (pol.) have
(Él/Ella)	Tiene	Tee-en-ney	He/She/It has
(Nosotros)	Tenemos	Teh-neh-mos	We have
(Uds.)	Tienen	Tee-en-en	You have (plural)
(Ellos/Ellas)	Tienen	Tee-en-en	They have

Expressing Hunger & Thirst and Hot & Cold With "*Tener*".

"*Tener*" also has the unusual job of expressing hunger and thirst and the physical characteristics of being hot or cold.

Where in English one might say "I *am* hungry" or "I *am* thirsty", in Spanish, you would say "I *have* hunger" or "I *have* thirst", i.e., "*tengo hambre*" (hunger: sounds like "*teyn_g-go ahm*-bray") or "*tengo sed*" (thirst: sounds like "*teyn_g-go said*").

Likewise, "I am hot" translates as "I have hot", i.e., "*tengo calor*" (sounds like "*teyn_g-go* kah-*lohr*"), and "I am cold" translates as "I have cold", i.e., "*tengo frío*" (sounds like "*teyn_g-go free*-oh").

Sometimes this use is difficult to remember, but that's just because it's foreign to the way we are accustomed to saying it. That's why I said at the beginning that interpretation is more important than translation.

If you translate, you'll want to say something like "*estoy hambre*" when that's not what you mean, and (pay attention) you'll sound really dumb.

Just remember that the way you say "I am hungry... thirsty... hot... cold... " is "*tengo hambre... sed... calor... frío...*", et cetera.

This is how you say it. Forget how it translates. This is how you say it. This is what it means. Now, you've got it!

Expressing Obligation With "*Tener que*".

"*Tener*" also is used to express obligation in much the same way as in English, i.e., "to have to... (... do something). This is accomplished in Spanish by following the verb form for "*tener*" with the word "*que*" (pronounced "kay") before the next verb. Let's look at some examples on the next page:

English	Spanish	Sounds Like
I have to eat	*Tengo* que *comer*	<u>Teyn</u>g-go kay koh-<u>mair</u>
She has to study.	*Tiene* que *estudiar*	Tee-<u>en</u>-ny kay es-tew-dee-<u>ahr</u>
We have to go now.	*Tenemos* que *ir ahora.*	Teh-<u>neh</u>-mos kay ear ah-<u>ohr</u>-ah

There are other ways, of course, of expressing obligation, but this is the most common and the most similar to English.

Also, notice that, in the preceding three examples, we used two verbs that you haven't learned in any other form than the infinitive, i.e., "*comer*" ("to eat") and "*estudiar*" ("to study").

Expressing obligation using "*Tener*" works just like English. The "*que*" can mean "to" or "that" or "which", but, <u>*in this usage*</u>, it's more important to recognize that, <u>more than anything else, *the "que" implies obligation*</u>.

EXERCISE 14:

Mentally refer back to your list of cognates, you know the one you are building from your dictionary. Pick ten and write 30 sentences, 10 each using "*ir*", "*tener*", and "*tener que*".

<u>"*ir*"</u>	<u>"*tener*"</u>	<u>"*tener que*"</u>

1.
2.
3.
4.
5.
6.
7.
8.
9.
10.

EXERCISE 15:

Meanwhile, TALK. Talk all the time. Make up sentences using all the cognates you can remember in combination with the verbs that you have already learned. Don't think them. Say them. OUT LOUD. Do it as often as you can remember. Remember? O.K.

Special Project: Let's Go to the Movies

If you have a DVD player, or can beg, borrow or steal one, go out and rent yourself a couple of really good movies that you've been dying to see.

Most DVD's today are multi-lingual, so check the label to be sure that the ones you rent have Spanish, as well as English, options for both dialogue and subtitles.

Then, sit back and watch your movie, first in English with Spanish subtitles, so you know what's going on in the movie, what it's all about, and essentially what's being said at each stage of the movie.

Then watch the movie again in Spanish with the English subtitles. See how much you can understand. Frankly, you shouldn't expect to understand very much. Don't be frustrated if you can't understand it all.

Remember, the dialogue was written for an audience of native speakers of Spanish. Also, you don't have the opportunity to ask actors to speak more slowly or to repeat what was said. And, you don't yet have enough vocabulary.

Your goal here is simply to understand as much as possible of what is said and to attempt to follow the movie IN SPANISH enough that you know basically what is going on.

MORE THAN ANYTHING this exercise will give you pronunciation, teach you some vocabulary, impart some nominal grammar and teach you the rhythm of the language.

It's especially good listening practice. Listening and understanding is just as important as speaking. You have to train your ear to hear to the Spanish sounds. Repeat this exercise as often as you would like. The more you do, the better you will train your ear.

This project will be a lot more fun and instructive than just following some structured conversation on a language learning tape. I promise.

Chapter XI.
The Auxiliary Verb "Haber".

The auxiliary or helping verb "*haber*" means "to have" and is used with past participles of verbs to construct a compound past tense called the pluperfect. When I was a youth studying English, we called it the "past perfect" tense.

When you say, "I have eaten", you are using the auxiliary verb "to have" and the past participle of "to eat". In Spanish, that would come out as "*(Yo) he comido*" (sounds like "ey koh-<u>mee</u>-dough").

Like the other Spanish verbs you have learned, it is specific as to person and is conjugated as follows:

English	Spanish		Pronounced
I have...	(yo)	*he...*	ey
you have...	(tú)	*has...* (familiar)	ahss
you have...	(Usted)	*ha...* (formal)	ah
we have...	(nosotros)	*hemos...*	<u>ey</u>-mohs
you have... (plural)	(Ustedes)	*han...*	ahn
they have...	(Ellos)	*han...*	ahn

<u>You can use "*haber*" with the past participle of *ANY* verb to form a perfect past tense</u> (that is, for an action completed in the past).

Formation of Past Participles.

All Spanish verbs appear in your dictionary in and are referred to always in the infinitive form, which is with the preposition "to" attached. In Spanish, the ending of the verb does this.

All Spanish verbs end in either "-ar", "-er" or "-ir".

The verb endings, "-ar", "-er", and "-ir" are equivalent to "to" in English in forming the infinitive of a verb.

Imagine that, in English, all verbs had the preposition "to" attached as a prefix, so that we would have, for example, "_togo_", "_toeat_", "_tohide_", "_todream_", et cetera. This would be the equivalent of the "-ar", "-er", and "-ir" endings of verbs in Spanish.

Then, let's imagine that, to form the past participle of "_togo_", we drop the "ending" to establish the "stem" of the verb, i.e., drop "_to_" and we're left with "_go_". Then, to complete the creation of the past participle, we have to add "_ne_" to the stem. Result? "_Gone_", the past participle of the verb "_togo_".

Now, let's look at the Spanish formation of the past participle.

For example, look at the verb you learned in the last chapter, "_tener_". "_TEN_" is the stem of the verb, and the ending "_ER_" is the infinitive form or ending of the verb (the equivalent of "to" in English).

To form the tenses, one "drops" the infinitive ending of "-ar", "-er" or "-ir" from the verb, and what remains is called the "stem" of the verb.

So, in the case of "_tener_", dropping the infinitive ending from the verb, we drop "-er" and we are left with the stem "ten-".

To form the past participle of ANY verb, one adds "-ADO" to the stem of verbs ending in "-ar" and "-IDO" to verbs ending in either "-er" or "-ir".

Let's look at some examples.

Spanish Infinitive	Spanish Past Participle	Sounds Like	English Infinitive or Past Participle
Comer	comido	koh-<u>mee</u>-dough	to eat eaten
Ir	ido	<u>ee</u>-dough	to go gone
Hablar	hablado	ah-<u>blah</u>-dough	to talk talked
Mirar	mirado	mee-<u>rah</u>-dough	to look at looked at
Participar	participado	par-ti-see-<u>pah</u>-dough	to participate participated
Aprender	aprendido	ah-pren-<u>dee</u>-dough	to learn learned
Entender	entendido	en-ten-<u>dee</u>-dough	to understand understood
Cultivar	cultivado	cool-tee-<u>vah</u>-dough	to cultivate cultivated
Tomar	tomado	toe-<u>mah</u>-dough	to take taken
Distinguir	distinguido	dis-ting-<u>gee</u>-dough	to distinguish distinguished
Vivir	vivido	vee-<u>vee</u>-dough	to live lived

Conducir	conducido	con-doo-<u>see</u>-dough	to drive driven
Eliminar	eliminado	ey-lih-mee-<u>nah</u>-dough	to eliminate eliminated

This is an extremely important part of your learning, yet, surprisingly, it is one of the simplest to learn and understand. Nothing complicated.

<u>My Heretical Rule No.19.</u>

Just drop the "-ar", "-er", or "-ir" ending from any verb and add "-ado" to verbs which end in "-ar" and "-ido" to verbs ending in "-er" and "-ir" to form the past participle; join this past participle with the right form of "haber" to form the past tense.

Verb Ending		*Past Participle Ending*
"-ar"	=	*"-ado"*
"-er"	=	*"-ido"*
"-ir"	=	*"-ido"*

One added advantage of knowing how to do this is that you can also create adjectives from verbs the same way, since the past participle can be used as a predicate adjective. Wow! Double duty and no work.

EXERCISE 16:

Using your cognates, this becomes a really great exercise. Take as many of your cognate verbs as you can recall or imagine, at this point, and convert the infinitive form to a past participle.

1.

2.

3.

4.

5.

6.

7.

8.

9.

10.

11.
And, keep going.

EXERCISE 17:

Look up the infinitives of ANY verbs whose Spanish equivalents you wish to know (for any reason). Create past participles for those verbs as you did above. Look up the past participles you have created in your dictionary to see if they exist in the form in which you have created them.

1.

2.

3.

4.

5.

6.

7.

8.

9.

10.

Putting it all together.

As in English, the auxiliary verb precedes the past participle. Therefore, you have "I have eaten, I have gone, I have spoken, I have looked at..., I have participated, I have learned, I have understood, I have cultivated, and so on, in English, and you have, respectively,

Spanish	Pronounced	Meaning
he comido	ey koh-<u>mee</u>-dough	I have eaten
he ido	ey <u>ee</u>-dough	I have gone
he hablado	ey ah-<u>blah</u>-dough	I have spoken
he mirado	ey mee-<u>rah</u>-dough	I have looked at...
he participado	ey par-tee-see-<u>pah</u>-dough	I have participated
he aprendido	ey ah-pren-<u>dee</u>-dough	I have learned
he entendido	ey en-ten-<u>dee</u>-dough	I have understood
he cultivado	ey cool-tee-<u>vah</u>-dough	I have cultivated

My Heretical Rule No. 20.

This works for (almost) ALL Spanish verbs, and you only need to know "haber" to make it happen, so make sure you know the auxiliary verb "haber" and it's conjugation really really well.

Any time you want to express something in the past, you can use this form. It is more common in Spain than other forms of the past tense, and it will be understood in Latin America (although they tend more toward simple past tense, as in American English).

In Britain, for example, one might say, "he has taken the bus", while in the States one would be more likely to say "he took the bus". With this form using "haber" plus a past participle, we're learning to say, "He has taken the bus". This way is the EASIEST way to form the past tense of any verb.

Here's another list of useful high frequency cognates:

English	Spanish	Pronounced
To Enter	entrar	ehn-<u>trahr</u>
Exception	excepción	ecks-sep-cee-<u>own</u>
To exist	existir	eks-sees-<u>teer</u>
Familiar	familiar	fah-mee-lee-<u>ahr</u>
Famous	famoso	fah-<u>moh</u>-sew
Fine	fino	<u>fee</u>-noh
To Force	forzar	for-<u>sahr</u>
Form	forma	<u>for</u>-mah
Group	grupo	<u>groo</u>-poh
Hour	hora	<u>oh</u>-rah
Human	humano	oo-<u>mahn</u>-oh
Human being	ser humano	<u>sair</u> oo-<u>mah</u>-noh
Important	importante	eem-pour-<u>tan</u>-tey
Individual	individual	een-dee-vee-doo-<u>all</u>
Interest	interés	een-tair-<u>eys</u>
Moment	momento	moh-<u>men</u>-toh
Move	mover	moh-<u>vair</u>
Name	nombre	<u>nohm</u>-bray
New	Nuevo	<u>noowey</u>-voh
Number	número	<u>noo</u>-mair-oh
Obvious	obvio	<u>ohb</u>-vee-oh
Opportunity	oportunidad	oh-pour-toon-ee-<u>dahd</u>
Part	parte	<u>pahr</u>-tey
Person	persona	pair-<u>sewn</u>-ah
Piece	pieza	pee-<u>ey</u>-sah

Chapter XII.
The Special Auxiliary Verb "Soler".

The auxiliary verb *"soler"* helps in *expressing habitual activities* and things that were continuing in the past, much as an imperfect tense would.

It is really only used in the present tense for things that are habitual now and in the imperfect tense for things that were habitual in the past.

The two tenses in which this verb is normally used are:

Present

1.) suelo (sounds like "<u>sway</u>-loh),   I usually...
    sueles (sounds like "<u>sway</u>-leys")   you usually...
    suele (sounds like "<u>sway</u>-ley")   he/she/it/usted usually...
    solemos (sounds like "sew-<u>lay</u>-mohs")   we usually...
    suelen (sounds like "<u>sway</u>-len")   they/ustedes usually...

Imperfect

2.) solía (sounds like "sew-<u>lee</u>-ah").   I used to...
    solías (sounds like "sew-<u>lee</u>-us")   you used to...
    solía (sounds like "sew-<u>lee</u>-ah")   he/she/it/usted usted to...
    solíamos (sounds like "sew-<u>lee</u>-ah-mos") we used to...
    solían (sounds like "sew-<u>lee</u>-un")   they/ustedes used to...

In other words, there is the "I usually...", "you usually...", "he/she/it/you usually...", 'we usually...', and "they/you usually..." forms in the present, and "I/he/she/it used to...", et cetera, in the imperfect past.

"*Suele*" is for things that are customary or habitual in the present.

For example, we might say that, where we live "it usually rains every afternoon".

In Spanish, you would then say, "*Suele llover por la tarde*" (sounds like "<u>sway</u>-ley yoh-<u>vair</u> pour lah <u>tar</u>-dey").

"*Solía*" is for things that were customary or habitual in the past.

For example, we might say, "we used to go there every summer".

In Spanish, you would then say, "*Solíamos ir allí todos los verános*" (or "*cada veráno*") (sounds like "Sew-<u>lee</u>-ah-mos ear ah-<u>yee</u> <u>toe</u>-dose lohs vey-<u>rah</u>-nohs").

So, in the sense of what is usual or customary in the present or the past, we have:

<u>English</u>	<u>Spanish</u>
It usually rains most afternoons	Suele llover por la tarde "<u>Sway</u>-lay yo-<u>vair</u> pour lah <u>tar</u>-dey"
I usually go for a walk after dinner.	Suelo dar un paseo después de la cena. "<u>Sway</u>-loh dahr oon pah-<u>say</u>-oh des-<u>pwais</u> dey lah <u>say</u>-nah"
He used to read stories to me.	Solía leerme cuentos. "Sew-<u>lee</u>-uh lay-<u>air</u>-may <u>kwen</u>-tohs"

They generally study together.	Suelen estudiar juntos. "Sway-len Es-tew-dee-<u>ar</u> <u>Hoon</u>-tohs"
We used to have a dog.	Solíamos tener un perro. "Sew-<u>lee</u>-ah-mos teh-<u>nair</u> oon <u>pai</u>-rro"

Distinguishing the perfect past from the imperfect past.

Sometimes it's difficult for people to understand the distinction between the perfect past and the imperfect past, so I'm going to give you an example which I hope will clearly illustrate this distinction for you:

"When he arrived (perfect), I was (imperfect) still mowing the lawn."

The *arrival* was at a fixed point in time. A person doesn't continue to arrive over a period of time (unless, of course, he/she is extremely large). Normally, someone simply arrives *all-at-once*, as it were.

However, *cutting the grass* is not something that happens all-at-once. Rather, it is something that *takes some period of time*, unless one has an extremely small garden.

That which happens at a fixed point in time *in the past* is "perfect".

That which happens over a period of time *in the past* is "imperfect".

"Perfect" simply implies that an action was completed, while *"Imperfect"* implies that the action was continuing in the past and may or may not have been completed.

Use *"haber"* and a past participle to give yourself the effect of the "perfect", and use *"soler"* to give yourself the sense of the "imperfect" for things you "used to do".

Soler won't create an imperfect for everything, but for those things that were customary or habitual, it's the easy way out.

Using *"haber"* and *"soler"* couldn't be simpler, and these solutions save you the trouble of learning 6 other past tenses which you don't absolutely need in order to be able to COMMUNICATE.

Expressing Past, Present and Future WITHOUT 14 Different Verb Tenses.

Have you ever heard a non-native speaker of English say something like, *"yesterday, I go to bank"* or have you yourself ever said something like, *"tomorrow, I am going to the bank"*?

In both these cases, *some time other than the present has been expressed using a verb in the present tense.*

"I go to the bank" (or, *"I am going to the bank"*) is present tense. It is happening NOW.

Yet, we can qualify the present tense by the judicious use of words like yesterday, day before yesterday, tomorrow, day after tomorrow, et cetera.

We can even be indefinite by saying *"Sometimes, I go to the bank"*. Right?

It may not necessarily be perfect, but it is expressive. When someone says this, YOU know what is meant, YOU understand it. Heck! You even do it yourself.

You can do the same thing, so let's learn those words, which will help to make that possible.

Come on!

Do you want to be perfect in 20 years, or do you want to communicate NOW?

English	Spanish	Pronounced
Today	Hoy	Oy
Tomorrow	Mañana	Mahn-*yah*-nah
Day after tomorrow	Pasado mañana	Pah-*sah*-doh mahn-*yah*-nah
Yesterday	Ayer	Ah-*yair*
Day before yesterday	Anteayer	*ahn*-tay-ah-*yair*
Someday	Algún día	Al-*goon dee*-ah
This year	Este año	Es-tay *ahn*-yoh
Last year	El año pasado	L *ahn*-yo pa*sa*do
Next year	El año que viene	L *ahn*-yo kay vee-*en*-ny
This week	Esta semana	Es-tah say-*mah*-nah
Next week	La semana que viene	Lah say-*mah*-nah kay vee-*en*-ny
Last week	La semana pasada	Lah say-*mah*-nah pah-*sah*-dah
This morning	Esta mañana	Es-tah mahn-*yah*-nah
Yesterday Morning	Ayer por la Mañana	Ah-*yair* pour Lah mahn-*yah*-nah
Tomorrow morning	Mañana	Mahn-*yah*-nah

English	Spanish	Pronounced
In the morning	Por la mañana	pour lah mahn-_yah_-nah
This afternoon	Esta tarde	E_s_-tah _tar_-dey
Tomorrow afternoon	Mañana por la tarde	Mahn-_yah_-nah pour lah _tar_-dey
Yesterday afternoon	Ayer por la tarde	Ah-_yair_ pour lah _tar_-dey
Day before yesterday	Ante ayer	_Ahn_-tay ah-_yair_
Tonight	Esta noche	E_s_-tah _noh_-chay
Tomorrow night	Mañana por la noche	Mahn-_yah_-nah pour lah _noh_-chay
Last night	Anoche	ah-_noh_-chay
Night before last	Ante anoche	_Ahn_-tay Ah-_noh_-chay
Next Tuesday	el martes próximo	L _mar_-tays _prohks_-ee-moh
	El martes que viene	L _mar_-tays kay vee-_en_-ey
Last Tuesday	el martes pasado	L _mar_-tays Pah-_sah_-dough
Sunday	el Domingo	L dough-_ming_-go
Monday	el Lunes	L _loo_-nays
Tuesday	el martes	L _mar_-tays

144

English	Spanish	Pronounced
Wednesday	el miércoles	L mee-_air_-koh-layss
Thursday	el jueves	L _hweav_-ehs
Friday	el viernes	L vee-_air_-nays
Saturday	el sábado	L _sah_-bah-dough
For (or during)	Durante	Doo-_rahn_-tey
Ago (perfect)	Hace	A_h_-say *

* Yes, it's the same verb, "hacer", used in a different time expression.

English	Spanish	Pronounced
Ago (imperfect)	Hacía	Ah-_see_-yah
Sometime	Alguna vez	Ahl-_goon_-ah Vez
Whenever	Cuándo quiera	_Kwan_-dough Kee-_air_-ah
At any time	En cuálquier momento	En _Kwahl_-kee-air Moh-_men_-toe
Shortly or momentarily	Ahorita	Ah-oar-_ee_-tah
Before	Antes	_Ahn_-teys
After	Después	Dez-_pweys_
At the same time	A la misma vez	Ah Lah _Mees_-mah Veyz
When	Cuándo	_Kwan_-dough
Until	Hasta	_Ahs_-tah

English	Spanish	Pronounced
Wee hours	Madrugada	Mah-droo-_gah_-dah
Midnight	Medianoche	Meh-dee-ah-_noh_-chey
Noon	Mediodía	Meh-dee-oh-_dee_-ah
Then	Entonces	En-_tohn_-seys
Now	Ahora	Ah-_ohr_-ah
Soon	Pronto	_Proan_-toh
At once	En seguída	En Sey-_ghee_-dah
Immediately	Inmediatamente	En-med-ee-ah-tah-_men_-tey
Later	Más tarde	Mahs _Tahr_-dey
Whenever	Cuándoquiera	_Kwan_-dough-kee-yeh-rah
Nowadays	Hoy en día	Oy En _Dee_-yah

It is important that you learn the days of the week with the masculine article, because the article is always expressed with respect to the days of the week in Spanish. It's not "_domingo_", it's "_el domingo_". Days of the week are never capitalized either.

EXERCISE 18:

Interpret the following:

1. *El martes pasado he acabado la investigación.*

2. *Mañana voy al banco.*
    ("*al*" is a contraction of "*a*" and "*el*"; "*banco*" means "bank").*

3. *Anteanoche hemos estudiado juntos.* (together)

4. *El jueves que viene vamos a estudiar el español.*

5. *Cuándo yo era estudiante solíamos estudiar hasta las tres de la madrugada.*

6. *En el mes que viene vamos a comer en el restaurante mejicano 'Pancho Villa'.*

7. *Hace dos años hemos ido a la playa (beach) en Tarifa.*

8. *La pelicula (film) del cine continua durante cuatro horas.*

9. *Esta mañana tengo que ir al banco.*

10. *Van a llegar (arrive) en cuálquier momento.*

---

* Anytime that the preposition "a" ("to") precedes the definite article "el" ("the"), as above, they form a contraction "al", much like "do not" becomes "don't" in English. Remember that the preposition "a" always follows the verb "ir" when there is a destination or a following verb. Likewise, the joining of the the preposition "de" with the definite article "el" is contracted to "del".

147

Explanation of Exercise 18:

1. Last Tuesday, I finished the research (investigation).

2. Tomorrow, I go (am going) to the bank.

3. Night before last we studied together.

4. This Thursday we're going to study Spanish.

5. When I was a student, we used to study until three in the morning.

6. Next month we're going to eat in the Pancho Villa Mexican restaurant.

7. Two years ago, we went to the beach in Tarifa.

8. The movie lasted for four hours.

9. This morning I have to go to the bank.

10. They will arrive any moment.

EXERCISE 19:

Construct 10 sentences using cognates and the time expressions above.

EXERCISE 20:

Construct 10 sentences each using cognates and "*Ser*", "*Estar*", "*Tener*", "*Haber*", "*Ir*", and "*Soler*".

At this point, you have learned in excess of 150 NON-COGNATE Spanish words, plus an untold number of cognates. How big is your vocabulary now?

Chapter XIII.
Forming the Progressive.

In Chapter XI, <u>we learned how to derive the past participle</u> from the infinitive form of a verb -- any verb.

Remember? Drop the "*-ar*", "*-er*", "*-ir*" ending from the infinitive and add "*ado*" to "*-ar*" verb stems and "*ido*" to "*-er*" and "*-ir*" verb stems.

<u>The Progressive.</u>

In this chapter, <u>we want to learn how to create the present participle</u> that can then be <u>used with the verb "*estar*" to form the progressive tense.</u>

Before learning how to do that, let's define progressive, because you might not remember this one from grammar school, since it's not really a "tense" in the conventional sense.

Let's take the verb, "*escribir*" (meaning to write) for our example. If I want to say, "I write", I can use "*escribo*" and be correct. On the other hand, if I want to say, "I am writing", I can still use "*escribo*" and be correct.

So, why would I want to use "*estoy escribiendo*" to say, "I am writing", when I could just as easily use "*escribo*".

"*Escribo*" does mean, "I am writing". I could say to you, for example, "I am writing a letter to the club president today" and use of the form "*escribo*" would be correct. I AM writing a letter today, but I am NOT writing that letter at this very minute.

If I want to convey that I am actually in the process of doing that very thing right this moment, then I would want to use the progressive in the form "*estoy escribiendo*", i.e., "I am writing right this moment."

So, the Progressive tells us that the action contemplated by the verb is actually in the process of happening *right this moment*. More importantly we can actually use this approach to express the present tense for any verb in Spanish.

Happily, to accomplish this with any verb, <u>we don't have to learn any new verb conjugations</u>. We can use a verb we already know how to conjugate, i.e., "*estar*".

In the same sense that "*haber*" is the auxiliary or helping verb to be used with *past* participles, we find that "*estar*" is the auxiliary or helping verb to be used with *present* participles.

Creating the Present Participle.

How do we create the present participle for use with "*estar*"?

Again, we look at the verb, "*escribir*". The two letters final are what make it an infinitive, so we have to drop the last two letters in order to arrive at the stem of the verb, the same as we did in Chapter XI to create the past participle.

To that stem, we add <u>"ando"</u> for verbs ending in <u>"-ar"</u> and <u>"iendo"</u> for verbs ending in <u>"-er" *and* "-ir"</u>.

Well, gosh! That was difficult, wasn't it?

The present participle is formed in exactly the same way as the past participle, but the present participle has an extra letter or two and "sounds" more active (because it is).

<u>Some examples:</u>

Infinitive	English	Spanish	Pronounced
escribir	I am writing...	estoy escribiendo	Es-<u>toy</u> Es-cree-bee-<u>en</u>-dough
hablar	I am talking...	estoy hablando	Es-<u>toy</u> Ah-<u>blahn</u>-dough
caminar	I am walking...	estoy caminando	Es-<u>toy</u> Kah-mee-<u>nahn</u>-dough
pasar	I am passing...	estoy pasando	Es-<u>toy</u> pah-<u>sahn</u>-dough
votar	I am voting...	estoy votando	Es-<u>toy</u> voh-<u>tahn</u>-dough
recibir	I am receiving...	estoy recibiendo	Es-<u>toy</u> rey-see-bee-<u>en</u>-dough
desarmar	he is disarming...	está desarmando	Es-<u>tah</u> des-arm-<u>mahn</u>-dough

---

My Heretical Rule No. 21.

To form the present participle, drop the last two letters in order to arrive at the stem of the verb. To that stem, add "ando" for verbs ending in "-ar" and "iendo" for verbs ending in "-er" and "-ir". Use the present participle with the auxiliary verb (in this case) "Estar" to create the Progressive Tense.

EXERCISE 21:

Now, you do some:

obedecer	they are obeying...
laminar	we are laminating...
consagrar	he is consecrating...
simpatizar	you are sympathizing...
anticipar	we are anticipating...
estimular	it is stimulating... *
duplicar	I am duplicating...
liberar	they are liberating...
practicar	I am practicing...
concentrar	you are concentrating...

*   Remember that there is no <u>subject</u> pronoun for "it".

<u>Additional high frequency cognates:</u>

<u>English</u>	<u>Spanish</u>	<u>Pronounced</u>
Position	posición	poh-see-see-own
Possible	posible	poh-see-blay
Practical	práctico	prahk-tee-koh
To prefer	preferir	prey-fair-eer
To Prepare	preparar	prey-pahr-ahr
Presence	presencia	prey-sen-see-ah
To Present	presentar	prey-sen-tahr
Price	precio	preh-see-oh
Private	privado	pree-vah-dough
Probable	probable	proh-bah-blay
Problem	problema	proh-blay-mah
To Produce	producir	proh-doo-seer
Program	programa	proh-grah-mah
Progress	progreso	proh-greh-sew
To Prove	probar	proh-bahr

Using the Progressive - One Step Beyond

You now know how to use the progressive to create a form of the present tense that will work with ANY verb, using only the present tense conjugation of *"Estar"*, plus the <u>present</u> participle of ANY other verb.

It's a brilliant short-cut to expanding your use of verbs in the present tense. It's almost like INSTANTLY knowing the present tense conjugation of ALL verbs, isn't it?

Now, I want you to think back for a moment to Chapter XII and to our discussions of the verb *"Soler"* for expressing things which we "used to do" in the past and, more specifically, to our discussions of the "imperfect past" (also known as the "continuing past").

In normal usage, the imperfect past tense of a verb is used to express both the "used to do" as expressed by *"Soler"* (But, not the 'usually do') AND the imperfect or continuing past. That's a separate verb conjugation for every single verb, as they would teach it in language school.

Using the Progressive, we can accomplish the expression of the "continuing" past by learning to use ONLY the verb *"Estar"* in the imperfect past tense.

Then, as in the Progressive (in the present) which you have already learned, you'll be able to express the "continuing" or "imperfect" past for ANY verb using:

"*ESTAR*" (imperfect tense) + Present Participle

"*Estar*" in the Imperfect tense conjugates as follows:

(Yo)	Estaba + PRESENT participle	I was... (going, doing, eating, etc.)
(Tu)	Estabas + PRESENT participle	You were... (going, doing, eating, etc.)
(El/Ella)	Estaba + PRESENT participle	He/She was... (going, doing, eating, etc.)
(Usted)	Estaba + PRESENT participle	You (pol.) were... (going, doing, eating, etc.)
(Nosotros)	Estabamos + PRESENT participle	We were... (going, doing, eating, etc.)
(Ellos/Ellas)	Estaban + PRESENT participle	They were... (going, doing, eating, etc.)
(Ustedes)	Estaban + PRESENT participle	You (pol.) were... (going, doing, eating, etc.)

Well, that wasn't difficult, was it?

So, now you know how to create the "continuing past" for ANY verb without having to learn a second conjugation for every verb you know.

Just learn this one conjugation of "*Estar*", and you will be able to use ANY verb in the "continuing past".

If you're not sure about the difference between using:

the IMPERFECT PAST (ESTAR Plus Present Participle)

versus

the PERFECT PAST (HABER Plus Past Participle),

then, go back and re-read the section of this book entitled "Distinguishing the Perfect Past from the Imperfect Past" which begins on page 141.

Use:

- "Haber" Plus Past Participle to express the "perfect" past,
- "Soler" to express things you "used to do" or which were "habitual" in the past, and
- "Estar" Plus Past Participle to express the "continuing" past.

Examples for Clarification:

Haber + Past Participle	We DID it (or, we have done it)
Soler + Infinitive	We USED TO DO it (or, we usually did it)
Estar + Present Participle	We WERE DOING it

Knowing the "Soler" and "Estar" in the imperfect is only TEN extra words for you to learn, yet those TEN extra words EMPOWER you and enable you to use ANY verb in Spanish in any of the three possible past conditions.

Are those TEN words worth the extra effort? You betcha!

Chapter XIV.
A Review.

At this point, I hope that you have determined that learning to communicate in Spanish isn't going to be as difficult as you thought.

I also hope you are talking to yourself constantly in Spanish and pronouncing English words with a Spanish accent (you'll be amazed at how many cognates you accidentally discover this way).

So far, you've learned:

1. The vowels.
2. The consonants.
3. The sounds of Spanish.
4. The alfabeto.
5. The verb "*Ser*".
6. The verb "*Estar*".
7. The principal difference between "*Ser*" and "*Estar*"
8. The verb "*Haber*".
9. How to form past participles.
10. How to use "*Haber*" and a past participle to create the past tense.
11. The verb "*Soler*".
12. Using the verb "*Soler*" to express actions in the present and in the past.
13. How to form present participles.
14. How to use "*Estar*" and a present participle to create the progressive tense.
15. The verb "*Ir*".

16. The verb "*Tener*"
17. Expressing obligation using "*Tener que...*".
18. The personal subject pronouns.
19. Words which express relationships of time.
20. Expressing something which will take place in the future using "*Ir*".
21. "Yo-ism".
22. The secrets to learning and remembering.
23. A substantial amount of cognate vocabulary (more than 500 cognates).
24. Some insights into the cultural aspects of the Spanish language.
25. Some words of courtesy and good manners so you're not viewed as a "*gringo*".
26. More than 150 non-cognate words.
27. Verbs of motion.
28. Words of position.
29. You have gone to the movies in Spanish.
30. More than 700 total words.

If you feel weak on any of these, you should go back and review the pertinent section. I want you to feel reasonably comfortable with what has preceded so that you will be able to apply it as we go into the next section.

Be honest with yourself now.

Have you been speaking? Have you been reading English words with a Spanish accent?

Have you sought out anyone who speaks even a little Spanish to help you with your pronunciations?

Have you been talking to yourself in Spanish?

If you have not been doing any of these things, ask yourself if you really want to learn to *speak* Spanish.

If you have been doing so, then congratulations. You are overcoming the most difficult aspect of learning to speak: *Speaking.*

We're going to pick up the pace now, because, in another thirteen lessons, you'll be finished with this course. Your only task then will be to continue to build vocabulary and to practice speaking at every opportunity.

Hang in there. You're almost a competent communicator in Spanish already!

EXERCISE 22:

From here on out and on a daily basis, take your dictionary in hand, begin at "a" in the Spanish to English side and use a highlighter to highlight ever word you see that is a cognate with which you would ordinarily be familiar and which you use in English.

Then, take your highlighted list and write the words and their definitions (the English cognate) in a wire-wound or other notebook. Keep building your list until you finish "reading your dictionary" with all of the "z" words. Maximum 50 to 75 per day.

Using a different colored highlighter, also mark regular, non-cognate vocabulary words in either section of the dictionary that you think you might want to use or might need. List them separately in your wire-wound notebook. Learn them well. They aren't as easy to remember as cognates.   Maximum 20 to 25 per day.

Your overall vocabulary should be about 60% to 65% nouns, around 30% verbs, and the rest (5% to 10%) spread among adjectives, adverbs, and prepositions.

Quiz Yourself:

Without reference to your notes or the text book:

1.   Make a list of all of the letters of the _alfabeto_. Name each letter on the list. Write out how that letter "sounds".

2.   Make a list of all of the cognates you can <u>remember</u>. Determine the total number of cognates you already recognize. If there are fewer than _50 cognates for every day since you started this course_, you aren't working hard enough.

3.   Make a list of all of the non-cognate, Spanish words you can <u>remember</u>. The more, the better. At least 10 per day since beginning this course.

4.   Explain from memory the differences between the verb "_Ser_" and the verb "_Estar_".

5.   Explain from memory how to express obligation using the verb "_Tener que..._".

6.   Conjugate the verbs "_Ser_", "_Estar_", "_Ir_", "_Tener_", "_Haber_", and "_Soler_".

7.   Make a list of all the verbs you can <u>remember</u> and write the past and present participles for each.

8.   List all of the subject personal pronouns.

9.   Explain "_Yo-ismo_".

10.   Pick 10 cognate nouns, 10 cognate verbs and 10 cognate adjectives and use each of them in a sentence using what you have learned. You may include any other vocabulary learned.

11.   **Extra credit exercise:**

Using what you know from the verbs you've learned to conjugate in the present tense and your knowledge from the conjugation template, you ARE ABLE to conjugate most other verbs in the present tense (*even if you don't believe it*).

If you do believe it, try to conjugate as many other verbs as you can. Do this only if you have purchased the 501 Spanish Verbs Fully Conjugated. Otherwise, you have no way of checking your work.

It's your quiz. Grade yourself. How did you do? Did you do well? Or, was it difficult? If you found it difficult, repeat the first nine chapters. If you did well, then proceed to the next chapter.

Chapter XV.
More of the Dynamic Dozen:
The Verbs "Saber",
"Hacer" and "Acabar (de)"

Although you don't absolutely have to know how to conjugate these verbs, it will be helpful to you if you do learn them.

"*Saber*" means "to know", but it's also used to express "how to", as in "I know how to swim".

"*Hacer*" means "to make" or "to do". It's also used in expressions about the weather, the passage of time and some useful idioms.

"*Acabar de*" means "to have just...", as in "I have just eaten" or "I just got back".

"*Acabar*" means "to finish".

<u>"*Saber*"</u> (Pronounced "Sah-bair") <u>is conjugated as follows:</u>

Pronoun	Spanish	Pronounced	Means
Yo	Sé	<u>Say</u>	I know
Tú	Sabes	<u>Sah</u>-base	You know(fam.)
Él	Sabe	<u>Sah</u>-bay	He knows
Ella	Sabe	<u>Sah</u>-bay	She knows
Usted	Sabe	<u>Sah</u>-bay	You know(pol.)
Nosotros	Sabemos	<u>Sah</u>-bay-mos	We know
Ustedes	Saben	<u>Sah</u>-bayn	You know(pl.)
Ellos	Saben	<u>Sah</u>-bayn	They know(masc)
Ellas	Saben	<u>Sah</u>-bayn	They know(fem.)

"I know that she is coming tonight" would be expressed using this verb as "*(yo) Sé que ella viene esta noche*". Or, "you know that I'm right" would be "(*Tú) sabes que tengo razón*" ("*tener razón*" means "to be right").

This verb is used in this sense exactly as it is in English.

However, it has another use. <u>It also expresses HOW to do something.</u> For example, in English, we might say, "I know <u>how</u> to swim". In Spanish, that is expressed as "*(yo) Sé nadar*". That is, "Sé ("I know [how to]") *nadar* ("to swim")."

Very simple. Using the present tense of "*Saber*", follow it with the infinitive of any verb that expresses what it is that you know how to do, and you've expressed that you know how to do it.

Don't make the mistake of trying inject the words "How to" (using "*como*") into this construction of "knowing how to do something". "How to" is implicit in the use of the verb.

Repeat:

"*Saber*" PLUS Infinitive of verb = "to know how to..."

Any questions?

EXERCISE : 23

Using your new verb, "*Saber*", construct 10 sentences using it in the normal sense, followed by 10 sentences that express things that you know how to do.

1.

2.

3.

4.

5.

6.

7.

8.

9.

10.

"Hacer" (Pronounced "Ah-sair") means "to do" or "to make" and is conjugated as follows:

Pronoun	Spanish	Sounds like	Means
Yo	Hago	<u>Ah</u>-go	I make/do
Tú	Haces	<u>Ah</u>s-ace	You make/do
Él/Ella/Usted	Hace	<u>Ah</u>-say	He/she/you make(s)/do(es)
Nosotros	Hacemos	Ah-<u>say</u>-mos	We make/do
Ellos/Ellas/Uds.	Hacen	<u>Ah</u>-sayn	They/You make/do

The verb is used as in English, except that it does double duty for "to do" and "to make".

<u>This verb is *irregular*; it's Past Participle is *"HECHO"*, but its Present Participle is *"HACIENDO"*, as expected.</u>

Examples:

"Do you do it?" "Yes, I do."
"*¿Lo˙ haces?*" "*Si, lo hago.*"

"Did you do it?" "Yes, I did."
"*¿Lo has hecho?*" "*Si, lo he hecho.*"

"Are you doing it now?" "Yes, I am doing it now."
"*¿Lo estás haciendo ahora?*" "*Si, lo estoy haciendo.*"

---

* This is the only kind of reference to "it" you will find in Spanish. "Lo" in this context means "it".

EXERCISE 24:

Create 10 sentences using "*HACER*" in all forms, i.e., the present tense (as conjugated above), the past tense, the progressive, and the habitual and using new vocabulary that you have learned.

1.

2.

3.

4.

5.

6.

7.

8.

9.

10.

"Acabar de" (Pronounced "Ah-kah-*bar* Day") means "to have just finished… (doing something)" and is conjugated as follows:

Pronoun	Spanish	Sounds like	Means
Yo	Acabo de...	Ah-<u>Kah</u>-bo Dey...	I just...
Tú	Acabas de...	Ah-<u>Kah</u>-bahs Dey...	You (fam.) just...
Él/Ella/Ud.	Acaba de...	Ah-<u>Kah</u>-bah Dey...	He/She/You just...
Nosotros	Acabamos de...	Ah-Kah-<u>bah</u>-mos Dey...	We just...
Ellos/Ellas	Acaban de...	Ah-<u>Kah</u>-bahn Dey	They just...

Like the verb, "*SABER*" used in the sense of "to know how to…:", "*Acabar de…*" takes the infinitive of another verb immediately following.

Examples:

"*Acabar de…*"

Acabo de comer	Ah-<u>Kah</u>-bo dey Koh-<u>mair</u>	I just ate
Acaba de llegar	Ah-<u>Kah</u>-bah dey yay-<u>gar</u>	He just arrived
Acabamos de jugar...	Ah-<u>Kah</u>-bay-mos dey hoo-<u>gar</u>...	We just finished playing...

"*Acabar*" by itself means "to finish" and is conjugated as follows:

Pronoun	Spanish	Sounds like	Means
Yo	Acabo	Ah-<u>Kah</u>-bo	I finish
Tú	Acabas	Ah-<u>Kah</u>-bahs	You (familiar) finish
Él/Ella/Ud.	Acaba	Ah-<u>Kah</u>-bah	He/She/You finish
Nosotros	Acabamos	Ah-Kah-<u>bah</u>-mos	We finish
Ellos/Ellas/Uds.	Acaban	Ah-<u>Kah</u>-bahn	They/You finish

Examples:

"Acabar"

¿Acabas el partido?	Did you finish the game?
	Ah-<u>Kah</u>-bahs L par-<u>Tee</u>-dough
Acabo las clases.	I am finishing the classes.
	Ah-<u>Kah</u>-bo lahs <u>Klah</u>-sace.
Acaban ahora.	They are finishing now.
	Ah-<u>Kah</u>-bahn Ah-<u>or</u>-ah

<u>*"Acabar"* when it is used to mean "to finish" does not require a following infinitive.</u>

EXERCISE 25:

Create 10 sentences each using *"acabar de"* and *"acabar"*, utilizing new vocabulary.

1.

2.

3.

4.

5.

6.

7.

8.

9.

10.

"Hacer" Used in Expressions of Weather and Time.

"Hacer" is a very useful verb to know, simply because it figures in so many idiomatic uses.

"Hacer" Idioms of Time.

Two simple uses of *"Hacer"* have to do with the expression which in English is rendered with "ago", "since...", etc.

Ago.

An important time expression in English has to do with when something happened in the past that we express with a time period plus the word "AGO".

For example, one might say in English, "I ate there two years ago".

In Spanish, this would be rendered by *"He comido allí hace dos años"*. *"Hace dos años"* is the operative time expression and in this context means "2 years ago". *"Hace"* stands for "ago" in this expression.

"Hace" makes just as much sense in this context as "ago" does in English, if you stop to think about it. I mean, what does "ago" really mean?

"Since" in the Past.

Another time expression regularly used in English has to do with the fact that something has been happening (or had been happening) for a given period, which is rendered in English with the word "SINCE" plus a time period or "FOR", plus a time period.

For example, one might say "I' have lived here for two years".

In Spanish, that would be rendered by *"desde hace"*.

"*He vivido aquí desde hace dos años*". "*Desde hace dos años*" is the operative time expression and, in this case, it means "for two years". It could also be interpreted in English as "since two years", something you may have heard said at sometime by someone who speaks English as a second language.

"Since" Continuing in the Past.

Elsewhere in this text, we addressed the distinction between a finite event in the past and some action continuing in the past. Again, "*Hacer*" has a valuable use.

For example, we might say, "I had been living there for two years when the baby was born".

In Spanish, we could say that "*hacía dos años que vivía allí cuándo nació el niño*". In this case, "*Hacía dos años...*" reflects that something had been continuing in the past when something else in the past happened.

In this sense, it is often interpreted as "for", as in "we had been doing it for two years". Or, "*hacia dos años que estudiamos el español cuándo hemos ido a pasar unos días de vacaciones en España*", "we were (or had been) studying Spanish for two years when we went to Spain on holiday."

"*Hacer*" In Idioms of Climate and Weather.

In English, we talk a great deal about the weather. Strangely enough, the same thing happens in Spanish. Everybody talks about the weather, but no one seems able to change it, especially on those days when it's 40° Celsius in the shade.

When we say in English, "it's hot" what do we really mean? "It" *what* is hot? This is an idiomatic expression in English, so it doesn't have to make sense. However, due to centuries of use, we know what "it" is intended to mean, even if "it" doesn't really make any sense.

In Spanish, one would say "*hace calor*", i.e., "it makes hot". Frankly, this makes more sense than "it is hot", since one can infer that it is the sun that is making it hot. Nonetheless, this too, is an idiomatic expression.

It doesn't have to make sense; we just have to get the sense of it.

For expressions having to do with weather, almost any climactic condition can be expressed with "*hace*". For example:

Hace calor	It's hot	<u>Ah</u>-say Kah-<u>lohr</u>
Hace frío	It's cold	<u>Ah</u>-say <u>Free</u>-oh
Hace fresco	It's fresh (or chilly)	<u>Ah</u>-say <u>Fres</u>-koh
Hace húmedo	It's humid	<u>Ah</u>-say <u>Oo</u>-mee-dough
Hace sol	It's sunny	<u>Ah</u>-say <u>Soul</u>
Hace nuboso	It's cloudy	Ah-say Noo-boh-sew

Other Idiomatic Uses of "Hacer".

Hacer caso.

"*Hacer*" has another interesting idiomatic use that you might find it valuable to know. That use couples "*Hacer*" with the noun "*Caso*" (Pronounced "Kah-sew").

Translating "*Hacer caso*" sounds like it would be "to make a case" out of something, right?

The fact is that the proper interpretation of "*hacer caso*" means "to pay attention".

For example, one might say in English "don't pay any attention to him".

---

* Don't confuse the contraction of the preposition "a" with the definite article "el" which means "to the…" with "a él", which means "to him". The article "el" (the) is not accented, the personal pronoun "él" (him) is accented. If you mean "him", then the contraction to "al" is not possible. If you mean "the", it is.

In Spanish, you would use *"Hacer"* and *"Caso"* together with the meaning of "don't pay any attention, as follows:

"No le haga caso (a él)", *"haga"* being the imperative form (polite) of the verb *"hacer"*. I used *"le"* in this example because it conveys the same thing as *"a él"* * but with an indirect object pronoun and implies the

same thing. So, *"No hacer caso"* means *"don't pay attention…"*

"Hacer caso" means "Pay attention to…"

"Hagas caso al mapa" means "pay attention to the map".

My favorite use, because at least part of the time it's true, is *"ella no me hace caso"*, that is, "she doesn't pay any attention to me".

And, on that note, you should have mastered this expression and use of *"Hacer"*.

You've now learned the uses of *"Saber"*, *"Saber"* Plus Infinitive, *"Acabar"*, *"Acabar de"* Plus Infinitive, and *"Hacer"*. In addition, you've learned some idiomatic uses of *"Hacer"*. So, now it's time to put them to good use with a little practice.

EXERCISE 26:

There follows a list of verbs in Spanish. Without going to your dictionary to look them up, write down what you think they might mean. When you have finished with the list, THEN look them up in your dictionary. Don't forget to record them in your notebook, too.

Spanish	Pronounced	Your Definition	Dictionary Definition
Promoter	Pro-moh-*tair*		
Communicar	Koh-moo-ni-*kahr*		
Atender	Ah-ten-*dair*		
Reembolsar	Ray-em-bowl-*sahr*		
Vindicar	Veen-dee-*kahr*		
Fomentar	Foh-men-*tahr*		
Abandonar	Ah-bahn-dough-*nahr*		
Abdicar	Ahb-dee-*kahr*		
Abolir	Ah-bow-*leer*		
Emitir	Ey-mee-*teer*		
Reducir	Ray-doo-*seer*		
Ventilar	Veyn-tee-*lahr*		
Mencionar	Men-see-own-*ahr*		
Marcar	Mahr-*kahr*		
Marchar	Mahr-*char*		
Estudiar	Es-too-dee-*ahr*		
Flotar	Floh-*tahr*		
Expander	Ex-pahn-*dare*		
Dictar	Deek-*tahr*		
Atribuir	Ah-tree-boo-*eer*		
Vomitar	Voh-mee-*tahr*		
Racionar	Rah-see-own-*ahr*		
Paginar	Pah-hee-*nahr*		
Identificar	Ee-den-tee-fee-*kahr*		
Liquidar	Lee-kee-*dahr*		
Tranquilizar	Trahn-kee-lee-*zahr*		
Traficar	Trah-fee-*kahr*		
Transportar	Trahns-pour-*tahr*		
Obligar	Oh-blee-*gahr*		
Normalizar	Nohr-mahl-ee-*zahr*		
Notificar	Noh-tee-fee-*kahr*		

Spanish	Pronounced	Your Definition	Dictionary Definition
Estrangular	Es-trahn_g-goo-*lahr*		
Evaporar	Ey-vah-pour-*ahr*		
Combinar	Kohm-bee-*nahr*		
Compensar	Kohm-pen-*sahr*		
Compilar	Kohm-pee-*lahr*		
Pilotar	Pee-loh-*tahr*		
Cementar	Say-men-*tahr*		
Aventurar	Ah-ven-too-*rahr*		
Refinar	Ray-fee-*nahr*		
Participar	Par-tee-see-*pahr*		
Averiguar	Ah-ver-ee-*gwar*		
Testimoniar	Tess-tee-moan-ee-*ahr*		
Consistir	Kohn-sees-*teer*		
Preparar	Preh-pahr-*ahr*		

175

EXERCISE 27:

Now, we begin to learn some of the words you're going to need to know that aren't cognates. These are words you need to know, so learn them well.

Spanish	Pronounced	Means
Comer	Koh-<u>mare</u>	to eat
Hablar	Ah-<u>blahr</u>	to talk
Decir	Dey-<u>seer</u>	to speak, to SAY
Conducir	Cone-doo-<u>seer</u>	to drive an auto (Spain)
Manejar	Mahn-ey-<u>har</u>	to drive a car (Lat. Am.)
Beber	Bey-<u>bear</u>	to drink
Dormir	Door-<u>meer</u>	to sleep
Leer	Ley-<u>Air</u>	to read
Ver	<u>Vare</u>	to see
Mirar	Mee-<u>rahr</u>	to look AT
Oír	Oh-<u>eer</u>	to hear
Escuchar	S-koo-<u>char</u>	to listen
Escribir	S-cree-<u>beer</u>	to write
Pintar	Peen-<u>tahr</u>	to paint
Fumar	Foo-<u>mahr</u>	to smoke
Vestir	Vess-<u>teer</u>	to dress
Pasar	Pah-<u>sahr</u>	to pass, to HAPPEN
Dar	<u>Dahr</u>	to give
Botar	Bvoh-<u>tahr</u>	To throw out
Echar	Etch-<u>ahr</u>	To pour, throw out
Chocar	Choh-<u>kahr</u>	To bump into, to wreck
Cuchara	Koo-<u>char</u>-ah	Spoon
Tenedor	Ten-ey-<u>door</u>	Fork
Cuchillo	Koo-<u>chee</u>-yo	Knife
Plato	<u>Plah</u>-toh	Plate
Taza	<u>Tah</u>-zah	Cup
Periódico	Pear-ee-<u>ode</u>-ico	Newspaper
Coche	<u>Koh</u>-che	Automobile (Sp.)
Auto	<u>Auw</u>-toh	Automobile (Lat.Am.)

Carro	Cah-rrho	Automobile (Carib.)
Camisa	Cah-mee-sah	Shirt
Blusa	Bloo-sah	Blouse
Pantalones	Pan-tah-loh-neys	Trousers
Bragas	Brah-gahs	Panties
Calzoncillos	Kahl-sewn-see-yos	Men's underwear
Calcetines	Kahl-sey-tee-neys	Men's hosiery
Medias	Meh-dee-ahs	Ladies' stockings
Falda	Fahl-dah	Skirt
Gorra	Goh-rrah	Hat
Pneumático	New-mah-tee-koh	Auto tires
Volante	Bvoh-lahn-tey	Steering wheel
Camión	Cah-mee-own	Truck
Furgoneta	Fur-goh-neh-tah	Panel truck
Niño	Neen-yoh	Little boy
Niña	Neen-yah	Little girl
Cuarto de Baño	Kwar-toh dey Bahn-yo	Bathroom
El Servicio	L Sair-vee-see-yo	Restroom
El Lavabo	L Lah-vah-boh	Washroom, wash basin
El Bate	L bah-tey	The actual toilet (throne)
Una Plancha	Ooh-nah Plahn-chah	An iron (for clothes), Also, a grill for cooking

EXERCISE 28:

Go to your dictionary and look up ten words, which you feel you need to know the meaning of and which are NOT cognates. Learn those 10 plus the 50 plus words given above. Two days from now, give yourself a Self-Test on these words to see how many you remember.

Chapter XVI.
More Dynamic Dozen: The Verb "Decir".
Object Pronouns.   Idiomatic Uses of Verbs.

The veb "*DECIR*" means "to speak" or "to say". In past tense, it means, "told."

"*Decir*" (Pronounced "Day-seer") is conjugated in the present tense as follows:

Spanish	Sounds Like	English
Decir	Dey-<u>seer</u>	Infintive of "to say"
Digo	<u>Dee</u>-goh	I say
Dices	<u>Dee</u>-sace	you (familiar) say
Dice	<u>Dee</u>-sey	he/she/it/you (polite) say/s
Decimos	Dey-<u>see</u>-mohs	we say
Dicen	<u>Dee</u>-sehn	They/You (plural) say

This is a really easy verb to use and it's pleasant to the ear.

Como Se Dice.

Probably one of the most useful idiomatic expressions you can know involves the verb "dec*ir*". It means "how do you say?" and it is "*¿como se dice?*", pronounced as "*Koh*-mo Say *Dee*-say?". If you don't know how to pronounce a word you find in your dictionary, show it (point) to a Spanish speaker and ask "*¿como se dice?*" You'll find out very quickly how to say what you want.

Likewise, it is very helpful and more appropriately used with a Spanish speaker who speaks some English when you don't know the word you want to use. You can then ask, for example, "*¿como se dice en español la palabra 'mechanic'?*" which means "how do you say in Spanish the word 'mechanic'?"

This is an exceptionally helpful idiomatic expression. Use it liberally when in a Spanish speaking environment.

Personal Object Pronouns.

Before we take a look at a few Idiomatic verb uses, let's take a closer look at Spanish Pronouns, that is, direct object pronouns and indirect object pronouns. Please see the table of pronouns given below.

Subject Pronouns	Direct Object Pronouns		Indirect Object Pronouns	
Yo	Me	Me	Mi	to me
Tú	Te	You	Ti	to you
Él	Lo	Him	Le	to him
Ella	La	Her	Le	to her
Usted	Lo/La	You	Le	to you
(depends on whether male or female)				
Nosotros	Nos	Us	Nos	to us
Ustedes	Los/Las	You	Les	to you
(depends on whether male or female)				
Ellos	Los	Them	Les	to them
Ellas	Las	Them	Les	to them

Mastering object pronouns in Spanish is *one of the most difficult aspects of the Spanish grammar*; in my opinion, it is even more difficult than mastering verb tenses which (once you learn the basics) are relatively simple by comparison.

Indirect object pronouns, in particular, can be especially taxing to the brain.

However, there is a way to simplify the indirect object pronoun problem, so that it isn't the nightmare it could be.

Direct object pronouns, on the other hand, don't have such a simple solution. Still, there is ALWAYS a solution.

Before we go any further, especially for those whose recollections of grammar from childhood studies may be slightly dimmed by the passage of time, let's review what these pronouns do in a sentence and what they do to clarify the meaning of a sentence.

Direct Object.

A direct object is the receiver of action within a sentence, as in "He hit the ball." "Ball" is the direct object. If we substitute "it" for "ball", "it" becomes the direct object, i.e., "he hit it".

Indirect Object.

An indirect object identifies to or for whom, by whom or for what the action of the verb is performed. For example, "he hit the ball to him". "To him" is the indirect object. "Ball" is still the direct object. Again, substituting "it" for "ball", we end up with "he hit it to him". In this case, "it" is the direct object and "him" is the indirect object.

The direct object and indirect object are different; they represent people or places or things.

Examples:

Let's look at the example above, "he hit the ball", but let's change it to read, "He hit the ball to me". In the latter sentence, "ball" is the direct object which could be replaced by "it". The indirect object is represented by "me".

If we change the sentence to, "he hit it to me" we then have both a direct object pronoun and an indirect object pronoun in the same sentence.

If we go through the same exercise in Spanish with "He threw the ball", we end up with "*Él tiró la pelota*". Next, "he threw the ball to me", i.e., "*él (me) tiró la pelota a mí*". *

Then, finally, we end up with "he threw it to me", i.e., "*él me lo tiró (a mí)*".

Now, we know from the above list that "*ME*" is a direct object pronoun, but in this example, it is an indirect object pronoun. The way we know that is because we can clarify this sentence to read "*me lo tiró a mí*"; that is, he hit it "to me" As soon as we do this, we have a form almost equal to English, and it is clear that "*me*" is used as an indirect object.

The problem with indirect object pronouns is that, if we place them in front of the verb (which is very common), they change to the form of the direct object pronoun. So, unless we attempt to apply the "to me" solution, we are never sure. But, if the "to me" solution works, then we can be confident that it is an indirect object pronoun.

That's a lot to try to do in the middle of a conversation, especially with our limited conversational experience at this point. So, that leads us to our next rule.

---

* "Me", in this instance, could replace the "a mí" in the sentence. That's one of the things that make indirect object pronouns so confusing.

My Heretical Rule No. 22.

For Indirect Object Pronouns, Just Do It Like In English.

So, the solution on indirect object pronouns is quite simple. Use the English grammar to accomplish your purpose. For example, in any case where you could say:

"to" me, you, him, her or them,

or where you could say "by" or "for" or "at" me, you, him, her or them,

then you know to use "a" plus the appropriate pronoun, the same as you would in English, as follows:

"to me" ("a mí"),

"to you" ("a tí"),

"to him" ("a él"), "to her" ("a ella"), "to you" polite form ("a usted"),

"to us" ("a nosotros"),

"to you" ("a ustedes), "to them" ("a ellos/ellas").

Therefore, in our example above, you could change "él me lo tiró" to read "él lo tiró a mí". That solves the problem with the Indirect Object.

For Direct Object Pronouns, It's A Hybrid Solution.

In the preceding example, "*lo*" represents the direct object "it".

The question is: what is "it"? We can refer to it by its name, i.e., "ball".

So, instead of saying "he threw it to me", we could say, "he hit the ball to me" (as we did at the beginning), using the actual noun (instead of pronoun) for the direct object.

We then have "*él tiró la pelota a mí.*" That's pretty much English grammar, isn't it? So, do it like in English.

A Spaniard would say "*él me lo tiró*", but he would know what YOU meant with your form.

The problem arises from your interpretation of what HE said to you. This makes it a case of doing what Mary Jane said and focusing on the context and "the gist" of what is being said, then asking for clarification, if needed.

Get Clarification.

Where you will find problems with personal pronouns is in interpretation of what is said to you by native speakers.

Let me say this about that. More often that you can imagine, they confuse themselves and have to clarify what is meant by what is said.

Therefore, it is not unusual for someone, even Spanish speakers, to seek clarification of what is meant by what is said where there is any chance for confusion because of the object pronouns.

Hence, if the Spaniard says to you "me lo tiró", you might ask, "What was thrown?", "Who threw it?"

Who can blame you for wanting clarification? More often than not, however, when you hear "lo", it will be standing for "it", especially if it precedes the verb.

As we proceed through the material in this text, we will be giving you real life examples of things you might say (or hear) involving the use of pronouns, and you will begin to get more comfortable with them, bit by bit. We just don't want you to lose your mind over them.

On a worst-case basis, you can always ignore them entirely.

It will detract from your speech and make understanding somewhat more difficult, but it is possible to do. I watched my wife in the past (and others) get along quite well without having any clue as to how to use the pronouns for quite some time. Frankly, I was amazed, but I had to agree finally that it **is** possible.

Now, when all of the traditional language teachers come back from the loo after being ill, we'll continue with the rest of this lesson.

Personal "a".

You will recall that a direct object is a noun or pronoun that receives the action dictated by the verb of a sentence. "He threw the ball to me". "Ball" is the direct object, "He" is the subject of the sentence, and the indirect object, expressed as "*a mí*" means "to me".

In Spanish, this is rendered as "*Él tiró la pelota a mí*".

Similarly, "*Él pidió su comida*" (he ordered his meal), "*el*" is the subject, "*pedir*" is the verb, and "*comida*" is the direct object.

However, *when the direct object is a person, Spanish requires the use of the "personal" preposition "a" that doesn't really translate into English.*

"He calls me (on the phone)". Based on the way we did the previous examples, one would think that this would translate as "*el (me) llama mí*". That would be WRONG.

When a person is involved, it must be translated as "*el (me) llama **a** mí*". Or, for example, "I gave it to John" would be expressed as "*lo dí **a** Juan*".

Now, prepare yourself. I know that I told you that grammar wasn't important. But, I also remember that I told you that when it was important, really important, there might be a rule of grammar.

Well, on the next page you will find:

AN ACTUAL REAL RULE OF GRAMMAR.

The personal "a" applies to people.

The personal "a" applies to animals.

When the <u>direct object</u> of a verb is a <u>person</u>, you <u>MUST</u> use the personal "a".

When the <u>direct object</u> is a pet or other domesticated animal (such as a horse) about which some personal feelings exist, the personal "a" <u>MUST</u> be used.

It may seem like an extra, unnecessary word in English, but it is a VERY NECESSARY word in Spanish.

<u>A Spanish speaker will truly perceive you as a barbarian if you fail to use the personal "a".</u>

It is NOT used after a direct object that is NOT a person or other living being.

It is NOT used after the verb "TENER".

It is NOT used after the verb "HAY".

And, it is NOT used if the direct object is an "indefinite person". "I need a doctor (in this case any doctor)", as opposed to "I need Dr. Charles" (specific doctor). "Necesito medico" (indefinite); "Necesito ver <u>a</u> Dr. Charles" (definite).

Please don't disappoint me by forgetting this one single rule of grammar in the entire book that I insist you remember. I don't want anyone to think YOU are a barbarian. We'll give you more examples in the exercises at the end of the chapter.

People Say. *"Se Dice Que"*.

The verb *"DECIR"* also has another idiomatic use.

In English, we say things such as "they say", "people say", and "everybody says". In Spanish, the same is done using the same verb, *"DECIR"*, but in an even simpler fashion. This is very common and heard everywhere.

"Se dice que" means "people say (that)...", such as *"se dice que es alcohólico"* ("they say he's an alcoholic") or *"se dice que va a llover"* ("they say it's going to rain").

Let's look at some other idiomatic uses of verbs. These will come up regularly. They don't make any sense if one tries to translate them, so we have to know what is intended to be interpreted and accept it as that.

"Hacer Falta". Huh?

This is one of my favorites, simply because it was literally years before that little "light bulb" when on over my rather hard head and I finally understood it.

Early on in my studies of Spanish, I heard this term all the time... *"hace falta"* this and *"hace falta"* (Pronounced "Ah-say Fall-tah") that. I had inferred that it meant something wasn't quite right, but didn't quite have a handle on it.

I'd be in a restaurant and watch a waitress or waiter ask a customer if everything was all right, and I'd hear *"no hace falta"* or *"me hace falta..."*.

It drove me crazy. The worst part was that NO native speaker of Spanish ever could or did give me a satisfactory explanation.

The reason is "*hacer*", as you know, means "to make" or "to do". "*Falta*" means "defect", "lack", "mistake", "fault". This would imply that the expression means "to make a fault" or "to make a lack" or "to make a mistake". Nothing could be further from the truth.

The most common explanation I got from Spanish speakers on this one was "it makes a fault". WRONG!

There are three basic ways you'll hear this expression. They are:

"*Hace falta*" means "to be necessary", and you might hear it in an expression such as "*hace falta que venga él*" ("does he have to come" or "is it necessary for him to come")

"*ME Hace falta*" means "I need ..." something. As in our restaurant scenario earlier in this book, "*Me hace falta un tenedor*" meant "I need a fork".

"*No (me) hace falta*" simply means the opposite, "I don't need anything".

OR

"*No hace falta,*" meaning "nothing is needed".

In context, I always thought this one really meant something to the effect of "don't trouble yourself", and, in a sense, it does. But, it's really just an impersonal way of saying "we don't need anything right now."

"*Contar con*". Count with me.

By now, you have already figured out that you can count on me to give you the straight information when it comes to learning Spanish quickly.

The *expression* "*Contar Con...*" (cone-<u>tahr</u> cone) means exactly that; i.e., it means "to count <u>on</u>", not "with".

What do the *words* mean? "*Contar*" means "to count". "*Con*" means "with". So, the expression *translates* as "Count with…".

<u>What the expression "*Contar con*" really means is "to count on".</u>

For example, "*Cuento con él que me ayude*" (I'm counting on him to help me") or "*Cuento contigo*" ("I'm counting on you").

In the preceding example, it might be helpful for you to know that "*Contar*" is irregular and conjugates as "*cuento*" (<u>kwen</u>-toh), "*cuentas*" (<u>kwen</u>-tas), "*cuenta*" (<u>kwen</u>-tah), "*contamos*" (cone-<u>tah</u>-mos), "*cuentan*" (kwen-tahn).

Contigo, Consigo and Conmigo.

"*Contigo*" (Pronounced "Kone-<u>tee</u>-goh") is a contracted form of "*con*" ("with") and "*ti*" ("you"). The "*go*" is added to the combination to enhance the sound of the word in speech.

"*Consigo*" (Pronounced "Kone-<u>see</u>-goh") is a contracted form of "*con*" ("with") and "*se*" and means "with oneself", "with himself/herself", et cetera.

"*Conmigo*" (Pronounced "Kone-<u>mee</u>-goh") is a contracted form of "*con*" ("with") and "*mi*" and means "with me".

Darse Cuenta. Give yourself the count.

Literally (translated), this means "to give oneself the count". <u>What it really means is "to realize"</u>, as in "I just realized that it's raining" ("*Acabo de darme cuenta que está lloviendo*"). Did we just make a complete, grammatically correct sentence using things you have learned already? Wow!

The key with this one is that the suffix "*SE*" is impersonal and/or refers to a third person. If you are referring to yourself, substitute "*me*" for "*se*". You already know how to conjugate the verb "*dar*". If you don't know, you'll learn how on the next page.

See the explanation below to get a more complete handle on how to use this idiomatic expression.

<u>Just remember when it's YOU who is "realizing" something you must change "*se*" to "*me*".</u>

<u>Also, "*se da cuenta*" can mean "it is realized", an impersonal expression.</u>

It might also be useful to at least take a look at how the verb "*Dar*" is conjugated. Continue to see how "*Dar*" and "*Darse*" are conjugated.

The verb "*DAR*" itself conjugates exactly like "*Estar*", as does "*Darse*", so you should have no problem.

The verb "*DAR*".

<u>Verb ("dar" and "darse")</u>	<u>Meaning</u>
Doy	I give
Me <u>doy</u> cuenta	I realize
Das	You give
Te <u>das</u> cuenta	You realize (familiar)
Da	He/She/you gives
Se <u>da</u> cuenta	He/She/Usted realize/s
Damos	We give
Nos <u>damos</u> cuenta	We realize
Dan	They give
Se <u>dan</u> cuenta	They/Ustedes realize

A Pesar De. Hmm.

"*Pesar*" means to weigh. So, can you figure this one out? Probably not. It means "in spite of", as in "*a pesar de la lluvia, vamos al cine*" ("in spite of the rain, we're going to the movies").

It always precedes whatever it is that is spiting one, as in the rain in the example. Or, "in spite of his attitude, he is still good at his work" ("*a pesar de su actitud, hace bien su trabajo*").

Tomar Por. Take me, take me!

What do you take me for? Some kind of fool?

"*Tomar por*" means "to take for...", as in "do you take me for a fool" ("*me tomas por tonto?*") Or, he takes me for granted" ("*me toma por supuesto*").

Dar Por Hecho. To Give by done?

Literally, this means "to give by (or, "for") done", but clearly that makes no sense in translation.

"*Dar por hecho*" actually means "to take *something* for granted, as in "*lo doy por hecho*" (I take it for granted). It can also mean to "to consider it (something) finished or completed or done".

Tener Ganas. Got that special feeling.

You'll hear this one a great deal. "*Gana*" means "appetite", but should be construed to mean an "urge", so "*tener ganas*" means "to have the urge".

For example, "*tengo ganas ir al cine*", meaning "I feel like going to the movies" or "I have the urge to go to the movies".

Another example you'll hear quite often is "*él hace lo que le dé la gana*", figuratively meaning "he (just goes around and) does whatever he feels like" or "he does whatever he wants to do".

Observation.

Beware of saying simply "tengo ganas". You may convey an impression you didn't intend. A very suggestive one...

EXERCISE 29:

Each one of the following sentences uses a phrase or idiom with which you are not familiar. Using your dictionary to explain the unfamiliar words, what do you think these sentences are saying? Take your best guess. Don't worry about being perfect. Just try to figure them out. We'll explain them in a few minutes.

If you find that you can't solve the meaning because it seems insolvable, don't worry. Just go on to the next one. Don't drive yourself to distraction. We'll explain them to you shortly.

1. *Nos vemos esta tarde.*

2. *Te vuelvo a llamar.*

3. *¿Me hace favor abrir la puerta?*

4. *Es la más bella que he visto en mi vida.*

5. *Cuándo venga, yo te llamo.*

6. *A lo mejor él viene hoy.*

7. *Lo necesito cuánto antes.*

8. *¿Cuál es el numero para servicio de habitación?*

9.   *¿Me trae la carta de vino?*

10.   *No es nada.*

11.   *Es igual.*

Don't panic! Read on.

Explanation of Exercise 29:

Yes, we sneaked up on you with some things you haven't been exposed to YET. It was deliberate.

We wanted you to try to figure them out, even though we're pretty sure you didn't (for the most part).

It was just another step in introducing you to idioms and verb endings different from those you already know in a way that won't confuse you -- with explanations.

1.   *"Nos vemos esta tarde."* (Nohs *Vey*-mohs *Es*-tah *Tahr*-day)

"You will recall that "*Nos*" is an object personal pronoun for "us". "*Vemos*" is the 2nd person plural "we" of the verb "*ver*" ("to see"). "*Esta tarde*" you already know means "this afternoon". So, looking at the sentence "*nos vemos esta tarde*" you would translate this to mean "we will see us this afternoon".

What it really means is " we'll see each other (*nos*) this afternoon". So, remember, *"Nos vemos"* means "we'll see each other". This is a very common expression.

"¡*Nos vemos!*" can also be used on parting meaning "See you later".

2.   *"Te vuelvo a llamar."*   (Tay *Vwail*-voh Ah *Yah*-mahr)

You will recall that "*te*" is the object pronoun for "you". "*Vuelvo*" is the 1st person singular of the verb "*volver*" which means to return, so,

194

"*vuelvo*" means "I return". "*Llamar*" is the infinitive of the verb "to call".

So, literally, we have a sentence that translates to "you I return to call".

What it really means is "I'll call you back". This is one most foreigners don't figure out for a while. Now, you'll be one up.

I have heard children and grandchildren of Cuban immigrants in Miami and Gibraltarians both use the phrase "*te llamo p'atras*" in an attempt to say "I'll call you back", because they are trying to say (translate) "I'll call you back" in Spanish AS IF it were in English.

Oh, the risks of translation! In the lands of "Span-glish", to find such Americanization of the language is tragic.

3.   "*¿Me hace el favor de abrir la puerta?*" (May *Ah*-say Fah-*vohr* Ah-*breer* Lah *Pwer*-tah)

"*Me*" is the object pronoun for "me". "*Hace*" is 3rd person singular of "*Hacer*" (he/she/it/you). "*Favor*" is "favor". "*Abrir*" is the infinitive of the verb "to open" and "*la puerta*" is "the door".

So, what does it mean? "Would you <u>do me a favor</u> and open the door?"

4.   "*Es la más bella que he visto en mi vida.*" (Es Lah Mahs *Bay*-yah Kay Ey *Vees*-toh En Mee *Vee*-dah)

"*Es*" you will recall is 3rd person singular (he/she/it/usted) of the verb "*Ser*" which you already know means "to be". "*La*" is the definite article "the", "*más*" means more, and "*bella*" means "beautiful" "*que*" means "that". "*He*" you should recall is 1st person singular of the auxiliary verb "*haber*". "*Visto*" is the past participle of the verb "*Ver*" ("to see"). "*En mi vida*" literally means "in my life".

So, what do we have here? Most likely it would be "SHE is the most beautiful woman I have ever seen".

It could also mean, "IT is the most beautiful thing (feminine) I've ever seen" or "YOU (polite) are the most beautiful woman I've ever seen".

The point here is "en mi vida" means "ever" or "ever in my life" in this context.

5.   _Cuándo venga, yo te llamo."_   (*Kwan*-dough *Veng*-gah Yo Tay *Yah*-moh)

"*Cuándo venga*" is an idiomatic use of "*cuándo*" ("when") and "*venga*" a subjunctive form of the verb "*venir*" ("to come").

What it means is "when he/she comes...". "*Yo te llamo*" means "I'll call you".

So, this sentence means, "When she (he/usted/it) comes, I'll give you a call".

6.   "_A lo mejor él viene hoy._" (Ah Loh May-*hohr* L Vee-*en*-ney Oy)

"*A lo mejor*" is an idiomatic expression meaning "maybe" which uses a following verb in present tense, rather than requiring a more complex subjunctive verb form. That Cuban professor wasn't <u>all</u> that wrong about the subjunctive, you know.

So, in the case of this sentence, we have "maybe he'll come today".

7.   "_Lo necesito cuánto antes._" (Loh Ney-say-see-toh Kwan-toh Ahn-tays).

"*Lo*" is an object pronoun that, in this instance, means "it". "*Necesito*" is 1st person singular of "*Necesitar*" ("to need"). "*Cuánto antes*" is an idiomatic expression meaning "as soon as possible".

This sentence means "I need it as soon as possible". In other words, ASAP in English might be a somewhat less exciting "CA" in Spanish.

8. _"¿Cuál es el número para servicio de habitación?"_ (_Kwal_ Ehs El _Noo_-mare-oh _Pah_-rah Sair-_vee_-see-yo Day Ah-bee-tah-see-_own_).

"_¿Cuál?_" is an interrogative word meaning "which" (or, "what") among several choices. "_Servicio de habitación_" is "room service".

This question means, "what is the number for room service?"

Remember, however, that the word for "what?" is "_Qué?_", not "_Cuál?_". "_Cuál?_" can only be used as "what?" when it is with respect to a choice among several choices or when more information is needed or required. It can also be used to mean "which", as in "_cual?_" ("which (one)?").

9. _"¿Me trae la carta de vino?"_ (May Try La _Kahr_-tah Day _Vee_-noh).

"_Trae_" is the 3rd person singular of "_traer_" meaning "to bring". "_La carta de vino_" is "the wine list".

Therefore, this sentence means "would you bring me the wine list?"

And, in any case, you would use, "_¿me trae.....?_" anytime you want to request something in the form "would you bring me...?"

10. _"No es nada."_ (No Ehs Nah-dah).

This is the perfect example of the double negative in Spanish. "_No_" negates "_es_" which gives us "it isn't" and "_nada_" means nothing – "it isn't nothing". Unlike in English, double negatives are permitted in Spanish.

What this expression means is "it's nothing" or "it's not a big deal" or "it's not important" or even "don't worry about it".

11.   *"Es igual."*   (Es Ee-*gwahl*).

"Es igual" is one of the most versatile expressions in Spanish. It *translates* as "it's equal", but it really means, in effect, "it's all the same to me".

You can use it on just about any occasion. It can mean anything from "it's all the same to me", "I don't care", "it doesn't matter", "don't worry about it", "no big deal", et cetera. It's a really useful expression.

A Word on Sentence Structure.

For the most part, sentence structure in Spanish is very similar to English.

However, placement of the pronouns is problematic for Anglophiles, since they can come before or after the verb, as we have already discussed.

Also, the subject of a clause, especially a question, can come at the end of that clause.

As much as possible, we're going to try to keep the sentence structure to "English Format" to reduce your confusion. Using *"a ti"*, for example, as we pointed out earlier is in keeping with that purpose, since it enables you to handle the indirect object pronoun as in English with similar placement in the sentence.

In questions, however, even English changes the placement of the subject. For example, in the question "Has John arrived yet?" we have placed the auxiliary verb "has" in front of the subject, John. In Spanish, you would say it in the form "Has arrived yet John?"

You could, if in doubt, put it in the form "John has arrived?" and still be understood.

The first form sounds better to the practiced ear. Sometimes, how something sounds is critical to it's being understood.

198

We will try to maintain a balance between what's easiest for you, what's most easily understood and what sounds best, so that you make the most of your opportunities to communicate.

Suffice to say that *Spanish is much more flexible* on sentence structure than is English, so, to some extent, it's more difficult for you to make a mistake.

Forming Questions.

Word order in questions is generally inverted, so that the subject falls at the end of a phrase. The example above, "has arrived yet John?" is the perfect example. The initial focus of a question is on the action designated by the verb, secondarily on the subject of the question.

But, if we want to ask, for example, "did it rain yesterday?", then we would have the same form in Spanish as in English, i.e., "*¿ha llovido ayer?*"

When in doubt, do it as in English and add the upward inflection at the end of the sentence to indicate that it is, in fact, a question.

Interrogatory Words.

"*¿Quién?*" means "who?".
It is pronounced "Kee-*yehn*$_g$".

"*¿Cuál?*" means "which (one)?" or "what (one)?" from a selection of choices.
It is pronounced as "Kwahl?".

"*¿Por qué?*" means "why?"
It is pronounced as "Pour K*ay*?"

"*¿Cuándo?*" means "when?"
It is pronounced as "K*wan*-dough?"

"*¿Como?*" means "how?"
It is pronounced as "*Koh*-moh?"

"*¿Qué?*" means "what?"
It is pronounced as "Kay?"

"*Preguntar*" means "to ask a question".
It is pronounced "Prey-goon-*tahr*".

"*Pedir*" means "to ask for (something)", as in ordering a meal or making a request.
It is pronounced ""Pay-*deer*".

"*Hacer preguntas*" means "to pose (a) question(s)".
It is pronounced "Ah-*sair* Prey-*goon*-tahs"

Remember that the word order in Spanish is typically reversed when a question is posed (although you can still just make a straight declarative sentence with a vocalized question mark on the end). That's right? That's right.

Chapter XVII.
More Words You Need to Know.

There are all kinds of situations in which you'll find yourself that will drive you to distraction if you don't have the right vocabulary handy. We're going to explain how we used to solve this problem, and then we'll solve part of the problem for *you*.

Occasionally, like everyone, I've had to take my car to the shop. Due to the type of vehicle I had, the only available dealership had NO English speakers in the shop. After my first visit there for service on my car, I realized that I had to know the all of the right words to be able to communicate with the auto mechanics with regard to my vehicle.

So, I sat down with my trusty dictionary, and I made a list of all of the words that pertained to the particular automotive problem, as well as automotive problems and issues, in general.

You know the words I'm talking about. "Squeaks" and "clunks" and "brake shoes", et cetera. I made a list of every word I thought would come up in that situation and tried to learn them before my appointment at the service bay. I carried the handwritten list with me, so that I would have the words handy just in case memory failed me. And, of course and as usual, it did. I was really glad I had that list.

This was such a successful enterprise that I began to do it with everything, much the same way my wife had had me teach her the names of all of the things she typically purchased at the supermarket and the vocabulary she needed to communicate with the cleaning person to be sure the house got properly cleaned.

Making these kinds of lists can save you from nightmare situations. Even if you don't LEARN the words, just having a list handy can be a lifesaver when it's really needed, such as my automotive list.

Other lists you may want to learn, because they deal with everyday things like buying groceries. We're going to give you some lists in this chapter, but these lists won't be exhaustive of all the lists you may want to make. Others that you may need you'll have to ferret out on your own.

In the lists that follow, you'll acquire more than 350 new words. This lesson is one which will be a real eye opener.

These lists will also pay you very big dividends if you photocopy the ones you are most likely to need, take them to a print shop or Mailboxes, Etc. or somewhere similar and have them laminated. You can then carry the laminated list in your purse, wallet, briefcase, or pocket for when you are reasonably certain you'll need to have them available.

These lists are extensive. They begin on the next page.

At the Super Market.

Let's begin with vegetables, fruits and nuts (dried fruit). We'll try to give you as complete a list as possible, in case you rent a flat for holiday with a full kitchen and want to do your own cooking.

English	Spanish	Sounds Like
Foodstuffs		
Apple	Manzana	Mahn-<u>zahn</u>-ah
Orange	Naranja	Nah-<u>rahng</u>-hah
Grapes	Uvas	<u>Oov</u>-ahs
Plum	Ciruela	Seer-oo-<u>ey</u>-lah
Pear	Pera	<u>Peh</u>-rah
Raisins	Pasas (de Uva)	<u>Pah</u>-sahs
Banana	Plátano	<u>Plah</u>-tah-noh
Watermelon	Sandía	Sahn-<u>dee</u>-ya
Strawberries	Fresas	<u>Frey</u>-sahs
Peach	Melocotón	Mel-oh-koh-<u>tone</u>
Carrot	Sanahoria	Sah-nah-<u>or</u>-ee-ya
Green beans	Habichuela	Ah-beetch-<u>wey</u>-lah
String beans	Judeas	Hoo-<u>dee</u>-yahs
Any of a variety of soup beans	Alúbias	Ah-<u>loo</u>-bee-ahs
Beans (Lat. Am.)	Frijoles	Free-<u>hole</u>-eys
Lettuce	Lechuga	Leh-<u>choo</u>-gah
Cabbage	Cól	Cole
Onion	Cebolla	Say-<u>boh</u>-ya
Chili peppers	Guindillo	Geen-<u>dee</u>-yoh

Green or Red Peppers	Pimiento	Pee-mee-_en_-toh
Black pepper	Pimienta	Pee-mee-_en_-tah
Salt	Sal	Sahl
Basil	Albahaca	Al-bah-_ah_-kah
Oregano	Orégano	Oh-_reg_-ah-noh
Rosemary	Romero	Roh-_mare_-oh
Cinnamon	Canela	Kah-_ney_-lah
Coffee	Café	Kah-_fey_
Chocolate	Chocolate	Choh-koh-_lah_-tey
Watercress	Berro	_Beh_-rrhoh
Parsley	Perejíl	Pear-ey-_heel_
Biscuits (UK)	Galleta	Gah-_yeh_-tah
Cookie (US)	Galleta	
Biscuits (US)	Panecillo	Pahn-ey-_see_-yoh
Scones (UK)	Panecillo	
Yeast	Levadura	Leh-va-_doo_-rah
Yogurt	Yogúr	Yoh-_goor_
Egg Yolk	Yema	_Yey_-mah
Eggs	Huevos	_Wey_-vohs
Yucca	Yuca	_You_-kah
Cream	Nata	_Nah_-tah
Walnut	Nuez de Nogal	Nooh-_eys_ dey Noh-_gahl_
Greens	Verduras	Vair-_doo_-rahs
Garlic	Ájo	_Ah_-hoh
Tomato	Tomate	Toh-_mah_-tey
Water chestnuts	Castaño de agúa	Kahs-_tahn_-yo deyah-_gwah_
Juice (fruit & vegetable)	Zumo (Sp)	_Soo_-moh
Juice (fruit & vegetable)	Jugo (Lat.Am.)	_Hoo_-goh
Juice (meat)	Jugo	_Hoo_-goh

Vinegar	Vinagre	Vee-<u>nah</u>-grey
Vegetable	Vegetal	Veh-heh-<u>tahl</u>
Peanuts	Cacahuetes	Kah-kah-<u>weh</u>-teys
Cashews	Anacardos	An-ah-<u>kar</u>-doughs
Pecans	Pecanos	Pey-<u>kah</u>-nohs
Dried Fruit (nuts)	Fruto seco	<u>Froo</u>-toh <u>Sey</u>-koh
Candies	Caramelos	Kahr-ah-<u>mey</u>-lohs
Meat	Carne	<u>Kahr</u>-ney
Beefsteak	Biftek	Beef-<u>teyk</u>
Fillet (of any meat)	Solomillo	So-lo-<u>mee</u>-yoh
Pork	Cerdo	<u>Sair</u>-dough
Beef	Carne de Vaca	<u>Kahr</u>-ney dey <u>Vah</u>-kah
Lamb	Cordero	Core-<u>dey</u>-roh
Chicken	Pollo * *	<u>Poh</u>-yo *
Ham	Jamón	Hah-<u>moan</u>
Fish	Pescado	Pehs-<u>kah</u>-dough
Filet of Sole	Lenguádo	Lin-<u>gwa</u>-dough
Prawns (shrimp)	Gambas (Sp)	<u>Gahm</u>-bahs
	Camarones (Carib)	Kah-mah-<u>roh</u>-nays
Halibut	Mero	<u>Mey</u>-rhoh
Minced meat (UK)	Carne picada	<u>Kahr</u>-ney Pee-<u>kah</u>-dah
Ground Meat (US)		
Bread	Pan	Pahn_g
Butter	Mantequilla	Mahn-tey-<u>kee</u>-yah

---

* Be very careful of this pronunciation. Be sure that you pronounce "pollo" so that you end it in "O" if you mean chicken; an "A" ending signifies a certain male-exclusive appendage. We know an English woman who went to the butcher shop and asked for a "polla" sliced up "just so". It took the butcher two weeks to stop laughing.

Olive Oil	Aceite de oliva	Ah-<u>say</u>-ee-tey dey Oh-<u>leeve</u>-ah
Sunflower Oil	Aceite de girasol	Ah-<u>say</u>-ee-tey dey Hee-rah-<u>soul</u>
Beer	Cerveza	Sair-<u>vey</u>-sah
Coca Cola	Coca Cola	<u>Coh</u>-Kah <u>Coh</u>-lah
Pepsi	Pepsi	<u>Pek</u>-see
Sugar	Azucar	Ah-<u>soo</u>-kahr
Wine	Vino	<u>Vee</u>-noh
Ice Cream	Helado	Ey-<u>lah</u>-dough
Cake	Tarta	<u>Tahr</u>-tah

Cleaning & Paper Products:

Handsoap	Jabón de baño	Hah-<u>bone</u> dey <u>Bahn</u>-yo
Detergent	Detergente	Dey-tare-<u>hen</u>-tey
Paper towels	Toalla de Papél	Toh-<u>ah</u>-ya dey Pah-<u>pell</u>
Paper napkins	Servilleta de papél	Sair-vee-<u>et</u>-ah Dey Pah-<u>pel</u>
Shampoo	Champú	Chahm-<u>poo</u>
Toilet Paper	Papél Higiénico	Pah-<u>pell</u> Eee-hee-<u>en</u>-ee-koh
Toothpaste	Pasta dentifrica	<u>Pahs</u>-tah Den-tee-<u>free</u>-kah
Mouthwash	Lavado bucál	Lah-<u>vah</u>-dough Boo-<u>kahl</u>
Toothbrush	Cepillo de dientes	Say-<u>pee</u>-yo dey Dee-<u>en</u>-teys
Bleach	Lejía	Lay-<u>hee</u>-ya
Hairspray	Espray de Pelo	Es-<u>prye</u> de <u>Pay</u>-loh
Hair brush	Cepillo de Pelo	Say-<u>pee</u>-yah de <u>Pay</u>-loh
Comb	Peine	<u>Pay</u>-ee-ney
Cleaning rags	Trapo de limpieza	<u>Trah</u>-poh dey Lim-pee-<u>ey</u>-zah
Fabric softener	Suavizante de Ropa	Swah-vee-<u>zahn</u>-tey dey <u>Roh</u>-pah

---

*   In the case of Peine, be sure that you pronounce it "<u>pay</u>-ee-ney" and not "<u>pay</u>-ney"; otherwise, you make reference again to that same male exclusive appendage and not to a comb.

At the Pharmacy/Chemist.

Decongestant	Decongestante	Dey-cone-hest-ahn-tey
Cough Syrup	Jarabe anti-tos	Hahr-ah-bey An-tee-tohs
Antibiotic **	Antibiotico	An-te-be-oh-te-coh
Medicine *	Medicina	Meh-dee-see-nah
Tissue Paper	Pañuelo de Papél	Pahn-you-wey-loh dey Pah-pell
Tampons	Tampón	Tahm-pone
Acid Indigestion	Acidéz	Ah-see-dess
Common cold	Un catarro	Oon Kah-tahrr-oh
Flu	El grippe	L Gree-pey
Diarrhea	Diarrea	Dee-ah-rey-ah
Vomiting	El Vomitar	L Voh-mee-tahr
Pain	Dolor	Dough-lore
Toothache	Dolor de dientes	Dough-lore dey dee-en-teyss
Cramps	Calambres	Kah-lahm-brace
Menstrual cramps	Calambres menstrual	Kah-lahm-brace mains-troo-all
Menstruation	Menstruación	Mains-troo-ah-see-own
Cotton	Algodón	Al-goh-dough
Hydrogen Peroxide	Agúa Oxigenada	Ah-gua Oxi-hey-nah-dah

** Most antibiotics, as you may already have realized earlier, are going to be cognates. In any case, you can ask for the antibiotic by name and most pharmacists will know what you want. Unlike the UK, USA, Canada, et cetera, most "farmácias" will give you these medicines and many more without a doctor's prescription, so long as you know what you want, why, and sound like you know what you're talking about.

** As to medicines other than antibiotics, to the extent that they are brand name or well known pharmaceuticals, they will go by the same or a very similar name in Spanish. So, for example, if you want Losec or Viagra, ask for Losec (Low-seck) and Viagra (Vee-ah-grah). Also, most vitamins will go by the same name; for example vitamin B-6 would be "*vitamina b-6*" (pronounced "vee-tah-*mee*-nah Bay *Say*-ees").

Unguent or Salve	Ungüento	Oon-gwen-toh
Diaper (s) (US) Nappy (ies) (UK)	Pañal (es)	Pahn-yahl (-eyss)
Cream	Crema	Krey-mah
Condom	Condon	Kohn$_g$-doughn
	Preservativo	Pray-sair-vah-tee-voh
Contact lenses**	Lentillas**	Lain-tee-yahs
(Contact lens) cleaner	Limpiador de Lentillas	Leem-pee-ah-door dey Lain-tee-yahs
Contact lens wetting solution	Agúa purificada (de Lentillas)	Ah-gwah Poo-ree-fee-kah-dah (Dey Lehn-tee-yahs)
Eyedrops	Gotas para los ojos	Goh-tahs Pah-rah Lohs oh-hohs
Eyeglasses	Gafas (Sp)	Gah-fahs
	Espejuelos (Lat. Am.)	Es-pay-whay-lohs
Sunglasses	Gafas del sol	Gah-gahs dell soul
Tablet	Pastilla	Pahs-tee-yah
Capsule	Cápsula	Kahp-soo-lah
Drops	Gotas	Goh-tahs
Nasal spray	Espray nasal	Es-*pry* Nah-*sahl*
Rash	Erupciones	Ey-roop-see-own-eys
Wart	Verruga	Veh-*rroo*-gah
Cyst	Cysto	*Sees*-toh
Spots (pimples)	Grano	*Grah*-noh
Blemish (skin)	Mancha	*Mahn*-chah
Make-up	Maquillaje	Mah-kee-*yah*-hey

** In many countries, including Spain, you will not find eyeglasses or contact lenses or any products associated with them in a pharmacy. They are sold exclusively by opticians in a "*Tienda Optica*" (Optical Store and pronounced "tee-*en*-dah *ohp*-tee-kah").

At the Auto Mechanic.

<u>Auto Parts:</u>

Shock Absorber	Amortiguador	Ah-more-tee-gwah-<u>door</u>
Spring	Muelle	<u>Mwey</u>-yey
Tire	Pneumático (Sp)	Neuw-<u>mah</u>-tee-coh *
	Llanta (Lat.Am.)	<u>Yahn</u>-tah
	Goma (Carib.)	<u>Goh</u>-mah
Brake	Freno	<u>Frey</u>-noh
Brake shoes	Zapata de freno	Sah-<u>pah</u>-tah dey <u>Frey</u>-noh
Brake drum	Tambor de freno	Tahm-<u>bore</u> dey <u>Frey</u>-noh
Brake lining	Forro de freno	<u>Foh</u>-rrho dey <u>Frey</u>-noh
Brake fluid	Fluído de freno	Floo-<u>ee</u>-doh dey <u>Frey</u>-noh
To brake	Frenar	<u>Frey</u>-nahr
Gasoline	Gasolina	Gahs-oh-<u>lee</u>-nah
Oil	Aceite	Ah-<u>say</u>-ee-tey
Oil Filter	Filtro de aceite	<u>Feel</u>-troh dey ah-<u>say</u>-ee-tey
Carburetor	Carburador	Kahr-boo-rah-<u>door</u>
Fuel Injection	Inyección de combustible	Een-yek-see-<u>own</u> dey Kohm-boos-<u>tee</u>-bley
Auto Jack	El gato (the cat)	L <u>Gah</u>-toh
Screw	Tornillo	Tohr-<u>nee</u>-yo
Bolt	Perno	<u>Pair</u>-noh
Nut	Tuerco	Too-<u>ehr</u>-koh
Headlamps	Fároles	Fah-<u>roll</u>-eys
Taillamps	Faroles traseros	Fah-<u>roll</u>-eys trah-<u>sair</u>-ohs
Windscreen Windshield	Parabrisa	Pah-rah-<u>bree</u>-sah
Windscreen wipers	Limpia parabrisa	<u>Leem</u>-pee-ya Pah-rah-<u>bree</u>-sah
Rearview mirror	Retrovisor	Rey-tro-vee-<u>sore</u>
Turn signal	Señalador	Sayn-yah-lah-<u>door</u>

Steering wheel	Volante (Sp)	Voh-<u>lahn</u>-tey
	Timón (Carib/Lat.Am.)	Tee-<u>moan</u>
Radio	Rádio	<u>Rah</u>-dee-oh
Speedometer	Velocímetro	Vey-loh-<u>see</u>-meh-troh
Temperature	Temperatura	Teym-pair-ah-<u>too</u>-rah
Guage	Metro	<u>Meh</u>-troh
Auto body	Carrocería	Cah-rrhoh-sair-<u>ee</u>-yah
Sheet metal	Chapa	<u>Chah</u>-pah
Fibreglass	Fibra de vídrio	<u>Fee</u>-brah dey <u>vee</u>-dree-oh
Horn	Kláxon (Lat.Am./Sp.)	<u>Klahx</u>-own
	Pito (Sp)	<u>Pee</u>-toh *
Paint	Pintura	Peen-<u>too</u>-rah
Paint & Body	Chapa y Pintura	<u>Chah</u>-pah ee Peen-<u>too</u>-rah
Side windows	Elevaluna	El-ey-vah-<u>loo</u>-nah
Accelerator	Acelerador	Ah-sell-air-ah-<u>door</u>
Clutch	Embrague	Em-<u>brah</u>-ghey
Transmission	Transmissión	Trahns-mees-see-<u>own</u>
Gear Changes	Cambio de velocidades	<u>Kahm</u>-bee-oh dey Vey-loh-see-<u>dah</u>-deys
Gear Shift	Palanca de cambios	Pah-<u>lahng</u>-kah dey <u>Kahm</u>-bee-ohs
Diesel fuel	Gasoleo	Gahs-oh-<u>lay</u>-oh
Battery	Batería	Bah-tair-<u>ee</u>-yah
Block	Bloque	<u>Bloh</u>-kay
Cable	Cable	<u>Kahb</u>-lay
Carburetor	Carburador	Kahr-boo-rah-<u>dohr</u>
Chassis	Chasis	<u>Chah</u>-sees
Cylinder	Cilinidro	See-<u>leen</u>-droh

---

* Guys, don't drive into the auto shop and tell them your "pito" isn't working. They'll refer you to a doctor. "*Pito*" is more common in Spain than "*klaxon*", but one should say my " '*pito*' doesn't sound"; that is, "*no suena el pito del coche*" (meaning the "*pito*," on the car's horn, doesn't make any noise" and pronounced "noh <u>sway</u>-nah el <u>pee</u>-toh dell <u>coh</u>-chay").

Differential	Diferencial	Dee-fair-ehn-see-<u>all</u>
Disk	Disco	<u>Dees</u>-koh
Generator	Generador	Hen-air-ah-<u>dohr</u>
Glove Box	Guantera	Gwan-<u>tair</u>-ah
Hub Caps	Tapacubos	Tah-pah-<u>koo</u>-bos
Odometer	Odómetro	Oh-<u>dough</u>-meh-troh
Ignition	Ignición	Eeg-nee-see-<u>own</u>
Indicators	Indicador	Een-dee-kah-<u>dohr</u>
Piston	Pistón	Pees-<u>tone</u>
Pump	Bomba	<u>Bohm</u>-bah
Radiator	Radiador	Rah-dee-ah-<u>dohr</u>
Muffler	Silenciador	See-lehn-see-ya-<u>dohr</u>
Valve	Válvula	<u>Vahl</u>-voo-lah

<u>Noises & Problems:</u>

Not working properly	Tener avería	Teh-<u>nehr</u> Ah-vey-<u>ree</u>-ah
Problem (out of order)	Avería	Ah-vey-<u>ree</u>-ah
Noise	Ruido	<u>Rooee</u>*-dough
Squeak	Chirrido	Chee-<u>ree</u>-dough
Knock	Golpe	<u>Goal</u>-pay
It's knocking	Está golpeando	Es-<u>tah</u> Goal-pay-<u>ahn</u>-dough
It sticks	Se pega	Say <u>Pay</u>-gah
Vibration	Vibración	Vee-brah-see-<u>own</u>
The jack's missing	No tiene gato	Noh Tee-<u>en</u>-ney <u>Gah</u>-toh
(The tire is) Flat	Reventada	Rey-vehn-<u>tah</u>-dah
Whistle	Silbido	Seel-<u>bee</u>-dough
Adjustment	Ajuste	Ah-<u>hoos</u>-tey
Alignment	Alineación	Ah-leen-ey-ah-see-<u>own</u>

---

*Try to pronounce the two letters as if they were a single letter.

Antifreeze	Anti-congelante	<u>Ahn</u>-tee Kohn-hel-<u>ahn</u>-tey
Charge (battery)	Carga	<u>Kahr</u>-gah
Grease	Grasa	<u>Grah</u>-sah
Inflate	Inflar	Een-<u>flahr</u>
Lubrication	Lubricación	Loo-bree-kah-see-<u>own</u>
Pressure	Presión	Preh-see-<u>own</u>
Petrol (gas) station	Gasolinera	Gah-so-lee-<u>nair</u>-ah
Garage	Garaje	Gah-<u>rah</u>-hey

In the Petrol Station/Service Station.

Tank	Depósito	Dey-<u>poh</u>-see-toh
Fill it up	Llene el depósito	<u>Yey</u>-ney El Dey-<u>poh</u>-see-toh
Unleaded	Sin Plomo	Seen <u>Ploh</u>-moh
Leaded	Con Plomo	Cone <u>Ploh</u>-moh
Oil	Aceite	Ah-<u>say</u>-ee-tey
Weight	El Peso	El <u>Pay</u>-soh
How's the oil?	Como está el aceite?	<u>Koh</u>-moh es-<u>tah</u> El Ah-<u>say</u>-ee-tey
Can you clean the	Puede limpiar la…	<u>Pwey</u>-dey Lim-pee-<u>ahr</u>
…Windscreen?	…Parabrisa?	…la Pah-rah-<u>bree</u>-sah
Is there a car wash?	Hay lavado de Coches/carros?	Eye lah-<u>vah</u>-doh dey koh-chays/<u>kah</u>-rrhos
Where do I pay?	En Dónde lo pago?	En <u>Doughn</u>-dey Low <u>Pah</u>-goh
Car wash	Lavado del coche	Lah-<u>vah</u>-dough Dehl <u>Koh</u>-chay
Automatic	Automático	Ow-toh-<u>mah</u>-tee-koh
Do you accept…	Acceptan…	Ah-sep-<u>ten</u>
creditcards?	tarjeta de Crédito?	Tahr-<u>het</u>-ah Dey <u>Kreh</u>-dee-toe?

Pliers	Alicates	Ahl-ee-cah-tees
Screwdriver	Destornillador	Des-tore-nee-ah-door
Glue	Pegamento	Peh-gah-men-toe
Wrench	Llave	Yah-vay
Hammer	Martillo	Mar-tee-yo

In the Local Pub.

Drinking in Spanish speaking countries can be a unique experience, especially in Spain.

To begin with, the price of alcohol is much less than what you are accustomed to, both by the bottle and by the drink.

Secondly, although they are beginning to come down more on driving under the influence, especially in Spain, this isn't necessarily so for most of Latin America. And, you'll also find that they're not nearly so diligent about it as in your English speaking country, in either case.

You will also find that, often, there is no mandatory minimum drinking age. Even where there is, it is often flaunted without consequence.

In Spain and most of Europe, you will find young people having wine with dinner with their parents not to be any kind of big deal, and you will find people going to the pub with youngsters in a pram (stroller).

You also will see young people (age 13 or 14) at discos that cater to young people drinking beer, and you need have no fear of taking your teenagers with you to the pub and buying them a drink, if you are so inclined.

Observation.

Be warned: In Spain and in many other Spanish-speaking countries, the drinks are much stronger than what you are accustomed to. Especially in Spain and Cuba, you will often find that the bartender or waiter will bring the bottle to your table and pour your favorite libation into your glass until YOU say "stop", at which point, he'll add two or three drops of your favorite mixer. If you are not an experienced drinker, you could find yourself on your hands and knees after two or three drinks.

English	Spanish	Sounds Like
A drink	Un trago	Oon <u>Trah</u>-goh
Whiskey	Whiskey	<u>Wees</u>-kee
Gin	Ginebra	Hee-<u>ney</u>-brah
Tonic	Tónico	<u>Toh</u>-nee-koh
Bourbon	Borbón	Bore-<u>bone</u>
Vodka	Vodka	<u>Bvode</u>-kah
Gran Marnier	Gran Marnier	Grahn <u>Mar</u>-nee-air
Tia Maria	Tía María	<u>Tee</u>-ya Mahr-<u>ee</u>-ya
Southern Comfort	Southern Confort	Sew-<u>thern</u> <u>Cone</u>-ford
B-52	B cincuenta y dos	Bey Seeng-<u>kwen</u>-tah ee dose
Snacks	Tapas	<u>Tah</u>-pahs
Olives	Aceitunas	Ah-say-<u>too</u>-nahs
Chips	Crisps	Kreesps
Nuts	Frutos Secos	<u>Froo</u>-tohs <u>Seck</u>-ohs
Peanuts	Cacahuetes	Kah-kah-<u>wheh</u>-teys
Cashews	Anacardos	Ah-nah-<u>kahr</u>-doughs
Lemon	Limón	Lee-<u>Moan</u>

214

Lime	Lima	<u>Lee</u>-Mah
Beer	Cerveza	Sair-<u>vey</u>-sah
Tavern	Cervezería	Sair-vey-sehr-<u>ee</u>-ah
Bill (check)	Cuenta	<u>Kwen</u>-tah

The Toilet. The Loo. The Necessary.

When you're in a public place, such as a pub, and you need to use the restroom facilities, there are a number of ways to ask, depending on what makes YOU comfortable.

Knowing as many ways of requesting information about public restroom facilities as possible increases your chances of being able to find one with the minimum of difficulties. Remember, not everyone refers to them by the same term. Many people have never heard of the "loo", while others have never heard a public facility referred to as a "bathroom."

Take your pick, because, "when you gotta go, you gotta go."

<u>English</u>	<u>Spanish</u>	<u>Sounds Like</u>
Where is... ?	Dónde está... ?	<u>Dohn</u>-dey Es-<u>tah</u>
Toilet	El servicio	El Sair-vee-<u>see</u>-yo
Restroom	Aseo	Ah-<u>say</u>-oh
Crapper	Retrete	Rey-<u>treh</u>-tey
W.C.	W. C.	<u>Doble Oo</u>-vay Say
Bathroom	El Baño	El <u>Bahn</u>-yo
Washroom	El Lavabo	El Lah-<u>vah</u>-boh
Toilet Paper	Papel Higienico	Pah-<u>pell</u> Ee-hee-<u>ehn</u>-ee-koh
Hot Water	Aguá Caliente	Ah-<u>gwah</u> Kahl-ee-<u>ehn</u>-tey
Handsoap	Jabón	Hah-<u>bone</u>
Paper Towels	Toalla de papél	Toh-<u>ah</u>-ya Dey Pah-<u>pell</u>
Out of order	Averiado	Ah-vair-ee-<u>ah</u>-dough

Driving.

English	Spanish	Pronunciation
Traffic	Tráfico	_Trah_-fee-koh
Car/Auto	Carro	_Kah_-rroh
	Auto	_Ow_-toe
	Coche	_Koh_-chay
Traffic signal/ light	Semáforo	Say-_mah_-foh-roh
Traffic jam	Obstáculo de tráfico	Ohb-_stah_-koo-loh Dey _Trah_-fee-koh
	Atasco de tráfico	Ah-_tahs_-koh Dey _Trah_-fee-koh
Very fast	Muy rápido	Mooee _Rah_-pee-dough
Very high speed	Velocidad muy alta	Vey-loh-see-_dahd_ Mooee _Ahl_-tah
Slowly	Despácio	Des-_pah_-see-oh
Registration	Matriculación	Ma-tree-ku-lah-see-_own_
Vehicle plates	Placa de matriculación	_Plah_-kah dey…
Certificate of …	Certificado…	Sair-tee-fee-_kah_-dough …
Insurance	de segúro	Dey Say-_goo_-roh
Vehicle documents	Documentación de coche	Doh-ku-men-ta-si-_own_ Dey _Koh_-chey
Truck	Camión	Kah-mee-_own_
Delivery vehicle	Furgoneta	Foor-go-_neh_-tah
Motor home	Caravana	Kah-rah-_vah_-nah
Accident	Accidente	Ahk-see-_den_-tay
To crash or collide w/	Chocar	Choh-_kahr_
To skid or slide	Resbalar	Res-bah-_lahr_
To stop	Parar	Pah-_rahr_
Driving as in "in traffic"	Circular	Seer-koo-_lahr_

Driving as in "control of vehicle"	Conducir	Kohn-doo-_seer_
Driving permit	Carnét de conducir	Kahr-_neyt_ dey Kohn-doo-_seer_
Witness	Testigo	Tess-_tee_-goh
Alcolhol control checkpoint	Control de alcohol	Kohn-_trohl_ Dey Ahl-koh-_ohl_
Police roadblock	Control policial	Kohn-_trohl_ Poh-lee-see-_ahl_
Police	Policia	Poh-lee-_see_-yah
Civil Guard (Traffic Control)	Guardia Civil Tráfico	Gwahr-dee-ah See-_veel_ Trah-fee-koh
Hitchhike	Hacer Autostop	Ah-_sair_ _Ow_-toe Estop
Motorway/ Autobahn	Autopista	Ow-toe-_pee_-stah
Dual Motorway(UK) Divided Highway(US)	Carretera	Kah-rrey-_tehr_-ah
Street	Calle	_Kah_-yay
Alley	Callejón	Kay-yay-_hone_
Congestion	Congestión	Kohn-hess-tee-_own_
Crossing	Cruce	Kroo-say
Crossroads	Encrucijada	En-kroo-see-_hah_-dah
Curve	Curva	Koor-vah
Direct	Directo	Dee-_reck_-toh
Intersection	Intersección	Een-tair-seck-see-_own_
Median	Mediana	Mey-dee-_ah_-nah
Overpass	Paso superior	Pah-sew Soo-pair-ee-_ohr_
Parking meter	Parquímetro	Pahr-_kee_-meh-troh
Parking lot	Parking	Pahr-keeng
Pavement (Highway)	Pavimento	Pah-vee-_mehn_-toh
Ramp	Rampa	Rahm-pah

Route	Ruta	Roo-tah
Signal	Señal	Sane-yahl
Speed Limit	Límite de Velocidad	Lee-mee-tey dey Vey-loh-see-dad
Traction	Tracción	Trahk-see-own
Tunnel	Túnel	Too-nell
Sidewalk (US) Pavement (UK)	la Acera	Lah Ah-say-rah
Toll	Peage	Pay-ah-hey
Bridge	la Puente	La Pwen-tay
One-way street	Calle Unidireccional	Kah-yay Oon-ee-dee-reck-see-own-ahl
Underpass	Paso inferior	Pah-soh Een-fair-ee-ohr

Body Parts.

(Might come in handy for a trip to the doctor, pharmacist or hospital.)

Body	El Cuerpo	Kwehr-poh
Head	La Cabeza	Kah-bay-sah
Hair	El Pelo	Pay-loh
Face	La Cara	Kah-rah
Eyes	Los Ojos	Oh-hohs
Eyelids	El Párpado	Pahr-pah-dough
Eyelash	La Pestaña	Pess-tahn-yah
Eyebrows	Las cejas	Say-hahs
Nose	La Nariz	Nah-reess
Nostrils	Las Narices	Nah-ree-says
Mouth	La Boca	Boh-kah
Teeth	Los Dientes	Dee-ehn-teyss
Gums	La Encía	Ehn-see-ya
Lips	Los Labios	Lah-bee-ohs
Dimples	Los Hoyuelos	Oy-yu-wail-ohs

Chin	La Barbilla	Bahr-_bee_-yah
Beard	La Barba	_Bah_r-bah
Mustache	El Bigote	Bee-_goh_-tay
Neck	El Cuello	_Kway_-yoh
Chest or Breast	El Pecho	_Pey_-choh
Breasts	Las Mamas	_Mah_-mahs
	Las Tetas	_Teh_-tahs
Nipple	El Pezón	Pey-_sown_
Stomach	El Estómago	Es-_toh_-mah-goh
Navel (belly button)	El Ombligo	Om-_blee_-goh
Abdomen	El Abdomen	Ahb-_doh_-men
Groin	La Ingle	_Een_-glay
Penis	El Pene	_Pey_-ney
Testicles	Los _Testículos_	Tess-_tee_-koo-lohs
Scrotum	El Scroto	_Skroh_-toh
Vagina	La Vagina	Vah-_hee_-nah
Vulva	La Vulva	_Vool_-vah
Ovaries	Los Ovarios	Oh-_vahr_-ee-ohs
Back	La Espalda	Es-_pahl_-dah
Buttocks	Las Nalgas	_Nahl_-gahs
Rectum	El Recto	_Reck_-toh
Anus	El Ano	_Ah_-noh
Legs	Las Piernas	Pee-_air_-nahs
Thigh	El Muslo	_Moos_-loh
Knee	La Rodilla	Roh-_dee_-yah
Calf	La Pantorilla (Sp)	Pahn-toh-_ree_-yah
	La Canilla (Lat Am)	Kah-_nee_-yah
Shin	La Espinilla	Es-pee-_nee_-ya
Ankle	El Tobillo	Toh-_bee_-yoh
Foot	El Pie	_Pee_-ey
Hand	La Mano	_Mah_-noh

Fingers	Los Dedos	*Deh*-doughs
Thumb	El Pulgar	Pool-*gahr*
	El Dedo Grande (colloquial)	*Deh*-dough *Grahn*-dey
Toes	El Dedo del Pie	*Deh*-dough del *Pee*-ey
Big Toe	El Dedo Gordo	*Deh*-dough *Gohr*-dough
Fingernail	La uña	*Oon*-yah
Toenail	La uña del dedo del pie	See toes & fingernail
Elbow	El Codo	*Koh*-dough
Wrist	La muñeca	Moon-*yeck*-ah
Ears (outer)	Las Orejas	Oh-*rey*-hahs
Ears (inner)	Los Oidos	Oh-*ee*-doughs
Heart	El Corazón	Koh-rah-*sown*
Lung	El Pulmón	Pool-*moan*
Kidney	El Riñon	Reen-*yown*
Bladder	La Vejiga	Vey-*hee*-gah
Gall Bladder	La Vesicula Biliar	Vey-*see*-koo-lah Bee-lee-*ahr*
Intestines	Los Intestinos	Een-tess-*tee*-nohs
Spleen	El Bazo	*Bah*-soh
Pancreas	El Páncreas	*Pahn*-crey-ahs
Blood	La Sangre	*Sahn*-grey
Scar	La Cicatriz	See-kah-*treess*

In this lesson, you have learned roughly 350 new words, at least 140 of which are cognates. You can either commit all of them to memory or make wallet sized lists to carry with you for those times when you need these specific vocabulary packages. Over time and with use, you'll learn them anyway.

EXERCISE 30:

A.   From the grocery list, write down as many of the food items as you can FROM MEMORY.

B.   From the chemist list, write down as many of the items as you can FROM MEMORY.

C.   From the auto mechanic list, write down as many of the items as possible FROM MEMORY.

D.   From the petrol station list, write down as many of the items as possible FROM MEMORY.

E.   From the pub list, write down as many of the items as possible FROM MEMORY.

EXERCISE 31:

Make up your own lists for any areas you find of particular interest or where you think you might have a need, e.g., school terms, bullfights ("corrida de toros"), the beach, or music.

Chapter XVIII.
Expressions You'll Find of Value.

The most frustrating experience you'll ever have is needing or wanting to say something and not knowing HOW to say it, even when you know the words.

In this lesson, we're going to try to anticipate some of those times

Some of these examples will also be of help to you in getting more comfortable with understanding pronouns, even if you don't get comfortable using them.

Also, we will keep the sentence form as simple as possible in these expressions in order to prevent confusion and to facilitate recollection. You'll be correct; you just won't be elegant.

Finally, please notice that most of these expressions do NOT involve cognates.

English	Spanish

May I see that one?

¿Puedo ver ese?
Pwe-dough vare es-sey?

The "that" ("ese") is singular so doesn't require "one".

How much is it?

¿Cuánto es?
Kwan-toh Es?

Remember that there is no subject pronoun for "it".

I like this one.

Me gusta este.
Mey goos-tah Es-tey.

This one is a reflexive verb, so it comes with "me" built in. The sentence literally means, "this one is pleasing to me". Any time you want to say, "I like something", you would say "me gusta".

Do you like it?

Te gusta?
Tey Goos-tah?

Same as above. Reflexive verb "gustar". The pronoun is built-in. "Gusta" doesn't change.

She likes it.

Le gusta.
Lay Goos-tah.

Again, the pronoun is built-in. "Gusta" doesn't change.

We'd like to invite you …

Nos gustaría invitarles …
Noss goos-tah-ree-ah
een-vee-tahr-laze

Ditto on the pronoun.

…to dinner

…a cenar.
ah Say-nahr.

Why?	¿Por qué?
	Pour <u>Kay</u>?

Please distinguish this from "porque" which means "because". They sound alike, are written differently.

How? or	¿Como?
What was that again?	<u>Koh</u>-moh?

When are you coming?	¿Cuándo vienes? *Familiar form*
	<u>Kwan</u>-dough Vee-<u>en</u>-neys?

When will they get here? or	¿A qué hora llegan?
"What time do they arrive?"	Ah Kay <u>Oh</u>-rah <u>Yey</u>-gahn?

Can you come?	¿Puede venir? *Polite form*
	<u>Pwey</u>-dey Veh-<u>neer</u>?

When did it happen?	¿Cuándo pasó?
	<u>Kwan</u>-dough Pah-<u>sew</u>?

Again, "it" is the subject and has no pronoun. "Pasó" is past tense of "Pasar" ("to happen").

What happened?	¿Qué pasó?
	Kay Pah-<u>sew</u>?

"pasó" is the past tense of "pasar, "to happen".

What happened to him?	¿Qué le pasó?
"Le" represents "to him".	Kay Lay Pah-<u>sew</u>?

Why did you do that?	¿Por qué hiciste eso?
	Pour <u>Kay</u> Ee-<u>sees</u>-tey <u>es</u>-oh?

"hiciste" is "fixed" or preterit past tense of "Hacer". See the same expression utilizing the perfect tense on the following page.

Same expression as above.	¿Por qué has hecho eso?
	Pour Kay Ahs Etch-oh Es-oh?

"has hecho" is the perfect tense you learned in Chapter VIII. Literally, "why have you done that?"

Who is he?	¿Quién es él?
	Kee-eyn Es El?

Who are they?	¿Quiénes son?
	Kee-eyn-es Sown?

Who is it?	¿Quién es?
	Kee-eyn Es?

Hi. I'm John.	Hola. Soy Juan.
	Oh-lah. Soy Hwan.

Most people forget when they pronounce the name Juan that "J" sounds like An "h" and that "ua" makes a "w". Hence, they forget to pronounce this properly as "HWAN". Same for Juanita. Or Marijuana. Keep in mind that the word "what" in English is not pronounced "Wat"; rather it is "What".

My name is John.	Me llamo Juan.
	Mey Yah-moh Hwan.
	Mi nombre es Juan.
	Mee Nohm-bray Es Hwan.

Either of these gets the same result. Now we know who you are.

What's your name?	¿Como te llamas? *Familiar form*
	Koh-moh Tey Yah-mahs?
	¿Como se llama Ud.? *Polite form*
	Koh-moh Say Yah-mah
	Ooh-stead?

Auto dealership	Concesionario de autos Cone-sess-ee-oh-<u>nah</u>-ree-oh dey <u>Out</u>-ohs.
How are things?	Qué tal? Kay Tahl?
How's it going?	¿Como anda? <u>Koh</u>-moh <u>ahn</u>-dah?
Fill the tank, please.	Lléne el depósito. <u>Yey</u>-ney el Dey-<u>pose</u>-ee-toh.
Could you bring me the menu?	¿Me trae la carta? Mey Try La <u>Kahr</u>-tah?

Personal pronoun "me" before the noun. Could add "a mi" so it's indirect object pronoun. Right?

I would like to have... (to eat)	Yo quisiera comer... Yo kee-see-<u>er</u>-ah Koh-<u>mare</u>...

This is the very polite and very refined way to ask when ordering food in a restaurant.

I'd like to have...	Me gustaría tomar... Mey Goos-tah-<u>ree</u>-ah Toh-<u>mahr</u>...
a coffee	Un Café. Un Kah-<u>fey</u>.
Where is... ?	¿Dónde está... ? <u>Dohn</u>-dey Es-<u>tah</u>... ?
Can you direct me to... ?	¿Me puede dirigir a... ? Mey <u>Pwey</u>-dey dee-ree-<u>heer</u> ah... ?

I wish I knew!	¡Ojalá que supiera! Oh-hah-<u>lah</u> Kay Soup-ee-<u>er</u>-ah!
Call the police!	¡Lláme a la policía! <u>Yah</u>-mey Ah La Poh-lee-<u>see</u>-ya!
What number do I dial?	¿Qué número marco? Kay <u>Noo</u>-mehr-oh <u>Mahr</u>-koh?
I have nothing to declare.	No tengo nada para declarar. No <u>Teyn</u>-goh <u>Nah</u>-dah <u>Pah</u>-rah Dey-klahr-<u>ahr</u>.
I want to declare this.	Quiero declarar este. Kee-<u>air</u>-oh Dey-klahr-<u>ahr</u> <u>Es</u>-tey.
Where is the telephone?	¿Donde está el teléfono? <u>Doan</u>-dey Es-<u>tah</u> el Tey-<u>lay</u>-fo-noh?

Be sure you get the emphasis on the second "e" in Teléfono. The word is Tey-LAY-fo-noh, not Tey-lay-FO-noh.

Give me 2 kilos of...	Déme 2 kilos de... <u>Dey</u>-mey dose <u>kee</u>-lohs dey...

In most of the Americas, you would order by "libras", not kilos.

My job is...	Mi trabajo es... Mee Trah-<u>bah</u>-hoh Es...
I need a doctor.	Necesito un medico. Neh-sey-<u>see</u>-toh Oon <u>Meh</u>-dee-koh.

Do you speak English?	¿Habla inglés? <u>Ah</u>-blah Eeng-<u>lez</u>?
I'm sorry.	Lo siento. Low See-<u>en</u>-toh.
I don't understand.	No entiendo. No En-tee-<u>en</u>-doh.
Can you talk more slowly?	¿Puede hablar más despácio? <u>Pwey</u>-dey Ah-<u>blahr</u> Mahs Des-<u>pah</u>-see-oh?
Could you repeat that?	¿Puede repetirlo? <u>Pwey</u>-dey Reh-peh-<u>teer</u>-low?
I don't know.	No sé. No <u>Say</u>.
How does it work?	¿Como funciona? <u>Koh</u>-moh Foonk-see-<u>oh</u>-nah?
I would like…	Quisiera… Kee-see-<u>air</u>-ah…
my steak …	el solomillo… El So-low-<u>mee</u>-yo…
very rare.	casi crudo. <u>Kah</u>-see <u>Kroo</u>-dough.
well done.	bien hecho. <u>Bee-yen</u> <u>Eh</u>-choh.

Medium.	A su punto. Ah Soo <u>Poon</u>-toh.
Where is check-in (airport)?	¿Dónde está la facturación? <u>Doan</u>-dey <u>Es</u>-tah Lah Fack-too-rah-see-<u>own</u>?
What time is the flight?	¿Cuándo sale el vuelo? <u>Kwan</u>-dough <u>Sah</u>-lay El <u>Vwey</u>-low?
Can you take my luggage?	¿Puede llevar el equipaje? <u>Pwey</u>-dey Yey-<u>vahr</u> El Eh-kee-<u>pah</u>-hey?
Boarding pass.	Tarjeta de embarque. Tahr-<u>heh</u>-tah De Em-<u>bar</u>-kay.
Aisle or window?	¿El pasillo ú la ventana? Pah-<u>see</u>-yo oo Lah Ven-<u>ta</u>-na?
Ticket.	Billete. Bee-<u>Yey</u>-tey.
Flight attendant.	Azafata. Ah-sah-<u>fah</u>-tah.
Here to the right.	Aquí a la derecha. Ah-kee Ah Lah Dey-<u>reh</u>-chah.
to the left.	A la izquierda. Ah lah Ees-kee-<u>yehr</u>-dah
Go straight.	Sigué recto. <u>See</u>-gay <u>Reck</u>-toh.

Stop here.	Pare aquí.
	<u>Pahr</u>-ey Ah-<u>kee</u>.
How much is it?	¿Cuánto es?
	<u>Kwan</u>-toh Es?
Why did you do that?	¿Por qué has hecho eso?
	Pour <u>Kay</u> Ahs <u>Etch</u>-oh <u>Es</u>-oh?
When will you do it?	¿Cuándo vas hacerlo?
	<u>Kwan</u>-dough Vahs Ah-<u>sair</u>-low?

One simple way to use the object pronoun is to attach it to the infinitive of a verb, as above.

In Spanish, I am a beginner.	En el castellano, soy principiante.
	En El Kahs-tey-<u>yah</u>-no
	Soy Preen-see-pee-<u>ahn</u>-tey.
It's expensive.	Es caro.
	Es <u>Kah</u>-roh.
It's cheap.	Es barato.
	Es Bah-<u>rah</u>-toh.
What a bargain!	¡Qué ganga!
	Kay <u>Gahng</u>-gah!
Where do I pay?	¿Dónde lo pago?
	<u>Dóhn</u>-dey Low <u>Pah</u>-goh?

In effect, "at" where or "in" where do I pay?

Where are we going?	¿A dónde vamos?
	Ah <u>Dohn</u>-dey <u>Vah</u>-mohs?

If effect, "to" where or "at" where are we going?

| There's no hot water. | No hay aguá caliente. |
| | No Eye Ah-<u>gwah</u> Kahl-ee-<u>en</u>-tey. |

"hay" prounced like "eye (ball)" means "there is" or "there are".

| I'm glad to see you. | Me alegro de verte. |
| | May Ah-<u>leg</u>-roh dey <u>Vair</u>-tey. |

Here you see personal pronouns used in two ways. In the first, it's like "gustar", i.e., "me alegro" ("I'm happy", literally, "I make myself happy") and, in the second, we have the object pronoun attached to the infinitive verb ending "verte".

| He was robbed. | Se le robáron. |
| | Say Lay Roh-<u>bar</u>-own. |

This one is difficult to fathom, I must admit. Literally, it is "they have robbed themselves to him". Don't try to understand it. Just accept. This is how you say "he was robbed."

| I was robbed. | Se me robáron. |
| | Say May Roh-<u>bar</u>-own. |

| I'm washing my hands. | Me lavo las manos. |
| | May <u>Lah</u>-voh Lahs <u>Mah</u>-nohs. |

Again the pronoun "me" comes with the verb. "Me lavo, te lavas, se lava, nos lavamos" etc.

I'm pleased to meet you.	Es un placer conocerlo.
(said to a man)	Es Oon Plah-sair
	Koh-noh-<u>sair</u>-*low*.

I'm pleased to meet you.	Es un placer conocerla.
(said to a woman)	Es Oon Plah-sair
	Koh-noh-<u>sair</u>-*lah*.

Please try to pick up on this very distinctive use of the polite form direct object pronouns in the last two phrases.

We were mugged.

Quite literally, "they mugged us".

Nos atracáron.
Nohss Ah-trah-<u>kahr</u>-own.

It was that guy.

Era ese típo.
<u>Ehr</u>-ah <u>Es</u>-ey <u>Tee</u>-poh.

It was those guys.

Eran esos tipos.
<u>Ehr</u>-ahn <u>Es</u>-ohs <u>Tee</u>-pohs.

He was wearing a blue shirt.

Llevaba una camisa azúl.
Yey-<u>vah</u>-bah <u>Oon</u>-ah
Kah-<u>mee</u>-sah Ah-<u>sool</u>.

Past tense of "llevar". Also, "llevar" means to carry. You just have to get used to it and try to glean whether one is wearing or carrying something when you hear this verb. Context provides the clue.

Note: The next four examples should be reviewed together, because they represent 4 different uses of the verb, *"dejar"*:

Let me get dressed.

Déjame vestir.
<u>Dey</u>-hah-may Vehs-<u>teer</u>.

In the first instance, the verb "dejar" is used in the context of "allow" or "let" or "give opportunity. It also has the the indirect object pronoun attached. Used in conjunction with the infinitive of another verb to which is attached the direct object pronoun.

Let me do it.

Déjame hacerlo.
<u>Dey</u>-hah-may Ah-<u>sair</u>-low.

In the second instance, we have "dejar" used in the same context, seeking opportunity to do something not described (but understood) and the direct object pronoun attached to the second verb, "hacer".

Drop it, child.	Déjalo, niño.
	<u>Dey</u>-hah-low, <u>neen</u>-yo.

This sentence is to demonstrate the second USE of "dejar" which is to "drop" or "put something down" or "to leave" something as in "leave it alone".

My parents don't let me.	Mis padres no me dejan.
	Mees <u>Pah</u>-dreys no May <u>Dey</u>-hahn.

Again, we have "dejar" being used in the context of "allowing" to do something or "permitting it".

Pardon (me).	Perdóne (me).
	Pair-<u>doan</u>-ey (may)

Used in the sense of "Please forgive me for something I have done (or am about to do).

Excuse me.	Discúlpeme.
	Dees-<u>kool</u>-pay-may

My apologies.	Discúlpe.
	Dees-<u>kool</u>-pay

Used in the sense of apologies for something that one has done, e.g., bumping into someone.

I'm sorry.	Lo siento.
	Low See-<u>en</u>-toe

I'm very sorry.	Lo siento mucho.
	Low See-<u>en</u>-toe <u>Moo</u>-cho

I appreciate it.	Lo agradezco.
	Low Ah-grah-<u>dess</u>-koh

Excuse me.   Con permiso.

Cone-pair-<u>mee</u>-sew

Used in the sense of excusing yourself to get by or past someone, e.g., in a supermarket aisle.

EXERCISE 32:

A.   From the list of useful expressions, write down as many as you can FROM MEMORY.

B.   Using your dictionary, scan definitions of words that are familiar to you which are typically used in "expressions" in English. See whether or not a similar expression exists in Spanish. Make a list of those expressions.

C.   How many cognates have you discovered? The total? How many non-cognate words do you know? Do you know 2,000 words, 3,000? If you're at that level already, you're already a Spanish speaker, even if you don't realize it yet. Make a precise total so you will know.

Chapter XIX.
Verbs with "SE".

This next subject is sooo confusing to most people, yet it is relatively simple.

As we saw earlier, there are verbs, such as "*gustar*" which have a reflexive pronoun; that is, they come in a form in which the verb "reflects" back on itself, as they like to say in more academic environments than this one.

To us English speakers, this just sounds like so much gobbledygook, so let's see if we can shed some light on the use of "*SE*" with a verb.

Traditional Explanation.

Verbs that end in "SE" are referred to as REFLEXIVE verbs.

A verb like "*lavarse*" which means to "wash oneself", so we end up with forms such as "*me lavo*" ("I wash myself"), "*tú te lavas*" (you wash yourself). This is what the Spanish grammar books all say.

The reality is, it's just another way of saying "to wash up". "*Me lavo*" means "I'm washing up". It's as simple as that. Don't waste time trying to understand why it's this way. It doesn't TRANSLATE. Just interpret it that way.

In the last chapter, we raised this issue with the verb "*gustar*". "*Gustar*" means "to be pleasing to". However, when we want to say, "I like it", we are forced by the form of the verb to use "*gustarse*", and it comes out "it is pleasing to me" or "it pleases me". That is, "*me*" ("to me") and "*gusta*" ("to be pleasing"), and it means, "I like it". "*Me gusta*". I like it.

Butt & Benjamin's "Verbs of Becoming".

According to the best Spanish language grammar book in the world by Butt & Benjamin**, many of these reflexive verbs with "*se*" mean that "one is becoming" something, and they refer to them as "verbs of becoming".

Huh?

Let's look at the verb "*enfadarse*". Butt & Benjamin refer to this is as a verb of "becoming". That is, the verb "*enfadarse*" means "to become angry",

Well, think about it. When one is "making oneself", let's say, angry, we can say one is "becoming angry". True?

The proper form for this is with the verb "*enfadarse*" ("to become angry").

This is the simplest explanation I've ever seen in a grammar book, and, essentially, I agree with it.

My Way Means You're "Getting..." There.

There is a great deal of logic to the "verbs of becoming" issue, certainly more than the complete lack of logic in most grammar books. But, it is my opinion that there is an even simpler explanation which makes it miles easier to understand most of the time.

My explanation is that using "*se*" makes of a verb a verb of "getting..."

---

* A New Reference Grammar of Modern Spanish by Butt & Benjamin. The opinion stated is my own. I believe this to be the best Spanish language grammar book in print anywhere. Period.

That is to say, a verb like "*me lavo*" means "I'm getting washed up" or one like "*me enfado*" means "I'm getting mad" or "*me visto*" which means, "I'm getting dressed".

"*Acostumbrar*" means "to accustom", but, with "*se*", "*acostumbrarse*" means, "to get accustomed to..." ("Accustom oneself", literally).

"*Administrar*" means "to administer", but adding "*se*" results in "*administrarse*" or "to get administered". For example, you might hear "*él administra el programa*", meaning, "He administers the program". On the other hand, "*se administra el programa*" would mean, "the program is getting administered".

This last example also points to the fact that many verbs are used 'reflexively' in the passive third person (like "*se dice*") when we want "the program" to be, in effect, the subject and not the object of a sentence. The end result is the same, in any case. And, in fact, you would see "*se administra el programa*" (or hear it) more often than not. It is much more common to hear it this way than using "*ser*" to form the passive, i.e., "*es administrado el programa*".

In the preceding example, YOU would say "*es administrado el programa*", because that is how we have shown you to do it. The Spaniard would say "*se administra el programa*". You would still understand him, and he will definitely understand you.

Other verbs, such as "*acabar*", which you already know, can also be presented in the form "*acabarse*". This just means, in the form "*me acabo*" that "I'm getting finished". Well, gee, that was really complicated. So, now we have:

<u>My Heretical Rule No. 24.</u>

When you hear a verb being used with "se", just assume that it means someone or something "is getting..."

Contradictions?

Let's look at an example that is more difficult and that would seem to contradict <u>My Heretical Rule No. 24</u>.

The verb "*poner*" by itself means "to put" or "*to place*". If we make it reflexive, i.e., if we add the reflexive pronoun "*se*" it becomes "*ponerse*" and it means "to become".

So, if I say "*voy a poner la mesa*", I have said or "I am going to 'set' the table". Likewise, "*voy a ponerlo en la mesa*" ("I'm going to put it on the table").

However, as soon as I add "se" to the equation, I end up with another possibility entirely.

For example, "*él me pone enfadado*", i.e., "*he is making me angry*" (actually, "he is making me to 'get' angry"). Either is a correct interpretation, and this use therefore does nothing to void *My Heretical Rule No. 24*.

Let's go back to an earlier example, "*Se dice*".

"They say", "People say", "It is said". These are the examples given in every grammar book ever written for this form, and it is correct.

Can we reconcile that with my approach of "getting"? Sure. We may have to stretch a bit, but we'd end up with "*se dice*" meaning "it is getting said".

Now, for non-Americans, this may be a more difficult explanation.

Americans, however, use this form of expression regularly. For example, "I'm getting ready..." as in "I'm getting ready to prepare dinner" or "I'm getting ready to go out", et cetera.

An even more farfetched idiom in use in North America is the expression "I'm fixing to..." which is almost a future tense for "I'm getting..."

Examples: "I am ready". "I am getting ready". "I am fixing to get ready". Sorry, Yanks, this one does not exist in Spanish.

Certainly, the area of reflexive verbs (those that are *permanently* reflexive and those that are *sometimes* reflexive) is not a simple one. It is a way of expression that is totally unlike English, notwithstanding that the form exists in languages as diverse as German, Arabic, Italian, Spanish, Portuguese, French and Urdu.

No matter. This explanation of 'reflexive' verbs is SO SIMPLE, yet I've *never* seen a grammar book that makes it this simple. Just remember, if you hear a verb used with the subject pronoun and the verb in the same person, it means, "getting..." or, as Butt & Benjamin would say, it's a "verb of becoming".

If you do, you'll make far fewer mistakes in *interpretation* than people with far better educations than yours.

This applies to any verb (with nominal exceptions, of course) that 'comes with' an attached pronoun "*se*".

A Couple of REAL Exceptions?

The most obvious exception to the idea of "getting..." with a reflexive verb is that of "*gustarse*". You remember that one.

However, with this verb, you rarely see "*me gusto*", meaning "I am pleasing to myself"; rather, you almost always see or hear "*me gusta*", meaning "I like... ". For example, "*me gusta mucho la carne*", meaning "I really like the meat". Or, "*a él le gusta la carne*" (meaning "he likes the meat").

No matter how I slice this one, I can't reconcile it with the "getting... " approach, unless I take the great intellectual leap to presume that "the meat really is 'getting liked by me'".

But, then, in that case, I wouldn't have an exception, would I? Still, I think I prefer to interpret it as "I really like the meat. What about you?

The other obvious exception is the reflexive form of "*ir*". You will recall that "*ir*" means "to go", so "*voy*" means "I am going" or "I go".

However, when we use it in its reflexive form, "*irse*", we end up with "to leave"; i.e., "*me voy*" means "I'm leaving" or "I leave". It's very difficult to reconcile this one to "I'm getting gone", but perhaps not so difficult to do with the interpretation of "I'm getting out of here".

All kidding aside, this one should be interpreted as either "I'm leaving" or, in certain circumstances, "I'm getting out of here".

Recommendation.

For your purposes in learning to converse in Spanish, I would suggest that you not take this "different" verb form too seriously. When you hear it, your first reaction should be that someone or something is "getting... " whatever. In time, you will learn to be more discerning and more adept at interpreting the subtleties of reflexive verbs.

Also, in terms of expressing yourself, it's fairly easy to know when to use the reflexive form of a verb (if you want) and that is when you intend to say, "I am getting... ", use the reflexive form of the verb. For example, "*me enfado*" for "I am getting angry".

OR

Use "*ponerse*", which means "to become", i.e., "to be getting... ", and say, for example, "*me pongo enfadado*" or "*me pongo más estudiosa/o*" for "I am getting mad" or "I am getting more studious", respectively.

The main thing is this: *No matter what you hear or what you are told or what you read, you cannot allow yourself to be intimidated by this verb form. It's just not that complicated and it's not that critical for you to master in order to be able to communicate.*

A Few More Carefully Chosen High Frequency Cognates for Your Lists follow on this page:

English	Spanish	Pronounced
Public	público	*poo*-blee-koh
Pure	puro	*poo*-roh
Quality	calidad	kahl-ee-*dahd*
Quantity	cantidad	kahn-tee-*dahd*
Reality	realidad	rey-all-ee-*dahd*
To Recognize	reconocer	rey-kohn-oh-*sair*
To Reduce	reducir	rey-doo-*seer*
To Repeat	repetir	rey-pey-*teer*
Rich	rico	*ree*-koh
Separate	separado	say-pahr-*ah*-dough
Service	servicio	sair-*vee*-see-oh
Situation	situación	see-too-ah-see-*own*
Social	social	soh-see-*all*
Special	especial	eh-spey-see-*all*
State	estado	es-*tah*-dough
Style	estilo	es-*tee*-loh
Time	tiempo	tee-*em*-poh
Type	tipo	*tee*-poh
Typical	típico	*tee*-pee-koh
United	unido	oo-*nee*-dough
Value	valor	vah-*lohr*
Visit	visita	vee-*see*-tah

Chapter XX.
Nouns, Adjectives, Adverbs and Prepositions.

These are the things that add detail to your speech and modify nouns and verbs, and indicate how and by what means, giving greater details to enable us to draw a mental picture of something that is more precise and more accurate, et cetera. These are simple, yet they are not. We'll try to keep it as simple as possible.

Nouns and Adjectives Shouldn't Argue.

Adjectives are words that modify nouns; in other words, they tell you something about the words that represent people, places and things.

"Girl" is a noun.

"Pretty girl", a noun modified by an adjective, tells us something more about the subject. Mentally, although we recognize "girl" to be a young female, modifying "girl" with "pretty" brings to mind a totally different image -- well, for me, anyway.

We know the "girl" has eyes, but if we further add "a pretty girl with big blue eyes", we know even more about the subject and can visualize even better how she might look. You know what adjectives are.

In English, a noun is a noun and an adjective is an adjective, and, although they may reflect the gender of the person or animal that they are used to describe, they themselves (nouns and adjectives) are without gender.

Not so in Spanish. In Spanish, every noun has its own gender, so every adjective changes as to gender. Obviously, if we're talking about people, we know generally if they are male or female. The same is true for animals.

However, when we start to talk about things that are not human or animal, rather inanimate or abstract, the concept of gender gets complicated. It's a complication that English doesn't have.

Obviously, even in Spanish, women are female and men are male. But, what about rocks or beaches or umbrellas? In English, they are just things, as they are in Spanish, but without gender.

Why Spanish nouns have genders I cannot say, because I have absolutely no clue other than from their derivations from Latin or Greek that also reflect gender specificity for things and concepts. Nonetheless, it's something we need to deal with.

From a practical point of view, here are some general guidelines (call them RULES we may break from time to time):

Masculine Nouns:

A.   Names of male humans and animals are almost automatically masculine.

B.   Nouns ending in "o" are masculine, with some exceptions."La mano" ("hand") and "La radio" ("radio") are two of those exceptions.

C.   Days of the week, months, rivers, oceans and mountains are all masculine.

D.   Most nouns ending in "-L" or "-R" and those adjectives derived from Greek ending in "-ma" are masculine. There are some notable exceptions, such as "honey" ("la miel"), "flower" ("la flor"), "salt" ("la sal").

E.   Nouns with positive connotations are generally masculine.

Feminine Nouns:

A.   Names of female humans and animals are almost automatically feminine.

B.   All the letters of the alfabeto are feminine.

C.   Nouns ending in "-cion", "-tad", "-dad", "-tud" and "-umbre" are feminine.

D.   Nouns ending in "a" are feminine with certain exceptions such as "el problema" ("problem"), "el mapa" ("map"), "el dogma" ("dogma"), "el programa" ("program").

E.   Diseases and nouns with negative connotations are usually feminine.

Why a rock ("piedra") should be feminine and paper ("papél") masculine is beyond me.

Even more striking is the fact that all euphemisms with which I am familiar render the male sexual equipment as feminine gender, while most euphemisms for the female genitalia are male gendered. As to logic there is none.

There are some nouns that change gender, such as the professions. There are others that never change, even when the gender of the person to whom it applies is of a different gender.

And, that will bring us to:

My Heretical Rule No. 25.

1.   Go with what feels right, with what feels natural. Don't worry about it.   Even Spanish speakers make mistakes. The also recognize that foreigners generally have a hard time with this aspect of their language, so they make the necessary allowances.

2.   However, when you modify a noun with an adjective, please make sure that the ending of the adjective agrees with the ending of the noun. That is, if the noun ends in "o", so should the adjective end in "o". Likewise, those nouns ending in "a" should have adjectives ending in "a".

3.   Even if you have the WRONG ending for the noun, the adjective should still agree.

Some Feminine Nouns and Adjectives of Importance.

Mujer	Woman	Moo-<u>hair</u>
Esposa	Wife	Es-<u>poh</u>-sah
Media Naranja	Other Half	<u>Me</u>-dee-ah Nah-<u>ran</u>-hah
Chica	Young girl	<u>Chee</u>-kah
	Teenager	
Niña	Little girl	<u>Neen</u>-yah
Querida	Dear(est)	Kay-<u>ree</u>-dah
Bella	Beautiful	<u>Bay</u>-yah
Belleza	Beauty	Bay-<u>yay</u>-sah
Bellísima	Very Beautiful	Bay-<u>yiss</u>-ee-moh
Linda	Pretty	<u>Leen</u>-dah
Guapa	Good Looking	<u>Gwah</u>-pah
Novia	Girl Friend	<u>Noh</u>-vee-ah
Prometida	Fiancee	Pro-may-<u>tee</u>-dah

Enamorada	Beloved	En-ah-mo-<u>rah</u>-dah
Mi Amor	My Love	Mee Ah-<u>more</u>
Mi Vida	My Life	Mee <u>Vee</u>-dah
Mi Cielo	My Heaven	Mee See-<u>ail</u>-oh
Amante	Lover	Ah-<u>mahn</u>-tay
Gorda	Fat	<u>Gore</u>-dah
Delgada	Slender	Dell-<u>gah</u>-dah
Animada	Lively	Ah-nee-<u>mah</u>-dah
Estudiante	Student	Es-too-dee-<u>ahn</u>-tay
Alumna	Student	Ah-<u>loom</u>-nah
Puta	Slut, hooker	<u>Poo</u>-tah
Prostituta	Prostitute	Pros-tee-<u>too</u>-tah
Bruja	Witch	<u>Broo</u>-hah
Embarazada	***Pregnant***	Em-bah-rah-<u>ssah</u>-dah
Avergonzada	Embarassed	Ah-vair-goan-<u>sah</u>-dah
Madre	Mother	<u>Mah</u>-dray
Tia	Aunt	<u>Tee</u>-yah
Hermana	Sister	Air-<u>mah</u>-nah
Sobrina	Niece	Sew-<u>bree</u>-nah
Hija	Daughter	<u>Ee</u>-hah
Prima	Cousin	<u>Pree</u>-mah
Viznieta	GreatGrandaughter	Bveese-nee-<u>et</u>-ah
Abuela	Grandmother	Ah-<u>bway</u>-lah
Monja	Nun	<u>Moan</u>-hah
Enfermera	Nurse	En-fair-<u>mair</u>-ah
Dama	Lady	<u>Dah</u>-mah
Señorita	Miss	Seyn-yor-<u>ee</u>-tah
Señora	Mrs.	Seyn-<u>yor</u>-ah
Nieta	Granddaughter	Nee-<u>eh</u>-ta
Vizabuela	GreatGrandmother	Bveese-ah-<u>bway</u>-lah
Cuñada	Sister-in-law	Koon-<u>ya</u>-do
Suegra	Mother-in-law	<u>Sway</u>-grah

| Madrina | Godmother | Mad-<u>dree</u>-nah |

Some Masculine Words and Adjectives of Importance.

Hombre	Man	*Ohm*-bray[**]
Esposo	Husband	Es-<u>poh</u>-soh
Marido	Husband	Mah-<u>ree</u>-dough
Media Naranja	Other Half	<u>Meh</u>-dee-ah Nah-<u>rahn</u>-hah
Chico	Young man Teenager	<u>Chee</u>-koh
Niño	Little boy	<u>Neen</u>-yoh
Querido	Dear(est)	Care-<u>ee</u>-dough
Chulo	Cocky	<u>Choo</u>-low
Guapo	Handsome	<u>Gwah</u>-poe
Novio	Boy Friend	<u>No</u>-vee-oh
Prometido	Fiancee	Pro-may-<u>tee</u>-dough
Enamorado	Beloved	En-ahm-oh-<u>rah</u>-dough
Mi Amor	My Love	Mee Ah-<u>more</u>
Mi Vida	My Life	Mee <u>Vee</u>-dah
Mi Cielo	My Heaven	Mee See-<u>ehy</u>-low
Amante	Lover	Ah-<u>mahn</u>-tay
Gordo	Fat	<u>Gore</u>-dough
Delgado	Slender	Dell-<u>gah</u>-dough
Animado	Lively	Ahn-ee-<u>mah</u>-dough
Estudiante	Student	Es-too-dee-<u>ahn</u>-tay
Alumno	Student	Ah-<u>loom</u>-noh
Cabrón	Cuckold (lit.), SOB (fig.)	Kah-<u>brone</u>
Avergonzado	Embarassed	Ah-vair-goan-<u>sah</u>-dough
Padre	Father	<u>Pah</u>-dray

[**] Please pronounce this word as "*ohm*-bray", not "*ahm*-bray". "Hombre" is man; "hambre" is hunger. There IS a difference. Forget your cowboy movies. It's "O", not "A".

Tío	Uncle	<u>Tee</u>-oh
Hermano	Brother	Air-<u>mah</u>-noh
Sobrino	Nephew	Sew-<u>bree</u>-noh
Hijo	Son	<u>Ee</u>-hoh
Primo	Cousin	<u>Pree</u>-moh
Nieto	Grandson	Nee-<u>eh</u>-toe
Viznieto	Greatgrandson	Bveese-nee-<u>eh</u>-toe
Abuelo	Grandfather	Ah-<u>bway</u>-low
Vizabuelo	Greatgrandfather	Bveese-ah-<u>bway</u>-low
Cura	Priest	<u>Coo</u>-rah
Caballero	Gentleman	Kah-bah-<u>yair</u>-oh
Señor	Mister	Seyn-<u>yore</u>
Cuñado	Brother-in-law	Koon-<u>yah</u>-dough
Suegro	Father-in-law	<u>Sway</u>-grow
Padrino	Godfather	Pah-<u>dree</u>-noh

<u>Changing Genders.</u>

No, no, it's nothing so kinky as that. I'm talking about nouns and adjectives, not people.

As you can see from the two preceding lists, for nouns and adjectives which end in "a" and "o", changing the gender of the word is fairly simple. If it's an "a", drop the "a" and add the "o" or vice versa.

For others, such as nouns that end in vowels OTHER THAN "a" and "o", i.e., is for vowels that end in "e", "i" and "u", the ending is invariable. The ending does not change, regardless of gender.

For example, someone who is *"fuerte"* ("strong") is *"fuerte"* regardless of gender, so you don't have to change anything. Well, that saves some time, doesn't it?

Remember, if it ends in a vowel that isn't "a" and isn't "o", it doesn't change.

Last but not least, for nouns of nationality, those ending in a consonant simply add "a" for feminine, e.g. *"aleman"* (german) changes to *"alemana"*.

That's all there is to it.

Comparatives.

Mucho	Much	Moo-choh
Más	More	Mahss
Menos	Less	May-noss
Poco	Little	Poh-koh
Alto	Tall	Ahl-toe
Bajo	Short	Bah-hoe
Pequeño	Small	Pay-cane-yoh
Menor	Smaller	May-nore
Grande	Large	Grahn-day
Mayor	Larger	Mah-yore
Malo	Bad	Mah-low
Peor	Worse	Pay-oar
Bueno	Good	Bway-noh

Superlatives.

El Mejor		El May-hore
La Mejor	The best	La May-hore
El Peor	El Pay-oar	
La Peor	The worst	El Pay-oar

252

El Mayor	El Mah-<u>yore</u>	
La Mayor	The largest	La Mah-<u>yore</u>
El Menor		El May-<u>nore</u>
La Menor	The smallest	LaMay-nore
Muy Bueno	Very good	M<u>ooee</u> <u>Bway</u>-noh
Buenisimo	The best	Boh-<u>neese</u>-ee-moh
Muy Malo	Very Bad	M<u>ooee</u> <u>Mah</u>-loh
Malisimo	The worst	Mah-<u>leese</u>-ee-moh
Muy Grande	Very big	M<u>ooee</u> <u>Grahn</u>-day
Grandisimo	Biggest	Grahn-<u>deese</u>-ee-moh
Muy Pequeño	Very Small	Mooee Pay-cane-yoh
Pequeñisimo	The smallest	Pay-cane-<u>yeese</u>-ee-moh

Prepositions.

Encima	Above, over	En-<u>see</u>-mah
Encima de	On top of	En-<u>see</u>-mah D<u>ay</u>
Sobre	On top of or Over	<u>Sew</u>-bray
Under	Bajo	<u>Bah</u>-hoh
Underneath	Debajo de	Day-<u>bah</u>-hoh D<u>ay</u>
To	A, Al	Ah, Ahl
From	De	D<u>ay</u>
Down	Abajo	Ah-<u>bah</u>-hoh
Up	Arríba	Ah-<u>rree</u>-bah

In	En, A	Ain, Ah
Into	En	Ain
Out	Fuera	Fway-rah
Outside	Fuera de	Fway-rah Day
At	A, De	Ah, Day
Beside	Al lado de	Ahl Lah-dough Day
Of	De	Day
About	Sobre, De	Sew-bray, Day
Before	Antes	Ahn-tayss
After	Después	Des-pwayss
Behind	Detrás	Day-trahss
In front of	Delante (de)	Day-lahn-tay
In front of	Enfrente (de)	En-frehn-tay
In front of	Ante de	Ahn-tay
By	Por	Pore
Through	Por, por atraves	Pore, Ah-trah-vayss
In front opposite	Ante a	Ahn-tay Ah
Toward	Hacía	Ah-see-ah

Adverbs.

As we have previously noted in the section on Cognates, many adverbs are formed by placing the suffix "-mente" on the end of the word. "Fácil" ("easy") becomes "fácilmente", "efectivo" ("effective') becomes "efectivamente", et cetera.

Comparative of adverbs is done by placing "more" or "less" in front of the adverb, so that we have "*más tarde*" ("more late") or "*menos tarde*" ("less late"), or "*más efectivamente*", and so on.

The superlative of adverbs is accomplished by "very" in English, as it is in Spanish, so we end up with "*muy tarde*" ("very late"), much, "*mucho*" becomes "*muchísimo*" (an exception), "a little", "*poco*" becomes "*muy poco*", and "*efectivo*" becomes "*muy efectivo*", et cetera.

The most familiar superlative of an adverb is with the word "well" in Spanish that is "*bien*", made superlative by "muy" with the result "*muy bien*", i.e., "very well".

Admittedly, this is probably the most difficult chapter so far, simply because of the vocabulary and the "rules" of grammar. Still, it's not so difficult you can't handle it.

If you know the word, you can communicate the thought, EVEN IF your grammar is incorrect.

So, don't be frustrated if it seems a little more difficult than I promised. You CAN do it.

Remember: Success only comes in cans.

Chapter XXI.
Conversation.

Truth.

Now, comes your moment of truth. I know you. I know how you are. You do, too. And, you know what you have NOT been doing. Don't you?

You have NOT been speaking Spanish. You've been going through this book, page by page, expecting to arrive at the end, flipping a switch and, suddenly, being able to speak Spanish with fluency you've only dreamed of. Am I right?

Fear.

You have been putting off the opportunity to try to converse with someone else in Spanish. I know you have. It's natural. It's normal. You're afraid. I know you are.

And, it's always more difficult if the only person you can find is someone you know well.

You're naturally embarassed by your "beginner's status". We have all put off the real conversational aspect of learning a language out of fear.

Change.

But, now, it's time. It's time to change all that. You cannot learn to speak Spanish unless you start talking, and NOW is past the right time to start.

That's a change you can handle quite well, at this point, even if you don't quite believe it. *I* know you can do it.

You have the tools, you have the knowledge, you have the vocabulary, and, I hope, you still have the "want to's".

Action. Find Someone to Talk With.

This lesson is an action lesson. Seek out a social group, e.g., the local Spanish Heritage group, or the Cuban or Dominican social group in your town, or seek out another Spanish student.

The best thing you can do is to find a kindergarten that caters to the Hispanic community in your town. Volunteer. Speaking with children is the most non-threatening way you can find to begin your life as a Spanish speaker. They won't make fun of you. They're still learning, too, AND you can learn FROM them and WITH them.

Seek out someone, preferably a native speaker of Spanish, or a fluently bi-lingual person, with whom you can have daily conversations.

Action. Spend Time Talking.

For the next 30 days, I want you to spend a minimum of 30 minutes a day speaking Spanish with someone. The more you talk, the better your skills in the language will become and the greater will be your confidence in your ability to communicate.

Action. Don't Give Up.

Initially, it will be uncomfortable, and you're "all of a sudden" going to feel like you can't remember a thing you've learned from this course.

Trust me, everything you need is in your brain. You just have to be determined enough and confident enough to ALLOW IT TO SURFACE.

Relax, and let it happen. The more you talk, the easier it will be.

Living in a Spanish Speaking Community.

If, by chance, you have recently moved to Latin America or Spain, and you're taking this course so that you can communicate with the locals, then you have the best opportunity of anyone.

Go out and spend as much time as you can every day talking to as many people as you can.

More importantly, try to find ONE person with whom you can have extended conversations. I suggest a neighbor, or a waiter or waitress in your favorite "*cafetería*". People who don't normally get a lot of attention from foreigners will be delighted to have extended conversations with you. Trust me on this.

It's the extended conversations that give you fluency. The little conversations give you comfort, but they don't go a long way in really and truly enhancing your fluency in the language.

But, for all of you, dare to break out of the mold.

Dare to tackle some difficult subjects, too, because, with your knowledge of cognates, you DO have the vocabulary to handle it.

Chapter XXII.
More on Culture.
The "Ugly" American Syndrome.
Life with a Spanish Flavour.

I did not coin the term "*The Ugly American*".

William J. Lederer and Eugene Burdick, authors of a book by the same name, coined it back in 1958. That book was written, in part, to address the issue of why Americans were not liked in foreign places and why American foreign policy was naíve, in particular, in Asia.

In 1993, there was an article written in USA Today also addressing the issue of "*The Ugly American*". Essentially, this article addressed the things one should <u>not</u> do, in order not to be perceived as the "*ugly American*".

The point of this article was that too often Americans, in particular, tend to think that only their culture has any value, that "nice, new, clean and modern" beats "old, used, dirty, and historical" any day and that "the way we do it back home is the only way."

I will tell you that Americans are NOT the <u>only</u> ones, in my experience, who can be "ugly" in this sense. But, the name is representative of a mindset that is not conducive to getting along well in a foreign country.

Allow me to elucidate with a couple of examples of things you don't want to do, whether you're from the U.S. or the UK or from Timbuktu.

Everybody Takes Greenbacks.

Diego is a good friend of mine in Spain. He owns a Mexican restaurant. It doesn't matter that he's never been to Mexico, maybe never even seen a Mexican. He's the proud owner of a pretty good Mexican restaurant. And, he's a really laid back, casual, friendly kind of guy and a really nice man. Nothing ruffles him.

But, I saw Diego go apoplectic with anger the day the Americans came to his restaurant.

It seems that 5 Yanks ate "*tapas*" ("snacks") and had drinks on the terrace of his restaurant. They asked for the check (which wasn't all that big), and then wanted to pay the check (which was then in *Pesetas*) with U.S. dollars.

I saw all this from an adjacent table and thought it was pretty funny.

Diego didn't see it as funny at all, and he suggested that they might want to walk about 50 feet to the nearest ATM and get *Pesetas*. He told them, "This is Spain. Here, you pay in Spanish money".

The Americans insisted "come on, everybody takes American money", and I overheard one of them comment that "they don't want it now, but they damned sure wanted it when we gave it to them after World War II".

In the all the years I've known him, this was the only time I have ever seen Diego angry. He was livid.

The fact is that "*everyone*" doesn't accept American Dollars -- or the British £ sterling.

The U.S. dollar is widely accepted in Canada, the Dominican Republic and most former British colonies in the Caribbean, as well as in Cuba. It's even the legal currency in Panama. (Interestingly, only American money is accepted <u>inside</u> the U.S.)

These Americans were unreasonable and offensive. And, the comment about Spain accepting American dollars at the end of WWII not only expressed a total lack of knowledge about the 20th century history of Spain and Europe, as well as WWII, it was gratuitous, rude and arrogant.

Spain was a neutral non-combatant, like Portugal, Switzerland and the Vatican. It was neutral. America didn't give any money to Spain at the end of WWII.

So, always make sure you have plenty of the local currency. And today, in Spain, as in all of Europe, the currency in use is the Euro (€).

How Old Is Your Country?

On another occasion, in Paris, I was playing tourist. My wife and I were across the street from Notre Dame cathedral admiring how beautiful a cathedral it really is, when an American next to us commented negatively on how "dirty" and "old" it was inside.

Americans have a reputation of believing that "nice, new, clean and modern (and big)", is better and more desirable than "dirty, old and historical". Their sense of history too often appears to be too in favor of a history "more recent".

In any case, the remarks of this American struck me as both rude and ignorant, as well as devoid of any sense of history. I couldn't help myself and remarked aloud to her as to the fact that the cobblestone pavement in front of Notre Dame is probably older than the United States.

In this instance, I couldn't help being rude any more than these Americans could help being ignorant.

The Ugly Catalána.

Even Spanish Speakers can be "ugly".

A few years ago, my wife and I were on holiday in Mexico and staying in "*un hotel de gran lujo*", a magnificent luxury resort hotel in Puerto Vallarta.

On our way to a late lunch, we ran into an elderly lady we knew from Barcelona who was staying in the hotel, too. Since she was alone, we invited this dowager Catalána to join us, little knowing what was in store.

When the waiter came to take our order, she insisted that only a Spanish wine would do. The waiter brought three, two of which she dismissed out of hand as being of poor quality, reluctantly agreeing on the third.

The waiter then brought lunch and the wine she had chosen to accompany it. After lunch, he offered dessert, followed by coffee.

When we were clearly finished, the waiter, a young Mexican of around 25 years of age, came to the table and asked how everything had been and if we had enjoyed our meal.

Before we could say a word, the Catalána began her litany:

"*Era una miérda*", she said, anger in her voice. "*El vino era vinagre, la carne era de poca calidad, la ensalada era para peones, el postre era una miérda, y el café aún más miérda. Y encima de todo, hay demasiados mejicanos aquí.*"

I was looking for a place to hide, the waiter blanched, and my wife looked on in horror. In one '*fell swoop*', this woman had nearly reversed all the goodwill we had established with the wait staff during our stay in the hotel.

What she had said was that the meal "was s--t, the wine was like vinegar, the meat was of poor quality, the salad was for peasants, the dessert was s--t, the coffee even more s--t. And on top of everything else, there are too damned many Mexicans here".

I might point out that, even in Spain among other non-Catalán Spaniards, people from Catalunya are generally considered to be cold, unfriendly, rude, arrogant, and often not very nice.

A Catalán visiting anywhere else in Spain is considered a foreigner even by the Spanish, but I have never seen or experienced anything anywhere to equal the episode with the *La Vieja Catalána* in the "*hotel de gran lujo*" in Puerto Vallarta.

What can I say? Americans <u>*do not*</u> have a monopoly on ugliness in foreign countries.

Stereotypical Behaviour.

Please don't think that I relate these stories to be demeaning or critical of Americans, in particular, or even of *Catalans*.

Brits and Germans and Arabs are quite often just as bad. In fact, no nationality is exempt from having some "ugly" citizens who manifest their ugliness as tourists.

I'm always amazed to watch Brits trying to speak English with a non-English speaker and, with growing frustration, getting louder and louder and louder, as if by sheer volume they can penetrate the obvious veneer of stupidity with which this non-English speaker must be covered, in order that he/she might understand them.

Even Spanish speakers are capable of stereotyping people. The running joke in Spain is that you can always tell a Brit who's good in languages -- he just yells in English.

They also identify foreigners, Americans and Brits in particular, by wearing apparel.

A man in short pants and an ugly old T-shirt is a Brit, but one in short pants with a designer golf shirt is an American. Anybody wearing short pants with socks has to be a Brit. Likewise, those who wear sandals with socks or white patent leather shoes and belts.

Loud talking, especially in restaurants, tends to identify people as either Americans or Germans or Swedes, and loud, boisterous behaviour and conversation, especially in public places (e.g., hotel lobbies, etc.), is generally seen as a singularly American trait.

Remember that the people at the table next to yours in the restaurant might be on a romantic interlude in the midst of their trip of a lifetime. We wouldn't want to ruin that with a lot of loud and boisterous conversation, now would we?

Most Spanish speaking countries are or have been part of the third world, and the residents of those countries are used to Yanquis and other foreigners coming into their countries and treating them badly or taking advantage of them, all the while speaking English, Arabic, German or French, but never Spanish. They are very resentful of this kind of behaviour.

On the other hand, people who go the extra distance to be polite, who aren't boisterous, who try to fit in and, in particular, who try to speak to them in their own language will find that Spanish speakers the world over are generally a very warm, hospitable people.

Spanish Speakers Have Their Own Idiosyncrasies.

Different cultures have different morés and customs. It will be beneficial for you to understand some of them.

Although most of my examples are from Spain, Mexico, Cuba, the Dominican Republic, and Panama, in my experience, they also apply in Costa Rica, Venezuela, Colombia, Argentina and Chile. The examples I'm going to give you are pretty much universal in the Spanish speaking world.

The Concept of Time?

First among all Hispanic idiosyncrasies is that one dealing with the concept of time, and it's most important one for you to understand that:

There is no concept of time.

You'd almost think they didn't realize that time is subject to measurement.

You generally cannot depend on native speakers of Spanish to show up when they say they will, nor can you ever expect them to call and say they're going to be late, or even that they aren't coming. They just show up when they get around to it, or, maybe, they don't show up at all. And, don't ever expect an apology.

The important thing for you to grasp is that what we as English speakers would construe to be inconsiderate behaviour is not meant in any way to be disrespectful. It's just the way things are. They do it to each other, so it's not like they've singled us out as foreigners in order to be disrespectful. So don't be offended.

For really serious business appointments, you can expect (especially in Latin America) that your appointment will either be followed by or preceded by lunch or dinner. I've had business meetings with Spanish speakers in Latin America which would have required five minutes to accomplish in an English speaking environment but which required 6 or 7 hours instead in the Spanish environment.

Typically, even for Spanish speakers trying to be punctual, punctuality means anywhere from an hour to an hour-and-a-half AFTER the appointed time.

In Miami, for example, they refer to being on "Cuban time". If one arrives within $1^{1/2}$ hours after the scheduled time, one is "on time", according to Cuban time.

Don't hold your breath for English/American style punctuality. It will not happen.

Just understand and expect it to be this way. Then, if it's better than what you expect, you can be happily surprised.

The typical way of dealing with this is to tell them you want to meet two hours before the time when you REALLY want to meet. Then, you can go late, still be on time, and your appointment will only be 'slightly' late.

Definite Appointments.

A definite appointment at a definite time does not exist for ANYTHING, other than for a doctor's appointment, court, or something extremely urgent, such as an audience with His Majesty King Juan Carlos I.

Otherwise, any definite appointment you might make really means "maybe".

Mañana.

This is a similar and related time concept.

We English speakers tend to think that "*mañana*" means "tomorrow" or "in the morning", but in Hispanic culture, it really means "whenever I get around to it".

Just because a Spanish speaker says he'll show up at your house "*mañana*" to fix the stove, you shouldn't believe it until you actually see it. After all, he didn't actually say which "*mañana*" he was referring to, did he?

I know that, to our Anglophile minds, these issues seem to be just too incredible to be believed, but they are true. What's worse, they will drive you totally crazy if you don't expect them, learn to accept them, and then disregard them. The custom is too prevalent to overcome, and life is too short.

Personal Space.

In most English speaking countries, we maintain a personal space around our personal selves of about 1 meter (3 feet) in diameter.

In Spanish speaking cultures, that is not the case, and you may find yourself becoming more and more uncomfortable as a Spanish speaker moves closer and closer to you until you are almost nose to nose while you talk. Personal space in Hispanic culture is much more contracted by comparison to what an English speaker is accustomed to.

Don't be offended when your personal space is violated. They don't see it as a violation.

Further, Spanish speakers like to talk up close and personal like this and on a direct eyeball-to-eyeball basis. They will look you directly in the eyes when they talk; you should reciprocate.

Holding Hands.

There is a holdover from 700 years of Moorish occupation in Spain of which you should also be aware.

In Arabic culture, it is not unusual for two men to hold hands. It is a sign of great friendship. You will quite often find that someone who feels you are his friend and who has great respect for you reaches out to hold your hand while you talk or while you are walking down the street.

If you jerk your hand away in some unjustified homophobic fear, you will offend your Spanish-speaking (or Arabic) friend deeply.

Kissy-Kissy, Huggy-Huggy.

Greetings, especially in Spain, between friends and acquaintances (i.e., women and anybody & between men and women) are almost always accompanied by a chaste "air kiss" on each cheek. Please, no groping and no saliva.

Between men a handshake and a hug is quite common and, occasionally and with good friends, a kiss on the cheek is not uncommon, especially after a long time since last seeing each other.

Standing in Queue.

Hispanic culture does not lend itself well to standing on line. I experienced this first hand the first time I ever went into a pharmacy in Spain. Just as it became my turn, an elderly woman moved herself to the front of the queue *"a codos"* (elbowing her way). She was quite indignant when I said to her, *"Disculpe, señora, pero me toca a mí"* ("Excuse me, Madame, but it's my turn").

Even when they queue up, they don't stand on line. Instead, they just cluster around, almost like loitering, but everyone knows who's in front and who's behind. It's a bit confusing until you get used to it. When you encounter this, just ask *"quién es el último?"* or "who's last (in line)?"

It's also quite common to be on line at the supermarket with a cart full of groceries and to have a local with one or two articles in hand walk up and tell you that they are going in line on front of you because they only have one or two items. They never give you the chance to offer.

And, of course, once they get in front of you, 12 members of their family come up from all directions bringing more "booty", so, by the time the dust settles, they've run more through the register than you will with your full cart. When it happens, don't say I didn't tell you.

Making change.

Although making change <u>properly</u> seems to be universally a problem these days, getting change at a McDonald's or at the supermarket after a purchase is almost an assault, more so in Spain than in Latin America.

Only in Cuba do they still seem to know how to make change the old fashioned way.

The computerized cash register tells the clerk how much change to give back, and that's what they give you. But, no one has ever taught them to "make change" properly, i.e., counting it back starting with the change.

Instead, what happens is they hurriedly count it out, place the paper money in the palm of your hand and the change on top of it and move on to the next customer. Invariably, I always drop some or all of the coins before I can get out of the way.

If you question the change, even before you've taken two steps, you're likely to be told, "I gave you correct change". Since they don't count it out, you can neither prove nor disprove the count. So, count it right at the moment it is given to you, before you take a single step.

Pride.

Pride is a big thing in all Spanish-speaking countries. In Spain, they have raised it to an art form. There, the best there can be in the world can ONLY come from Spain.

Even if the person you are speaking with has never been out of his/her pueblo, he or she will tell you that the best wine, the best strawberries, the best whatever is from Spain. They will not even consider the possibility that anything could be better than what they have there.

A prime example of this comes from a discussion I had one day with a very good Spanish friend with the *Policía Nacional*. Juan was insisting that the crayfish from Spain were the best in the world, fatter, juicier and more succulent than any other. He went on and on praising the virtues of the Spanish crayfish.

Then, another of our mutual friends, Antonio, said, "Juan, Spanish crayfish are extinct. There haven't been any for 15 or 20 years. They've been replaced by Louisiana crayfish from America."

"It doesn't matter," said Juan. "When we had them they were the best, and, if we still had them they would still be the best."

To which I quipped, "well, it appears to me that if the crayfish in Spain are the best in the world, then the best crayfish in the world must really come from Louisiana".

The shouts of protest could be heard all the way into the next *pueblo*.

I have had this same discussion in more than one city in Spain with more than one person. Apparently, there is a great deal of sensitivity over the bringing of Louisiana crayfish into Spain, on the part of a Louisiana State University professor.

I have even heard it suggested by some Spaniards who are most passionate on the subject that the Spanish crayfish would not be extinct if the Louisiana crayfish had not been introduced and "eaten all the Spanish ones".

Invitations.

In English speaking cultures, we love to entertain in our homes.

In Hispanic countries, if you receive an invitation to dinner, it doesn't necessarily mean in someone's home. In fact, it most probably will not. Dinner invitations are generally to restaurants.

We in our family are well plugged in (*enchufado*) in the Spanish speaking community. Yet, in all of our more than 10 years of living in Spain, we've actually been to a Spanish person's home for lunch or dinner but rarely, and only a few times just for drinks and hors d'oevres (*"tapas"*).

In part, I think it's a function of the small size of their living quarters and, in part, a function of the inviolability of the family home. There is a much more Arabic approach to having visitors into the family home, so, if you actually do get an invitation to someone's house, you will know that your relationship with them is very *"intimo"*.

They will come to your home for lunch or dinner reluctantly, and, initially at least, they are not very comfortable in doing so. It's just not a custom to which they are accustomed.

The exception to this rule can easily be found Cuba or the Dominican Republic.

One of the best meals I've ever eaten in my life I enjoyed in a private home of some friends in La Habana Vieja. Their home was extremely humble, but their hospitality was world class and so was the food. And, of course, the rum was the best.

Grandparents.

In Spanish speaking countries, the idea of sending elderly parents to a nursing home or a retirement home is almost a blasphemy. It's never even considered, except in case of those who are totally unable to care for themselves and where the family has no other choice.

One of the reasons for this is the fact that usually both members of a couple work. Where there are children, grandparents are the most important things in the world, because they are the built-in child minder (baby sitter), the ones who give the child all the love and attention it wants or needs because grandmothers, at least, tend to be home all day for this express purpose.

More often than not, you'll find the grandparents living with their children and grandchildren, or, if not, then living very near by.

The Hispanic culture recognizes that the elderly often have more to offer to children than a child's parents do, especially when it comes to spoiling the children, and it also frees the parents to focus their energies on earning a living to benefit the whole family.

Old Fashioned Ideas.

On the first of September, sweaters and long pants for the children, and jackets and all the other accoutrements of autumn and winter for the whole family come out of the closet or wardrobe. And, all of the summer clothes get packed away not to see the light of day again until June 1 of the following year.

Nothing is more frustrating for me than to see a child wearing shorts and a T-shirt one day and long corduroy pants and a sweater the next day (temperatures and climatic conditions being the same), simply because of a change in the date. However, that's the way it works.

Spanish speakers generally believe that one should not drink cold drinks of any kind (except beer, of course) because they aren't good for the throat, especially in wintertime, and that they'll make one sick. If you're ill, they say, you shouldn't drink soft drinks either, because they're bad for the throat.

The same is true of ice cream that, in countries like Spain, Argentina, Chile, is eaten only in summer, June, July and August.

Técnicos.

This is one of my favorites. Anybody with a vocational skill that requires more than three hours of education is a *"técnico"*.

One of the funniest of the tecno-idiosyncrasies I have seen in Spain has to do with dry wall (sheet rock). Just about anyone in an English speaking country knows what dry wall is and how to put it up, at least in general terms.

In most of Spain, where even the interior walls are generally made of brick, dry wall is a recent (maybe since the year 2,000) occurrence.

When I had a dry wall partition installed in the basement of my house in Spain, I had to hire two Ukrainian chaps, because there were no Spaniards around who knew what it was, let alone how to hang it.

Then, just recently, I had the laugh of the year when I saw a truck driving through town with painted on advertising for *"Técnicos en Pladur"*, i.e., "drywall technicians". I laughed until I cried. It turned out that the two Ukrainian chaps who had hung my drywall had shown a couple of Spanish guys how to do it. Now, they're *"tecnicos"*.

Where in America, for instance, unions restrict certain jobs to members of a certain union, in Spain, at least, jobs are restricted to those trained *"técnicos"* who know how to DO the job.

I guess this is a by-product of the fact that the vast majority of Spanish men don't even finish secondary school. The ones who do finish, obviously, get most of the training to become *"técnicos"*, instead of just *"obreros"* or *"jardineros"*, i.e., "workmen" or "gardeners".

Sidewalk Superintendents.

On another occasion, shortly after having moved to Spain, we discovered a leaking pipe in the basement (*"sótano"*) of our new home. It wasn't a terrible leak, but it was consistent. Since it was a 'new' house, we called the builder to come and resolve the problem. He assured us that he would send someone over right away.

Bright and early the next morning, our bell rang five times within 30 minutes to allow for 6 supervisors and one workman to enter the premises.

While the workman worked in the basement resolving the problem, the six supervisors stood around discussing the character of the problem and assessing whether or not they were implementing the best solution, whether the solution was being implemented in the best possible manner, and whether or not there were any other solutions to the problem other than the one being implemented.

Finally, they found that they had to consider what other possibilities might exist if, in fact, they were solving the wrong problem.

By the time they had finished their discussions, along with coaching the workman from time to time, the workman was finished with the job. Most interesting of all, the workman had totally ignored them from the beginning to the end. He just came in, indentified the problem for himself, and set about solving it. When he was finished, they all congratulated themselves on doing such a masterful job of supervision and left.

Some years later, the empty lot next to our house was slated for the construction of a new chalet. On the day the footers for the foundation were to be laid, a backhoe was *driven* to the property by its operator (That's right. Right down the motorway, right through the neighborhood and up our street).

While the operator began digging in the area designated for laying of the footers, the architect, the contractor, and three other supervisors all stood around and watched to be sure that it was being done properly. All the while, they were arguing about whether he was doing it properly, whether he was doing it in the right place, whether or not it was deep enough, etc.

And, of course, the backhoe driver ignored them all. That was just as well, since they couldn't seem to agree on anything anyway.

It is my considered opinion that, although sidewalk superintending may not have been invented in Spain, members of the Spanish construction industry have managed to turn it into an art form without equal anywhere in the world.

Ferias & Saints.

Every *pueblo* has its own patron and its own festivals to celebrate and venerate that saint (or "The Virgin"). Celebration time brings *"feria"*. Sometime during the week of *"feria"*, there is a procession with an effigy of the saint, with everyone dressed out in uniforms looking like something right out of the middle ages, which, of course, is what is intended.

Every store, business, bank and government office in the pueblo will be closed (or on shortened hours) during the week of *"feria"*. No work this week – just fun.

Starting around mid-day each day, there are all kinds of events going on in the town square and surrounding streets, an almost *'carnaval'* kind of feeling. This usually will continue during daylight hours until around 5:00 p.m. or 6:00 p.m. Then, everyone seems to take a break until perhaps 10:00 p.m., at which time everyone heads to the fairgrounds where one can find the typical traveling carnival show with rides and games and animals. This last entertainment and frivolity lasts until daylight.

Drinking is the norm, and everyone takes his or her turn at the total fun and abandonment of things.

Every *"feria"* is different and typically includes an exposition of local produce, product or whatever. For example, in wine country, the wine sampling is a really big event, where in others it's the cider or the strawberries, or the leather goods. It just depends on what the locals think puts them on the map and makes them *"destacar"* ("standout") from the rest of the towns and villages.

Not all *"ferias"* are created equal, and you owe it to yourself to experience at least one or two just for the opportunity to share the pure exuberance of the event.

Siesta.

Yes, they DO take *"siesta"*. No, it doesn't mean everyone goes home and has a nap. Of course, many do take a nap, but most don't take a three or four hour nap. Instead, "siesta" is an interlude in the middle of the day during which one eats a leisurely lunch with a couple of glasses of wine or some beer, after which one *may* or *may not* take a nap.

There is one thing you can count on during the hours of the *"siesta"*. Except for large department stores, restaurants and petrol (gasoline) stations, there won't be much open for business.

Most businesses in the Spanish-speaking world close at either 1:00 p.m. or 2:00 p.m., depending on local custom and personal preferences of the shopkeeper, and they remain closed until either 4:00 p.m. or 5:00 p.m., again depending on custom and preferences.

This is a quaint custom UNTIL you live in a Spanish speaking country. Then, you discover that you can't run your daytime errands as you might in your English speaking country.

Nope! No can do. Won't happen.

You must either plan to do all of your errands in the morning between 10:00 a.m. (when most places open) and 1:00 p.m. OR after 4:00 or 5:00 p.m. and before 7:00 or 8:00 p.m. when they close again.

This can be very frustrating.

Still, the custom has its merits, and it's quite pleasant to share a long leisurely lunch with friends at some beachfront *"chiringuito"* or some sidewalk café in the pueblo or on the *"paseo"*. Worse things could happen to you in your life. This is a custom that I find to be occasionally a burden but, most times, a pleasure. You will, too.

"Siesta" is a time for food, friends, family and relaxation. All in all, it's not a bad custom to have. I just wish it were for only two hours!

In Summary.

Spanish speaking people the world over are passionate, flamboyant, proud, caring, spirited, and hardheaded.

They worship their children, they value the elderly, they're wild about football (soccer), and they love to dance, to party, to celebrate anything that needs celebrating.

They make great friends and implacable enemies.

Spanish culture is unique and offers an experience to English speakers that they just won't encounter at home.

And, historically, whether in Spain or in Latin America, you can't ask for more. Every visit to a Spanish speaking country is a close encounter with history, fabulous architecture, and the magic of legends.

In the western world, only England can compare to the historical and mystical sense which one encounters in Spain and many other Spanish-speaking countries.

All in all, Hispanic culture, whether in Spain or in Latin America, is unique, and I love it. I hope you will, too.

Chapter XXIII.
Numbers.
Time On Your Hands.

To this point, we have avoided dealing with numbers. Your comfort level at this point should be such that you can handle the concept of numbers and telling time all in the same lesson. So, here we go.

Nº	\underline{English}	\underline{Spanish}	\underline{English}	\underline{Spanish}
	The Cardinal Numbers are:		**The Ordinal Numbers are:**	
1	one	*uno*	first	*primero*
2	two	*dos*	second	*segundo*
3	three	*tres*	third	*tercero*
4	four	*cuatro*	fourth	*cuarto*
5	five	*cinco*	fifth	*quinto*
6	six	*seis*	sixth	*sexto*
7	seven	*siete*	seventh	*séptimo*
8	eight	*ocho*	eighth	*octavo*
9	nine	*nueve*	ninth	*noveno*
10	ten	*diez*	tenth	*décimo*
11	eleven	*once*	eleventh	*undécimo*
12	twelve	*doce*	twelfth	*duodécimo*
13	thirteen	*trece*	thirteenth	*décimotercio*
14	fourteen	*catorce*	fourteenth	*décimocuarto*

15	fifteen	*quince*	fifteenth	*décimoquinto*
16	sixteen	*diez y seis*	sixteenth	*décimosexto*
17	seventeen	*diez y siete*	seventeenth	*décimoséptimo*
18	eighteen	*diez y ocho*	eighteenth	*décimoctavo*
19	nineteen	*diez y nueve*	nineteenth	*décimonono*
20	twenty	*veinte*	twentieth	*vígésimo*
21	twenty-one	*veinte y uno*	*Ordinal numbers are seldom*	
30	thirty	*treinta*	*over 20th, i.e., vígésimo.*	
40	forty	*cuarenta*		
50	fifty	*cincuenta*		
60	sixty	*sesenta*		
70	seventy	*setenta*		
80	eighty	*ochenta*		
90	ninety	*noventa*		
100	one hundred	*cién*		
101	one hundred one	*ciento y uno*		
200	two hundred	*doscientos*		
300	three hundred	*trescientos*		
400	four hundred	*cuatrocientos*		
500	five hundred	*quinientos*		
600	six hundred	*seiscientos*		
700	seven hundred	*setecientos*		
800	eight hundred	*ochocientos*		
900	nine hundred	*novacientos*		
1000	one thousand	*mil*		

And so on.

One anomaly.

When one arrives at 1,000,000,000, there are two ways of expressing this. Brits will understand this better than Americans, simply because of the way "billion" is used in Britain.

In Latin America, with its more americanized way of doing things, you'll almost always hear "one billion" or *"un billón"*.

To an American, "billion" is always one thousand units of one million of something, but, in Britain, "billion" can simply mean more than one million (when used as an adjective) or one thousand million (when used as a noun).

So, in Spain, and in both English and in Spanish, one is more likely to hear "a thousand million" or *"un mil millónes"*.

Telling Time.

In Spanish, one has two choices: 1.) The 12-hour clock, or 2.) The 24-hour clock. Regardless of which you hear or which you choose to use, the RULES are the same.

First, in speaking or writing the hour, the verb "*SER*" is used exclusively to express time. Therefore, we have:

It's 12:00 a.m.	Son las doce…	("Es la medianoche").
It's 01:00 a.m.	ES la una…	(de la mañana)
It's 02:00 a.m.	Son las dos…	(de la mañana)
It's 03:00 a.m	Son las tres…	(de la mañana)
It's 04:00 a.m.	Son las cuatro…	(de la mañana)
It's 05:00 a.m.	Son las cinco…	(de la mañana)
It's 06:00 a.m.	Son las seis…	(de la mañana)
It's 07:00 a.m.	Son las siete…	(de la mañana)
It's 08:00 a.m.	Son las ocho…	(de la mañana)
It's 09:00 a.m.	Son las nueve…	(de la mañana)

It's 10:00 a.m.	Son las diez...	(de la mañana)
It's 11:00 a.m.	Son las once...	(de la mañana)
It's 12:00 p.m./mid-day	Son las doce...	(de la mañana/mediodía)
It's 01:00 p.m.	ES la una...	(de la tarde)
It's 02:00 p.m.	Son las dos...	(de la tarde)
It's 0:300 p.m.	Son las tres...	(de la tarde)
It's 04:00 p.m.	Son las cuatro...	(de la tarde)
It's 05:00 p.m.	Son las cinco...	(de la tarde)
It's 06:00 p.m.	Son las seis...	(de la tarde)
It's 07:00 p.m.	Son las siete.	(de la tarde)
It's 08:00 p.m.	Son las ocho...	(de la tarde)
It's 09:00 p.m.	Son las nueve...	(de la noche)
It's 10:00 p.m.	Son las diez...	(de la noche)
It's 11:00 p.m.	Son las once...	(de la noche)
It's 12:00 a.m./midnight	Son las doce.	(de la noche)

My Heretical Rule No. 26.

There is only one thing that you have to remember about telling time, besides the name of the number representing the hour. For all of the hours, except for ONE, the plural form "SON" is used. For the ONE O'CLOCK hour, the singular form "ES" must be used.

I'll never forget the day the young Spanish woman, Ani, who works for us told me she had to leave because *"SON LAS UNA"*.

I said, "Excuse me?" She repeated, *"son las una"*.

Thus, ensued the first real disagreement I had ever had with a Spanish speaker about how their language is spoken.

Now, I must say that, until that time, this young woman had never been out of her pueblo, but she had finished secondary school. For her generation and in her country, she is better educated than most people. Yet, she was unaware that the hour of one o'clock must be expressed by *"es la una"*. I had to pull out a grammar book and show her before she gave any credit to my argument.

About a week later, she showed up at my house with a Spanish "Spanish" grammar book, recently purchased, which she gave me for my library. She had purchased it, in fact, not just to confirm what I had told her but also to improve her own abilities in the language.

Interestingly, we both had discovered that my "knowledge" of her language exceeded hers in some respects, even though my skill in "using" the language was not nearly so well developed as hers.

These days, I am proud to say that she is a far more polished speaker of her native tongue, and so am I.

Interestingly, too, shortly after that argument, I heard her correcting some of her fellow Spaniards on how to say "it's one o'clock". My heart leapt for joy.

To further develop the issues of time, we have the hour and quarter hour and partially expired hours, as follows"

It's 130.   *Es la una y media.*

It's 2:15.   *Son las dos y cuarto.*

Up until the half hour, according to most grammar texts, one expresses the hour PLUS the minutes.

It's 4:25.   *Son las cuatro y veinte y cinco.*

After the half hour, one expresses the coming hour MINUS the minutes remaining.

It's 4:45.   *Son las cinco menos quince.*

In practice, it's very much like English. That is, I've often heard time expressions such as "it's 4:55", i.e., "*son las cuatro cincuenta y cinco*". It's not grammatically correct, but it does happen.

Doing Simple math.

2 + 2 = 4   *dos y dos son cuatro.*
       Dose ee dose sown <u>kwa</u>-tro.

4 − 1 = 3   *cuatro menos uno son tres.*
       <u>Kwa</u>-troh <u>meh</u>-noss <u>oo</u>-no sown trace.

.4 x 2 = 8   *cuatro por dos son ocho.*
       <u>Kwa</u>-troh pour dose sown <u>oh</u>-choh.

8 / 4 = 2   *ocho entre cuatro son dos.*
       <u>Oh</u>-choh <u>en</u>-tray <u>kwa</u>-troh sown dose.

"*Y*" (or "*Más*") means "plus". "*Menos*" means "minus". "*Por*" ("or, *multiplicado por*") means "times" ("or multiplied by"). "*Entre*" (or, "*Dividido por*") means "divided by".

If something is "two square meters", it would be "*dos metros cuadrados*". "Half" of something is "*la mitad*".

Other than that, it's "*la matematica*" as usual. Math is done just the same as in English. Only the jargon is different. It's easy.

Chapter XXIV.
Idiomatic Expressions
and Special Words.
Creating Descriptive Words
From Nouns.
The Last of the Dynamic Dozen.

Idiomatic Expressions.

It often doesn't occur to us that, in English, we have many idiomatic expressions. In fact, many of us may not even understand the term "idiomatic" expression.

Simply put, it's a form of slang, but not in the sense of "*cool, bro*" or "*that's righteous*".

Idiomatic expressions in English are really quite common and more numerous than one would expect. You probably know most of them -- for your country.

I know Americans won't recognize "*the Old Bill*" as being the police or "*Bob's your uncle*" as "That's it" or "It's done", and most Brits may not comprehend such expressions as "*tell yo' mama to park the car*".

And, when you hear it in Spanish, you may not comprehend such an expression as "*if my grandmother had a sprocket chain, she'd be a bicycle.*" It means "if, if, if…"

But, these are all idiomatic expressions. They add colour to the language. They define its character. To some extent, they clarify the cultural definitions within a country.

I've never heard the "*old Bill*" or "*Bob's your uncle*" in north America or anywhere else English is spoken other than the UK. Likewise, I've never heard "*tell yo' mama...*" in the UK or anywhere outside North America. And, "*my grandmother...*" is strictly a Cuban idiomatic expression. Even your average Spaniard has no comprehension of this one.

However, there are idiomatic expressions that are universal in English speaking countries that usually, but not always, have comparable idiomatic expressions in other languages. We are going to acquaint you here with some of those expressions which will be meaningful to you, regardless of your nationality, and which are used universally in the Spanish-speaking world, as well.

Beginning on the next page, we'll acquaint you with some of the more useful idiomatic expressions, or "*modismos*".

Useful Idiomatic Expressions.

Dutch treat	*A la americana*
At the same time	*A la vez*
By hand	*A mano*
On purpose	*A propósito*
Wholesale	*Al por mayor*
Retail	*Al por menor*
At your service	*A sus órdenes*
Dead drunk	*Borracho como una cuba*
Bon appetite!	*¡Buen provecho!*
The apple of my eye	*La niña de mis ojos*
To queue up	*Hacer cola*
To strike one as funny	*Hacer gracia*
To run an errand	*Hacer recado*
Round trip	*Ida y vuelta*
Much ado about nothing	*Mucho ruido, pocas nueces*
I don't give a hoot	*No me importa*
To set the table	*Poner la mesa*
I'll be right back	*Voy y vengo*
And a little bit	*Y pico*
You know it!	*¡Ya lo creo!*
Literally: I believe it already!	
I don't believe it	*No lo creo*
I don't think so	*Creo que no*
To take place	*Tener lugar*
In person	*En vivo*
So, what?	*¿Qué más da?*
	¿Y qué?
It's a (done) deal!	*¡Trato hecho!*
To be in a hurry	*Tener prisa*
To be in effect	*Estar en marcha*
I'm sorry	*Lo siento*
Better late than never!	*¡A buenas horas!*
To get late	*Hacerse tarde*
To match	*Hacer juego*
Rather	*Mas bien*

Special Words.

Some words are really important but just don't quite fit in to some of the categories we have covered. Some of those words will be considered on the following pages.

Hay.

A really important use of a derivative form of the verb, *"haber"* is the word *"hay"*. *"Hay"* means "there is" or "there are". So, if you want to say, "there are a lot of people on the street", you would say, *"hay mucha gente en la calle"*.

Likewise, if you want to ask a question such as "are there any oranges?" you would ask using *"hay"* as follows: *"¿hay naranjas?"* "Is there any petrol (gasoline)?" becomes *"¿hay gasolina?"* Remember to pronounce this word *"hay"* as "eye".

Hay que.

"Hay que" means "it is necessary", as in *"hay que comprar la entrada en el kiosco"* ("it's necessary to buy a ticket from the kiosk"), or *"hay que estudiar"* ("it's necessary to study"). It's very impersonal and has the effect of the English "one must…" or "you have to…" (meaning people in general "have to…").

Ojalá.

"¡Ojalá!" is a uniquely Spanish creation based on the Arabic *"Insha'allah"*, meaning literally "may God grant" or "when God wills".

In practice, it means "I wish…" You may remember from an earlier example, *"¡Ojalá que supiera!"*, meaning "I wish I knew". In a sentence, this word is properly followed by a verb in the subjunctive mood.

You don't know the subjunctive, so you may or may not choose to use it in a sentence. Most people will know what you mean, even if you don't use the subjunctive.

Still, it has great value just as an interjectory word, i.e., "¡*Ojalá*!" ("I wish!").

De and En.

Look in the dictionary. It says *"de"* means "of", "from", "about" or "concerning". *"En"* means "in", "on" or "upon". Literally, that's correct.

From an interpretative point of view, however, this is not always the case. Look at the example above under *"Hay que"*. "It's necessary to buy a ticket from the kiosk", i.e., "*hay que comprar la entrada en el kiosko.*"

From a practical point of view, we English speakers tend to get too hung up on which one of these to use in which situation. For example, "*it can*" can mean "in" after a superlative or "if" before an infinitive. It can also mean "with" and "than". It can even mean "from" or "out of".

When in doubt, do it the English way: *"en"* for "in" and *"de"* for "of" or "from". If you're consistent with this usage, you'll fare better, and your listener will know what to expect and what you mean.

Por and Para.

Here's another 'confuser' for most English speakers. Both of these words mean "for", so, let's make it simple.

If you what you mean can be construed to mean *"in order to..."* or if you mean that something (such as a gift) is *"for"* a specific person or something is to be used *"for"* a specific purpose, then use *"para"*.

Example: "This gift is for you" would be *"Este regalo es para ti"*.

If you mean *"by"* or *"through"* or *"because"* or *"on account of"* someone or something, then use *"por"*. Example: "I did it for (or "because of") you" (i.e., on your account of or for your benefit) would be expressed as *"te lo he hecho por ti"*.

In practice, it's simpler than it sounds.

Distinguish *"¿para qué?"* meaning "for what?" and *"¿por qué?"* meaning "why?" *"¿Para qué?"* connotes purpose; *"¿por qué?"* connotes cause.

Again, the issue here is to be consistent in your use. If you are using them incorrectly, I promise you that your listener WILL correct you.

I don't know why, but this is one usage where a Spanish speaker will almost always give you some help, even when they don't otherwise want to correct you for fear of offending. I guess they recognize the difficulties.

Amar and Querer.

"Amar" which is related to the noun *"amor"* means "to love". *"Querer"* also means "to love", or "to want".

So, if you want to say you love someone, which one do you use?

Let me enlighten you by way of a little story about my wife. Early on in her process of learning to speak Spanish, we were in the process of remodeling a flat.

The architect's son was a nice young 15-year-old secondary school student who actually spoke some English and helped my wife some with her Spanish in exchange for help with his English. He worked every afternoon after school with the workmen on our construction site, and he was a VERY nice boy and very well brought up.

One weekend afternoon, we passed by the architect's house to have a brief chat, and he and his wife, daughter and son all came out into the street to talk to us.

My wife, wanting to express to the architect's wife her appreciation for her son and all his help attempted to say to her "I just love your son".

However, what she actually said in her own inimitable and "grammatically insufficient" Spanish was "tengo mucho amor para" (sic) your son, i.e., "I have a lot of romantic love for your son" or, to call a spade a spade, "I'm having an affair with your son".

The response from the boy's mother was instantaneous.

"¿Como?!" she said. "¿Como?!" With a choice of fight or flight, this mother had no intention of leaving the scene. She was instantly into attack mode and ready to have a war in defense of her son's virtue.

Not catching on, my wife just kept on saying the same thing louder (typical foreigner), thinking she wasn't being understood.

It was only by my intervention with my wife and the architect's with his wife that we kept the two ladies from coming to blows. Before that day, they had gotten along fine. After that day, they never got along again, and the architect's wife never quite trusted my wife ever again.

Why do think that was?

In more than 40 years of studying this language, I have rarely heard (once or twice) the verb "amar" used in any context outside of poetry or song.

However, when and IF you hear this verb, think "romantic" or "carnal". I suggest that you forget your Latin on this one, and ignore this verb entirely. It's safer.

The noun, *"amor"* is another matter, because it is used in a harmlessly idiomatic form, *"mi amor"* meaning "my love" or "my darling" or "sweetheart" and is used by or with anyone, including children - in fact, especially with children - and between spouses, even between humans and pets.

So, if you want to tell someone you love him or her, be it spouse, girl/ boy friend, child, friend, grandparent or whomever, the proper form is *"(yo) te quiero"*.

Also, this (*"querer"*) is the verb predominately is used to express "want"; for example, "I want a new car" (*"quiero un coche nuevo"*) or "I want a hamburger" (*"quiero una hamburguesa"*). *"Quisiera"* is a more polite form of *"quiero"* which merely softens it to "I would like..."

And, if you want to master the double entendre in Spanish, think of the little dog selling Taco Bell Burritos in North America when he says, *"yo quiero Taco Bell"*.

Does he mean "I love Taco Bell" or does he mean, "I want Taco Bell"? It's a great play on words and, unfortunately, is probably completely lost on the vast majority of its North American audience.

Periódo and Punto.

Oftentimes, in English, to add emphasis to a point we're trying to make, we'll say something to the effect that "that's all there is. Period!" ("Full Stop"!)

In Spanish, we can do the same thing. However, we must use the word *"¡punto!"* not *"¡periódo!"*

Many years ago, I learned this lesson the hard way while in the company of a Cuban friend of mine as we were strolling the halls of a "clinica". I was trying to make my point, and I said *"¡Periódo!"* for the proper emphasis.

294

All conversation in the hallway stopped, and somewhere in the vicinity of 100 (felt like 1,000) elderly Spanish speaking old ladies looked at me and began to "fry eggs", you know, *"tsk, tsk, tsk"*.

I, of course, had no clue as to what was going on, until my friend explained to me. You won't make this same mistake, will you?

Making descriptive words from nouns.

Can you guess from the following list how to create an adjective from a noun?

wind - windy	*viento - ventoso*
storm - stormy	*tormenta - tormentoso*
rock - rocky	*roca - rocoso*
rain - rainy	*lluvia - lluvioso*
fame - famous	*fama - famoso*
marvel - marvelous	*maravilla - maravilloso*

In case you missed it, <u>drop the last letter of the noun and add "-oso"</u>. Now you have it.

More on Verbs. The Verb *"Poder"*.

You already know the verbs *"estar"*, *"ser"*, *"acabar"*, *"tener"*, *"haber"*, *"hacer"*, *"soler"*, *"saber"*, *"ir"*, *"decir"*, and *"dar"*. Now is the time to learn one more of the Dynamic Dozen.

"Poder" means "to be able". In practical usage, it means "can". "I can do it", "you can do it", et cetera. Let's look at the present tense of *"poder"* to see how it conjugates.

Pronoun	Spanish	Sounds like	English
Infinitive	poder	poh-_dair_	to be able
Yo	puedo	_pwey_-doh	I can
Tú	puedes	_pwey_-deys	you can (familiar)
El/Ella/Usted	puede	_pwey_-dey	he /she /you can
Nosotros	podemos	poh-_dey_-mos	we can
Ellos/Ellas/Uds.	pueden	_pwey_-den	They/you can

How does it stack up alongside the other verbs you've learned? Surprisingly, it's the same, right?

It should not be a surprise. You could have done this one with your eyes closed, except for the change from "_pod_" to "_pued_". Otherwise, it's just like "_tener_".

Now, with this last verb, you have the minimum number of verbs to be comfortable enough to say whatever you want to say with the proper present tense ending at your fingertips.

If you NEVER learn to conjugate another verb, you'll be able to get by with the 12 present tense conjugations that we've given you.

As we pointed out earlier, though, you should be able to conjugate just about any verb with the templates we gave you in an earlier chapter.

However, I'm going to assume you're not ever going to conjugate again and that from here on out, you'll only be using the infinitives of verbs you learn.

I do hope you'll consider conjugating other verbs that you use. Your Spanish will be all the better for it, you'll feel a greater sense of mastery over the language, you will sound more articulate, and, in the long run, you _will_ be glad you did.

Just remember, EVEN IF you master the conjugations, there are going to be times when the proper verb ending completely escapes you. When that happens, PANIC NOT. Just remember that you can ALWAYS use the infinitive form of the verb with a pronoun and be perfectly understood.

My Heretical Rule No. 27.

There are two important things to know about any additional verbs that you learn in the infinitive:

1.   Most of the verbs you will learn in the infinitive can be used in combination with one or more of the 12 verbs we've given you. That's why those 12 were chosen.

2.   Even where you can't find a way to use the infinitive of a newly learned verb in combination with one of the 12, you can always use that verb in the form: Pronoun + Infinitive, e.g. "yo poder beber" ("I can drink"), or "yo estar cansado" ("I am tired"), et cetera.

You should choose to TRY to conjugate all new verbs in the present tense (now that you know how easy it really is), but, even if you don't, you'll have no trouble with this approach, and no one will look down their nose at you for doing so, except maybe another foreigner who thinks he/she knows it all.

As long as you're talking and communicating, I really don't care whether you conjugate or you don't conjugate. Neither should you. It's not CRITICAL.

Chapter XXV.
Verbs of Liking.
Verbs of Understanding.

I n the last chapter, we touched on the use of the verb, *"querer"* which means "to like", "to love" or "to want".

There are six verbs, in particular, which deal with the concepts of "liking" and "importance" with which I'd like to acquaint you at this point, simply because they are very commonly used.

Verbs of Liking.

Querer.

As we have noted, *"querer"* means "to like". For example, in the segment dealing with dining, we used the expression *"yo quisiera..."* to mean "I would like...".

"Yo quiero ese" means "I want that one".

"Yo te quiero" means "I love you".

This is a particularly important verb to know.

Desear.

This verb means "to desire", and, though it is not that commonly used, some of its more derivative forms are.

Something *"deseoso"* is desirable, as in *"este lugar es muy deseoso"* ("this location is very desirable").

"Deseo" is more often expressed in its verb form in a sensual or sexual sense, or with respect to one's dreams and aspirations, wishing for the impossible, etc.

Preferir.

"Preferir" means "to prefer". It is a very commonly used verb. For example, *"prefiero un vino español"* ("I prefer a Spanish wine").

<u>The next three verbs are all used in a form that requires a pronoun.</u>

Gustar.

We have already previously discussed the verb *"gustar(se)"*, so you should not be unfamiliar with the concept. *"Me gusta"* means "I like it".

In the case of *"gustar"* the person doing the liking is denoted by the pronoun used, while the verb remains constant in its form. That is, *"gustar"*:

English	Spanish
I like	me gusta
You like	te gusta
He likes	le gusta
She likes	le gusta
We like	nos gusta
They like	les gusta
It is liked	se gusta

Likewise, the verbs *"encantar"*, *"importar"* are used in the same manner.

Encantar.

This is more often than not used in meeting someone or expressing how much one "loves" something.

For example, on being introduced to a lady, a gentleman might say *"me encanta conocerla"* which means "I am enchanted to know you" or *"encantado"* which is shorthand for the same thing.

Admittedly, this might sound a bit "flowery" in English, but it is quite common in Spanish.

Also, *"me encanta helado"*, means "I love ice cream".

Like *"gustar"*, this verb is constant. That is:

Me encanta	I am enchanted
Te encanta	You are enchanted
Le encanta	He/she/you (pol.) is/are enchanted
Nos encanta	We are enchanted
Les encanta	They are enchanted

Verbs of 'Importance'.

Importar.

This verb means "to be important" but is used more often in the sense of "to care". It is used in the same manner as *"gustar(se)"* above.

For example, one of the more common idioms using this verb that you will hear is *"no me importa un pito"*, meaning, literally, "I don't care a whistle". In English, we might say "I don't give a hoot" or "I could not care less".

Or, in a store choosing clothing or material or whatever, *"no me importa el color"* would mean "I don't care about the color".

Like *"gustar"* and *"encantar"* above, this verb remains constant in form. That is:

Me importa	It's important to me (or, I care)
Te importa	It's important to you (or you care)
Le importa	It's important to him/her/you (pol.)
	(or he cares, etc.)

Emphasis.

An interesting issue concerning these last three verbs is that of emphasis.

The emphasis is accomplish by using *"a"* plus the appropriate pronoun following the verb, as in *"me gusta a mí"* or *"me importa a mí"*.

You might find this usage in a situation where you are discussing with someone your interests or likes and you want to say, for example, "what is really important to me is…" You would render this as *"lo que me importa a mí"* in response to what the person with whom you've speaking has said.

For example, I say that what's important to me in a hotel is the cleanliness of the rooms, and you might respond with "what's really important to ME is… the food".

Verbs of Understanding.

Comprender.

Too many movies and television shows with American writers trying to write "Spanish" into their scripts have made *"no comprendo"* famous for "I don't understand".

"Comprender" is certainly a cognate synonym for " to understand". However, as in English, it has more to do with *"grasping"* or "getting the meaning (of something)" than with "understanding".

Let me clarify for you.

"I don't comprehend this math lesson". This implies one kind of understanding.

"I don't understand what you said." This implies a different kind of understanding.

"Comprender" expresses the former, and the verb which follows (*"entender"*) expresses the latter.

Entender.

For this latter kind of understanding, the most common, the verb most often used is *"entender"*. So, if I want to say "I don't understand" to the nice policeman who is telling me that my passport is expired, *"no entiendo"* would be the proper response.

"Comprender" is conjugated, in case you want to know, according to the templates.

"Entender" is different in terms of the spelling changes it undergoes to maintain the right "sound" of the word in its various forms. Very quickly, it is conjugated as:

Spanish	Sounds Like
Entiendo	En-tee-yen-dough
Entiendes	En-tee-yen-daiss
Entiende	En-tee-yen-day
Entendemos	En-ten-day-moas
Entienden	En-tee-yen-dehn

As you can see, except for the spelling change, it, too, follows the template.

More Clarification.

The flip side of the coin would be to say that you "understand" something (as opposed to "comprehend").

As you can see from the following lists of synonyms for each of these words taken from the <u>Collins English Dictionary</u>, there is a subtle but distinct difference in the two words even in English.

"I comprehend what you said" implies one thing. Synonyms for "comprehend" are:

know

realize

grasp

get

figure out

have a handle on

follow

understand

"I understand what you said" implies something slightly different. Synonyms for "understand" are:

appreciate

know

recognize

realize

be aware of

value

identify with

comprehend

The differences are subtle, but there are differences, and they can be seen in both languages. Be accurate with your language, whichever you are speaking, and use *"no comprendo"* when that's what you mean, and use *"no entiendo"* when that is what you mean.

Chapter XXVI.
False Friends.

F alse friends are words that LOOK LIKE COGNATES but ARE NOT COGNATES.

Let me give you some examples. I earlier mentioned *"decepción"*. It doesn't mean a *"deception"*; it means a "disappointment". Likewise, we pointed out that *"embarazada"* does not mean "embarrassed"; it means "pregnant". I'll leave it to you to speculate as to why.

So, in the interest of insuring that you always look up and confirm your cognates in the dictionary, we're going to give you a list of some of the more common FALSE COGNATES with explanations.

Using a false cognate thinking that it is a cognate (when it isn't) can lead you to make some pretty silly mistakes.

Actual.

I personally had a very difficult time with this one when I first began to converse seriously in Spanish. *"Actual"* and the adverbial form, *"actualmente"* only indicate that something is current, i.e., at the present time. So, the *"noticias actual"* is not the "actual news", it is the "current news".

To properly convey the English meaning of this word, you could use either *"real"* or *"verdadero"*. Don't get confused, though, because *"real"* also means "royal". You have to glean the meaning from the context.

Asistir.

I had a difficult time with this one when I first began my studies of Spanish. It didn't seem "logical". Every time I heard it, I thought "help" or "assist", but *"asistir"* means to attend (a meeting) or to be present. *"Asistieron mil personas al congreso"*, means "one thousand people attended the convention".

If you really want to convey the meaning of "assist" in the English sense of the word, you would use the verb *"ayudar"* ("help") which is a cognate for "to aid".

Atender.

This word conveys much the same meaning as "tend to" in English, e.g., "I'm tending to the baby". It means "to take care of", "to attend to" someone or something. If you're talking about attending a meeting or a class, use *"asistir";* or if you mean "attending to" a customer in a store, for example, you would use *"atender"*.

Bizarro.

This one is really different. It means someone who is courageous, not weird.

"Bizarre" in the English sense of the word is more commonly and better expressed by *"extraño"*.

Campo.

Even though I got a handle on this one early on as meaning an open field or out in the country, I was really stumped the first time I wanted to talk about "camping" in a conversation. *"Campo"* means a "field" or "the country".

For example, a friend of ours lives in her parent's old house in town, while the retired parents have moved to the *"campo"* house out in the country to get away from the hustle and bustle of town life.

I learned from my conversational experiences that "camping" is *"campamento"*.

Then, I nearly fell over with a bad case of the "huhs?" when I discovered that "tent" was *"tienda de campaña"*, (literally, "store of the campaign"). Stores used to be in tents, especially during Moorish occupation of Spain. Oh, yeah! Uh huh.

Carpeta.

You may actually hear this one improperly used by a native speaker, especially in Puerto Rico. A *"carpeta"* is a "file folder" or "file folio". It can even be like the file folders on your computer. It most definitely does NOT mean "carpet".

A "Carpet" or "rug" is generally referred to as an *"alfombra"*, while "wall-to-wall carpeting" is referred to as a *"moqueta"*.

Interestingly enough, I have heard Puerto Ricans say that they were going to *"vacumar la carpeta"* when what they actually meant was they were going to *"aspirar la alfombra"*. Trust me. *"Vacumar la carpeta"* is NOT Spanish.

Complexión.

"My *'complexión'* is bad", does not mean your face is full of spots. It would indicate that, perhaps, you are built rather strangely, physically, that is. If your face (your SKIN) is full of spots, you would want to use the word *"tez"* for English "complexion". In technical or beauty parlor terms, you might even use "cutis".

Compromiso.

This is another one that took me aback at the beginning. To me, when someone told me they couldn't make an appointment because they had a *"compromiso"*, I thought they meant they couldn't meet with me because it would compromise them somehow.

What it really means is that they have another "commitment" or that they are otherwise obligated.

The English form of "compromise" doesn't really exist in Spanish.

There are a number of other verbs one might choose to use, depending upon circumstances, to try to convey this meaning, but, frankly, I find it very difficult to capture the English sense in Spanish.

One of the reasons, I believe, is due to the influence of the Catholic Church and its historic tendency to teach things in absolutes, i.e., "either it's black or it's white", with no room anywhere for compromise (as in the English sense)…

-- or, maybe…?

Constiparse.

The first time someone recommended a cold remedy to me when I mentioned "constipation" completely took me aback.

I said something to the effect that I didn't realize that the particular cold medicine recommended was good for constipation. And, I was so earnest about it, and I actually thought they didn't know what they were telling me.

Well, they did; it's just that *I* didn't realize *what* they were telling me. "Oh, yes, it is excellent when you're constipated," my Spanish friend told me. And, she was correct. It is good for a "cold", but, when the old plumbing is clogged, the word to use is *"estreñimiento"*, not *"constipación"* and you'll need *"un laxativo"*.

Contestar.

This one makes no sense. It just is. *"Contestar"* means "to answer". If you want to have a contest of some sort, the right word is *"contender"*.

Corresponder.

"Corresponder" means "to correspond" in the sense of matching, not in the sense of communicating.

If you're talking about carrying on a correspondence with someone, you'll be well advised to *"mantener correspondencia"* with someone or to *"escribir con"* someone.

"This nut goes with this bolt" must use *"corresponder"*.

Decepción.

We've already mentioned this one previously as an example of false cognates. It means disappointment. I learned it the first time I had to chastise someone in Spanish, explaining that I was *"decepionado"*, i.e., "disappointed". It felt a bit strange, but now I'm used to it.

"Deception" in the English sense of the word would require the use of *"engañar a alguién"* or, more strongly, *"estafar a alguién"*. Something involving "deception" that is, something, which is "deceptive", is *"engañoso"*.

Delito.

This word means "misdemeanor", not a delight. It's pronounced "dey-lee-toh".

Departir.

This word means "to talk", not "to depart".

Desgracia.

This does NOT mean "disgrace". In Spanish, it's just "bad luck" or "misfortune".

"Disgrace" in the English sense would require *"una verguenza"* or *"una deshonra"* or, even more precisely, *"un escándolo"*.

Disgusto.

This word is the reverse side of the coin of the verb, *"gustar"*. That is, it is a derivation of the word *"gusto"*, meaning "pleasure" or "pleasing" with a prefix that means "not".

This word isn't strong enough to convey "disgust" in the English sense, just "dislike".

I would use it, for example, to indicate that I don't really like horror movies, like "Nightmare on Elm Street" and the like. They don't please me.

When I find something to be REALLY disgusting (such as maggots, for example), I generally find that *"me da asco"* works much better. *"Asco"* conveys the English sense of "disgust" perfectly. That example was *"asqueroso"*, wasn't it?

Destituido.

Why this word even exists is a puzzle to me. It doesn't mean "indigent", as one would expect. Rather, it just means "someone who has been removed from (political) office".

Do we even have such a word in English? I am sure we must, but what is it? Impeached is as close as I can come.

An "indigent" or "destitute" person in the English meaning would be conveyed by *"indigente"* in Spanish.

Emocionante.

Another "gosh, I'm surprised word". It is used to describe something which EVOKES emotion or which is really exciting.

If you want to say "emotional", you already have a good cognate in the word *"emocional"*.

En absoluto.

Even though I know this one when I hear it, I still find it difficult to use because it's so contradictory to English. It means exactly the opposite of what you would expect it to mean. It means "Absolutely NOT".

If we want to express "absolutely", we have to say *"totalmente"* or *"completamente"*. Somehow, those two don't convey the same feeling (at least for me) that "absolutely" conveys.

Éxito.

I learned this one early on, and now never give it a thought. It means "success". We're always talking about so and so's song is a "hit" in English. In Spanish, we would say that the song *"tiene exito"*, i.e., it's successful, it's a hit.

Finding your way out of a building? Look for a sign that says *"Salida"*.

Fábrica.

This word means "factory". If we want to discuss dry goods (fabrics), we would use *"tela"* or *"tejido"*. *"Tejido"* probably expresses the idea of dry goods, i.e., material or fabric, better than *"tela"*, but *"tela"* is the more commonly used.

Fútil.

This does not mean "futile". "Futile" is expressed as *"inutil"* or *"ineficaz"*. The word *"fútil"* really just means something that's *"trivial"* or *"insignificant"*.

Ganga.

This is a great word. It means "bargain". Don't confuse it with "gang" in the mafia or street gang sense. That would be expressed as a "*pandilla*".

Introducir.

Use this verb if you're "introducing" something in the sense of the introduction of fresh water into an arid place or "introducing" a constitutional amendment or something similar.

When you're talking about introducing one person to another, you must use "*presentar*". We already know how to do that in English. Remember your cotillion days, when you went around introducing your date to everyone saying "may I present my date, ... "?

Largo.

Remember the movie, "Key *Largo*" with Humphrey Bogart and the lovely Lauren Bacall. That's "long key" in English. And, THAT is what "*largo*" means: "*Long*". It does not mean "large." That would be "grande".

Molestar.

The word just means "to inconvenience" or "to bother". It isn't used in the sexual crime sense as in English.

"Sexual molestation" in the English sense is rendered in Spanish as "*abusar sexualmente*".

Fastidiar.

Related to "*molestar*" is the word "*fastidiar*". It does NOT mean "to be fastidious". It means "to aggravate", or "to annoy" or "to hassle".

Pretender.

I'm always amused when I hear a Spanish speaker say in English that he will "pretend" to do something, when he really means "to try" to do something. "*Pretender*" means "to try to do…"

"Pretending" to be an astronaut or something one isn't is either to "*simular*" or to "*fingir*". The verb "*fingir*" is probably more common, but I much prefer "*simular*". It just has a better ring to it.

Rapista.

This is a really unusual word for "a barber", i.e., a person who cuts hair. Where in English, we might tease someone about having gotten his hair cut by the lawnmower, in Spanish we admire his "*rape*" (*rah-pay*).

A "rapist" in the English sense is a "*violador*", and English "rape" is "*violación*".

Realizar.

The word is a fairly loose way of expressing that something "became real", "became manifest" or "was finished". "*Se realizó la pelicula*" just means that the film was made manifest, produced, or became real or finished.

When your phone call is "*realizada*", it means your "call went through".

You already know that "*darse cuenta*" means to "realize" in the cognitive sense.

Recordar.

This means "to remember", more often "to remind". It does not mean "record" in the sense of recording some on a tape recorder.

In that latter case, we would use the verb, *"grabar."* Also, you could *"anotar"* or *"tomar notas"* or *"escribir notas"* in the sense of, for example, taking (recording) the minutes of a meeting.

Ropa.

This means "clothing", not "rope". "Rope" is *"soga"* or *"cuerda"* or *"cordon"*.

Revolver.

This one is tricky and wears two hats.

On the one hand, it means "to revolve", or "stir things up".

On the other hand, if you were talking about a handgun with a rotating cylinder, the word would be *"revólver"*.

It looks the same, except for the accent mark, but it's meaning is totally different. More often, for handguns, the term *"pistola"* will be the more used.

Sano.

A person who is *"sano"* is NOT (necessarily) a person who has all his/her marbles. This means that the person is "healthy", "undamaged", or "sound". It has nothing to do with one's mental state. "Safe and Sound" is rendered as *"Salvo y sano"*.

Sensible.

Generally, *"sensible"* means "sensitive" in the sense of being able to experience feelings and emotions.

If you mean that a person is "sensible" in the sense that they have common sense, you would use the word *"sensato"*.

Sensiblemente.

Right. It doesn't mean "sensitively" in the same sense that *"sensible"* in Spanish doesn't mean "sensible" in the English sense. Instead it just means, "appreciably". Sometimes, it can mean "painfully" or "perceptibly".

If you mean sensibly as in common sense, you would use *"sesudamente"* or *"con sentido común"*.

Suceso.

Means an event.

"Success" in English is, as we have already seen, rendered in Spanish as *"exito"*.

Tuna.

"Tuna" in English is food. A *"tuna"*, in Spanish, is a "college (musical) glee club".

The fish you're thinking of is *"atún"* in Spanish, which in English, naturally, would sound like "a tune" or a song.

Reverse cognates, anyone?

A final note:

Especially in the United States, the border areas of Mexico, and the Caribbean, the Spanish language doesn't exist in a vacuum.

In these areas, you may hear some speakers, especially those who frequently speak *Spanglish*, use some of these false cognates in the English sense when speaking Spanish or, particularly, *Spanglish*.

A few of these Americanized usages may be creeping into the language elsewhere, although they would still be considered substandard by most native speakers.

In addition, a good many English words are being substituted in more bi-lingual communities and "Spanish-ized".

One of the worst examples of this I have ever heard was in Puerto Rico. It was *"está raínando"* (for "it is raining") instead of *"está lloviendo"*. That's almost as bad as *"voy a vacumar la carpeta"*.

If you have a choice, don't use an "americanismo". It does real harm to an otherwise truly majestic language.

Chapter XXVII.
Going Further With Your Study of Spanish.

If you ultimately decide that you want and intend to go further in your studies of Spanish, I want to make some recommendations to you.

First, with respect to your Spanish language library:

Dictionary.

The best and most useful dictionary I can recommend for you is the _University of Chicago Spanish Dictionary_ in paperback.

Not only does this dictionary provide the translations of words, English to Spanish and Spanish to English, it also provides a section on idiomatic expressions and their interpretations.

It gives an excellent overview and background on the development of the Spanish language in different parts of the world that have an effect on word usage in those places.

This is the only dictionary I've found that consistently provides good information on the word usage by country and by region.

For example, in Cuba with its trade route Spanish that was more prevalent 200 years ago, the verb for throwing out the trash is _"botar"_, but, if you use that word in Spain, they won't generally understand you, since they use the verb _"echar"_.

Obviously, Spanish has not evolved the same way in all places. Some Spanish dialects will have more "*americanismos*" and some less. This dictionary will give you all of those differences.

Cognates.

NTC's Dictionary of Spanish Cognates Thematically Organized by Rose Nash.

NTC's "Cognates" is truly the ultimate Spanish Vocabulary Builder and will give you more than 25,000 cognates between English and Spanish.

It's the proof, if you ever needed it, that you do indeed already have a substantial Spanish language vocabulary waiting to be discovered. This is a most wonderful, most enlightening book.

With 25,000 cognate words like these at your command, you'll have a really good handle on the Spanish language.

Grammar Book.

The absolute very best grammar book I have *ever* seen or used is *A New Reference Grammar of Modern Spanish*, published in 1995, by John Butt & Carmen Benjamin at Oxford.

This grammar book is the most complete and easiest to understand of any I have ever seen AND it also addresses the issues of regional dialects, as does the University of Chicago dictionary, but in a manner which clarifies the issues amazingly well.

If you decide, after taking this course, that you *really* want to learn Spanish grammar and become more polished in your use of the language, including conversational and reading and writing skills, this is the book for you.

I have been using my copy for ten years, and, every time I open it, I learn something new. It's been highlighted so many times, it's Technicolor. I just wish that John and Carmen would send me a new one before this one wears out.

This grammar book is also more practical than most. It's more oriented toward conversation and gives really good, real life examples in Spanish & English of the grammatical points it explains.

I have never seen any other grammar book in any language that was as good. It's like a tool kit for solving Spanish language conundrums.

Verbs.

501 Spanish Verbs Fully Conjugated by Christopher Kendris and Theodore Kendris.

The"501" will make sure you always have the right verb ending at hand, because it fully conjugates 501 verbs in every tense for every person, plus providing imperative and participle forms.

Armed with these four books, you will not need to buy any others, unless you want to spring for books on slang or specialized dictionaries for something like business or engineering or medicine.

In any event, I suggest you purchase the U of C dictionary to go with this course and the NTC Dictionary of Cognates, because they'll really help you -- in this course and for the rest of your life. You'll find them very helpful indeed and they're really all you'll ever need, besides this course to become an accomplished *communicator* in Spanish.

Immerse Yourself. Thinking in Spanish.

After you've been speaking for six months to a year, you may decide that you want to try reaching the point where the words roll trippingly off the tongue with the ease of a native speaker and to be able to THINK in your new language.

Thinking in a language is how you really know that you have achieved fluency.

The best way to accomplish this is either signing up for and taking an immersion type course or by living in and talking in an environment where ONLY Spanish is spoken for a period of at least three to four weeks.

It usually takes about three weeks in a language immersion program before you really start to think in the language. Once you start thinking in language, your speed and your mastery of grammar will come very very rapidly. But, you have to take the step of immersing yourself fully into the language for at least three weeks.

Master of the Language. Dreaming in Spanish.

You will know when you have achieved true fluency in the language when you start to dream in it. One of the most amazing revelations of my life was to discover that my dreams in English are in Black & White, while my dreams in Spanish are in "Living Color".

I first realized I was fluent from the influence of my dreams, because I realized from them that I was speaking (in the dreams) in rapid, grammatically correct and dialectically appropriate Spanish. It amazed me because I could do it in my dreams and couldn't do it in person when I was awake and conscious.

Then, I realized that, as Dr. Freud would have told me, my inhibitions were keeping me from being fluent when awake. That realized, it was just a matter of time to overcome most of those inhibitions and get on with it.

No matter what you do, no matter what approach you take, no matter what course you take -- the Most Important secrets to being a successful Spanish speaker are achieving a good vocabulary and -- talking.

No number of books or tapes or CDs can take the place of conversation with friendly, compatible Spanish speakers. And, from an academic point of view, you're well covered with the suggested library above.

Now, just go out and DO IT! At this point, you ARE a Spanish-speaker. You CAN "get by" in Spanish and quite well. Just remember, the more you talk, the better you'll be able to talk. Congratulations on getting this far. And, if you see me on the street some time, speak Spanish to me and let me know you learned it from me.

Now, go out and have some fun!

Good Luck!

Appendix I.
The 30 Most Often Used Verbs
In Spanish.

Spanish	English	Pronounced
Ayudar	To help	Eye-yoo-<u>dahr</u>
Estar	To be	Ehs-<u>tahr</u>
Decir	To speak, to say	Day-<u>seer</u>
Hacer	To make, to do	Ah-<u>sair</u>
Llamar	To call	Yah-<u>mahr</u>
Conocer	To know (someone)	Co-no-<u>sair</u>
Gustarse	To be pleasing to	Goos-<u>tahr</u>-say
Saber	To know (something)	Sah-<u>bair</u>
Ir	To go	<u>Eer</u>
Poder	To be able	Poh-<u>dair</u>
Ser	To be	<u>Sair</u>
Venir	To come	Vey-<u>neer</u>
Dar	To give	<u>Dahr</u>
Haber	To have (auxiliary verb)	Ah-<u>bair</u>
Mirar	To look at	Mee-<u>rahr</u>
Tener	To have	Teh-<u>nair</u>
Ver	To see	<u>Vair</u>
Querer	To want, to love	Keh-<u>rair</u>
Escribir	To write	Ehs-kree-<u>beer</u>
Leer	To read	Lay-<u>air</u>
Parecer	To seem, to appear	Pah-ray-<u>sair</u>
Entender	To understand	En-ten-<u>dair</u>
Usar	To use	Oo-<u>sar</u>
Tomar	To take	Toe-<u>mar</u>
Comer	To eat	Co-<u>mair</u>
Hablar	To talk	Ah-<u>blahr</u>

Cenar	To dine	Say-<u>nahr</u>
Trabajar	To work	Trah-bah-<u>har</u>
Estudiar	To study	Es-too-dee-<u>ahr</u>
Aprender	To learn	Ah-pren-<u>dair</u>

How many do you know? How many can you use?

How many can you conjugate?

Appendix II.
The 400 Most Used Spanish Words.

How many of them do you know? Look up the meanings of those you don't know or recognize.

Spanish Meaning	Spanish Meaning
El aguá	Vivir
Algún	Y
El Año	Estar
Alto/a	Ser
Cada	Poder
Con	Saber
La Cosa	Ir
Corto	Hacer
Cuánto	Haber
Cuántos/as	Acabar
Nuevo	Hablar
Otro/a	Decir
Parecer	Comer
Significar	Tener
Sin	Venir
Su	Soler
Suyo/Suya	Saltar
Solo/Solamente	Ayudar
El Sonido	Árbol
Tambien	Arbusto
Tan	Traer

Tanto	Pedir
Tantos	Preguntar
La Tierra	El Compromiso
El Tipo	La Cita
Todavía	Él
Tomar	El
La Vez	Ella
El Viejo	La
Ver	Le
Donde	Lo
Dónde	Porque
Entre	Por qué
Ese/Esa (adj.)	Aquello
Ése/Ésa	Cómo
Aquel/Aquella (adj.)	Eso
Áquél/Áquélla	Quién
Éste/Éstos	Cuyo
Ésta/Éstas	Áquellos
Ésto	Pasar
Esta/estas	Áquellas
Parar	Aquellos/Aquellas
La Manera	El Desayuno
Mía, Mío	Encima
Mismo	Sobre
La Cena	De
Por	Para
Yo	Tú
Usted	Nosotros
Atrás	En Frente
Detrás	Desde
El Coche	El Carro
El Accidente	La Policía

Rápido	Niño/a
Hijo/a	Padre
La Cabeza	Los Ojos
La Madre	El Abuelo/a
El Cielo	Estupendo
El Primero	La Farmácia
El Médico	El Colegio
El/La Estudiante	El Futból
El Futbolista	El Mar
La Playa	Nadar
Cocinar	Preparar
El Maquillaje	La Matriculación
El Carnét	La Música
El Cuerpo	Cuándo
Me	Te
Nos	Se
Bién	Bueno/a
Mal	Malo/a
Más	Menos
Mejor	Peor
Mucho/a	Muy
El Hombre	La Mujer
La Gente	El Marido
El Avión	El Vuelo
El Tiempo	La Hora
Llover	La Lluvia
Conducir	Manejar
Escoger	Encoger
El Auto	El Camión
La Casa	El Café
La Leche	Azúcar
La Sal	La Pimienta

El Teléfono	Tragar
Un Traguito	El Postre
Un/una	El Último
Al Fin	El Caso
Dormir	Jugar
Gracias	Por Favor
La Noche	El Día
La Tarde	Por
El Perro	Pero
El Juguete	Andar
La Prisa	El Paseo
Bailar	El Vaso
El Plato	El Tenedor
El Cuchillo	La Cuchara
La Mesa	La Cama
El Cigarillo	Fumar
Esperar	Grueso
El Trabajo	La Chaqueta
La Blusa	La Falda
La Camisa	Vestir(se)
La Vista	Mirar
A	Al (a el)
Del (de el)	Uno
Dos	Tres
Cuatro	Cinco
Seis	Siete
Ocho	Nueve
Diez	Cien
Bella	Guapo/a
El Gobierno	El Dinero
El Pelo	Bañar(se)
El Baño	El Sueño

La Siesta	El Cenicero
La Cerveza	La Gasolina
El Helado	La Primavera
El Verano	El Otoño
El Invierno	El Fuego
La Bicicleta	El Barco
El Ferrocarríl	El Cura
La Medicina	El Grippe
El Catarro	Guardar
Beber	La Ensalada
La Ropa	La Taza
El Abogado	El Dependiente
El Banco	El Cambio
Cambiar	El Parto
Partir(se)	Nacido
El Nacimiento	La Fecha
El domingo	El lunes
El martes	El miércoles
El jueves	El viernes
El sábado	La Semana
El Mes	La Canción
Cantar	Recibir
Marchar(se)	La Falta
Contigo	Pesar
La Gana	La Puerta
La Cuenta	Abrir
La Vida	Nada
El Número	Iguál
Ver	La Pregunta
Las Tapas	Ojalá
El Equipaje	Barato/a
Caro/a	Hay

Dejar	Alegrar(se)
Gordo/a	Feo/a
Embarazada	Pequeño
Poco	Mayor
(a) Fuera	El Provecho
A Propósito	La Cola
Encantar	El Placer
El Hambre	La Salsa
Aprender	Juntos
Hasta	Después
Ahora	El Chiste
Sucio/a	Aquí
Escrito/a	La Galleta
Cansado/a	Ahí, Allí, Allá
El Alfabeto	La Letra
Aparcado/a	La Burocrácia
La Carcel	El Burro
El Departamento	Flexible
Contento/a	Seleccionar
Todo/a	Harto
El Premio	Preferido/a
El Antibiótico	Bajo
Abajo	El Frío
Frio/a	El Calor
Caliente	A Compras
Participar	Espectáculo
Correr	Apagar
Encender	La Misa
La Iglesia	El Bautismo
La Féria	El Santo
La Santa	La Procesión
El Restaurante	El Camarero

El Jefe	El Contable
El Piloto	El Castellano
El Periódico	La Revista
Las Noticias	El Juez
El Juicio	El Juzgado
El Fiscal	Satisfecho/a
La Condenación	Vale
Valer	La Pena
La Verguenza	Verde
Dura	Suave
Poquito	La Peluquería
El Salon	La Belleza
De Lujo	Joven/a
Brillante	Las Joyas
Muerto/a	Fallecer
El Turista	Las Vacaciones
La Navedad	La Noche Vieja
La Semana Santa	Los Reyes
Los Árboles	Los Pájaros
La Cena	Aparte
El Costo	La Costa
Acordar(se)	El Talonario
Magnifico/a	El Cine
La Película	Distribuir
Marcar	Acostar(se)
Levantar(se)	Averiguar
La Hipoteca	La Venta
El Alquiler	Alquilar
La Traducción	Traducir
Interpretar	Intérpreto

Appendix III.
1,000 Frequently Used Cognates

Anthología	Atlas	Catálogo
Compendio	Diccionario	Enciclopedia
Manual	Referencia	Tesauro
Apéndice	Biblografía	Capítulo
Folio	Ilustración	Índice
Introducción	Margen	Notas
Página	Prefacio	Subtitulo
Texto	Titulo	Verso
Informativo	Interesante	Raro
Correción	Formateado	Idea
Manuscrito	Línea	Papel
Royalties	Trilogía	Comunitario
Circulante	Público	Archivo
Audiovisual	Microfiche	Microfilme
Video	Clasificación	Autor
Editor	Artículo	Boletin
Información	Medios	Noticias
Publicación	Sensacionalismo	Diario
Panfleto	Periódico	Radio
Tabloide	Televisión	Clasificado
Entretenimiento	Obituarios	Programación
Columna	Comentario	Despacho
Documental	Editorial	Revista
Testimonial	Censura	Confidencial
Corriente	Distorsión	Divulgar

Free-lance	Ilustración	Incidente
Libelo	Objetividad	Fotografía
Privacidad	Supresión	Circulación
Concernir	Edición	Gaceta
Numero	Serial	Suscripción
Censor	Columnista	Comentarista
Corresponsal	Editorialista	Entrevista
Publicista	Paparazzi	Reportero
Distorsionar	Expresión	Género
Humanidades	Influencia	Licencia
Literatura	Manera	Plagio
Poema	Popurrí	Trilogía
Alegoría	Drama	Épica
Literatura Erotica	Escapismo	Ficción
Juvenil	Narración	No ficción
Poesía	Prosa	Acción
Anticlimax	Carácter	Climax
Composición	Conflicto	Descripción
Diálogo	Forma	Hiato
Imagenes	Intriga	Localizacion
Motivación	Punto de vista	Historia
Estructura	Estilo	Tema
Tiempo	Tratamiento	Unidad
Aventura	Clasicismo	Contemporáneo
Esotérico	Futurismo	Histórico
Modernismo	Naturalismo	Neoclasicismo
Pastoral	Picaresca	Realismo
Romanticismo	Surrealismo	Simbolismo
Utópico	Epílogo	Episodio
Extracto	Pasaje	Prólogo
Caricatura	Comedia	Farsa
Humor	Ironía	Parodía

Sarcasmo	Sátira	Fábula
Literatura Fantástica	Leyenda	Misterio
Narrativa	Novela	Parábola
Romance	Saga	Ciencia ficción
Melodrama	Moralidad	Pasión
Tragedia	Soneto	Elegía
Copla	Idilio	Réquiem
Argumento	Autobiografía	Biografía
Comentario	Crítica	Diario
Disertación	Exposición	Historia
Monografía	Retórica	Sinopsis
Tesis	Adagio	Anécdota
Epgrama	Epitaph	Epiteto
Proverbio	Antagonista	Héroe
Ingenua	Narrador	Persona
Protagonista	Romántico	Villano
Androide	Marciano	Robot
Elfo	Genio	Gnomo
Monstruo	Ogro	Vampiro
Cuasimodo	Supermán	Metro
Pausa	Verso	Dramático
Lírico	Narrativo	Blanco
Masculino	Hypérbole	Metáfora
Personificación	Aliteración	Eco
Rima	Metafórico	Autor
Ensayista	Humorista	Novelista
Poeta Laureado	Sitírico	Celebración
Distracción	Diversión	Entretenimiento
Festividad	Frivolidad	Humor
Jovial	Pasatiempo	Placer
Recreo	Recreación	Relajarse
Espectáculo	Banquete	Camping

Cartas	Colección	Computadora
Escursión	Fiesta	Jardinería
Hobby	Puzzle	Mascarada
Numismática	Filatelia	Fotografía
Picnic	Turismo	Atracción
Burlesco	Cine	Circo
Concierto	Farsa	Hipnotismo
Imitación	Magia	Mímica
Pantomina	Pirotenia	Rodeo
Show	Striptease	Televisión
Variedades	Vodevil	Ventriloquia
Video	Arte	Danza
Música	Radio	Carnaval
Exhibición	Exposición	Feria
Función	Gala	Cabaret
Casino	Club	Discoteca
Ferial	Hipódromo	Museo
Club nocturno	Parque	Teatro
Zoologico	Cámara	Carrusel
Confeti	Marioneta	Máscara
Tienda	Trampolín	Trapecio
Acróbata	Amateur	Artista
Coleccionista	Comediante	Cómico
Contorsionista	Geisha	Maestro de Ceremonias
Ilusionista	Mágico	Humorista
Aficionado	Músico	Numismatista
Filatelista	Estpecador	Atleta
Competencia	Olimpiada	Deporte
Amateur	Profesional	Arena
Bolwling	Campamento	Pista (or Cancha) de Golf
Gimnasio	Ring	Coliseo
Estadio	Pista de Tenis	Campeonato

Copa	Derby	Favorito
Match	Fotofinish	Récord
Torneo	Trofeo	Descalificación
Campamento	Liga	Preliminares
Rally	Béisbol	Básquetbol
Criquet	Fútbol	Golf
Polo	Tenis	Vóleibol
Conotaje	Regata	Yate
Alpinismo	Ciclismo	Equitación
Boxeo	Judo	Darate
Aeróbica	Ejercicio	Isometría
Yoga	Base	Bloqueo
Drible	Nocaut	Servicio
Estrategía	Conceder	Conversión
Defensa	Dobles	Falta
Gol	Ofensiva	Bicicleta
Motocicleta	Aparatos	Pelota de Béisbol
Balón de Fútbol	Esnórquel	Tobogán
Trampolin	Boxeador	Golfista
Surfista	Campeón	Competidor
Entrante	Finalista	Medallista
Oponente	Billar	Backgammon
Bingo	Dardos	Lotería
Ping-pong	Ruleta	Bacará
Blackjack	Crupier	Canasta
Pinacle	Póquer	Solitario
Anagrama	Charadas	Dominó
Videojuego	Carta	Dos
Diamante	Espada	Descartar
Audio	Canal	Guía
Cinespcopio	Alineación	Programa
Recepción	Selección	Estudio

Transmisión	Adulto	Cable
Comercial	Educativo	Étnico
Independiente	Local	Nacional
Público	Satélite	Deportivo
Telemarketing	Adaptación	Dramatización
Episodio	Miniserie	Producción
Eventos Especiales	Antena	Coaxial
Contraste	Dial	Definición
Dirección	Instalación	Interferencia
Reajustar	Reconexión	Selector
Servicio	Estático	Control remoto
Videocámara	Videocasete	Camcorder
Descodificador	Receptor	Teleprompter
Tubo	Audiencia	Director (a)
Distribuidor	Talento	Edición
Matiné	Nominación	Caracterización
Escena	Suspenso	Animación
Interrupción	Montaje	Panorama
Secuencia	Efectos Especiales	Tecnicolor
Cowboy	Detective	Gángster
Científico Loco	Sex Symbol	Horror
Musical	Actor	Actriz
Extra	Ídolo	Aerofoto
Holgrama	Microfilm	Foto
Transparencia	Distancia	Tiempo
Imagen	Filtro	Flash
Reflejo	Rollo	Trípode
Zoom	Negativo	Papel
Reproducción	Solución	Radio
Banda	Emergencia	AM
FM	Mensaje	Radioemisora
Señal	Estación	Experto

Novato	Técnico	Amplificador
Circuito	Micrófono	Oscilador
Resistencia	Supresor	Transformador
Transistor	Audiofrecuencia	Amplitud
Eco	Fidelidad	Frecuencia
Modulación	Multibanda	Multiplex
Omnidireccional	Recepción	Estático
Volumen	Operador (a)	Radioaficionado
Computadora	Aplicación	Código
Comuniaciones	Cibernética	Electrónico
Hardware	Software	Lógica
Programa	Análogo	Digital
Multimedia	Portátil	Acceso
Adaptador	Chip	Disco Compacto
Cursor	Disco	Externo
Floppy	Formatear	Disco Duro
Memoria	Modem	Monitor
Escáner	Base de Datos	Formateado
Gráficos	Icono	Instalar
Inicializar	Macro	Mensaje
Procesamiento	Programación	Simulación
Ciberespacio	Interactivo	Internet
Protocolo	Remoto	Servidor
Destino	Turismo	Tránsito
Vacaciones	Crucero	Excursión
Expedición	Safari	Transatlántico
Visita	Hotel	Recepción
Suite	Aerolinea	Auto
Bote	Carro	Tren
Autobús	Limusina	Metro
Monorriel	Taxi	Trole
Agencia	Cancelación	Chárter

Itinerario	Pasaje	Reservación
Tarifa	Pasaporte	Ticket
Visa	Aeropuerto	Carrusel
Desembarcarse	Embarcarse	Exceso
Puerto	Estación	Terminal
Mapa	Ruta	Ruinas
Chófer	Conductor	Pasajero
Portero	Taxista	Turista
Vagabundo	Visitante	Estética
Creación	Criterio	Formalismo
Género	Ideal	Influencia
Manera	Obra Maestra	Patrocinio
Purismo	Calidad	Realismo
Estilo	Simbolismo	Técnica
Contraste	Diseño	Armonía
Proporción	Simetria	Unidad
Acústica	Órgano	Piano
Banjo	Chelo	Contrabajo
Guitarra	Arpa	Mandolina
Ukelele	Viola	Violin
Bugle	Clarinete	Corneta
Flaut	Armónica	Piccolo
Trombón	Saxófono	Trompeta
Marimba	Atonalidad	Acorde
Armonía	Meolodía	Notación
Nota	Escala	Tempo
Tono	Cromático	Diatónico
Mayor	Menor	Do
Re	Mi	Fa
Sol	La	Si
Do	Dominante	Tónica
Arpegio	Disonante	Cadencia

Coda	Conservatorio	Concierto
Recital	Acompañamiento	Instrumentación
Solo	Blues	Bugui-Bugui
Discoteca	Jazz	Rocanrol
Salsa	Casete	CD
Banda	Orquesta	Dueto
Filarmónica	Virtuoso	Abstracción
Causalidad	Concepto	Doctrina
Ética	Existencia	Forma
Ismo	Medieval	Moderno
Moralidad	Filosofía	Realidad
Socrático	Universal	Lógica
Metafísica	Cinismo	Epicureísmo
Hedonismo	Escepticismo	Estoicismo
(G)nosticismo	Empirismo	Existencialismo
Materialismo	Mentalismo	Nihilismo
Pragmática	Transcendentalismo	Anarquismo
Conservatismo	Liberalismo	Determinismo
Idealismo	Analítica	Argumento
Causa	Consecuencia	Efecto
Falacía	Proposición	Cuantificador
Racionalidad	Símbolo	Sistema
Validez	Contradicción	Antecedente
Conclusión	Predicado	Analizar
Aparente	Condicional	Contructo
Contrario	Erróneo	Implícito
Inválido	Negativo	Ramificación
Espurio	Adoración	Credo
Divinidad	Éxtasis	Gloria
Intolerancia	Misterio	Perdón
Persecución	Religión	Sobrenatural
Espiritual	Evangelismo	Creacionismo

Celibato	Ecumenismo	Fetichismo
Misticismo	Destino	Exoneración
Inmortalidad	Perdición	Purgatorio
Trinidad	Altar	Catedral
Confesionario	Convento	Misión
Sinagoga	Templo	Fantasía
Oculto	Paranormal	Predicción
Superstición	Hipnosis	Ilusion
Precognición	Aparición	Carisma
Manifestación	Misticismo	Ocultismo
Reencarnación	Tabú	Visión
Profecía	Revelación	Enigma
Invocación	Aura	Poción
Congestión	Crimen	Delincuencia
Densidad	Educación	Graffiti
Polución	Privacidad	Prostitución
Recreación	Esmog	Tráfico
Zonficación	Comercial	Industrial
Residencial	Sitio	Subterráneo
Centro	Gueto	Plaza
Privado	Público	Suburbio
Avenida	Bulevar	Isleta
Túnel	Bazar	Restaurante
Universidad	Club	Apartamento
Bunalow	Condominio	Mansión
Palacio	Penthouse	Residencia
Sinagoga	Monumento	Cementerio
Clínica	Garaje	Hospital
Estación	Viaducto	Indigente
Habitante	Prostituta	Policía
Decoración	Confortable	Metal
Funcional	Plástico	Sofá

Bidé	Urinario	Candelabro
Lámpara	Floreado	Linóleo
Paneles	Parqué	Placa
Barbacoa	Hamaca	Cremoso
Delicioso	Exótico	Fresco
Granulado	Insipido	Aditivo
Apetito	Digestión	Menú
Nutrición	Banquete	Bufet
Picnic	Cacerola	Cereal
Condimento	Confección	Extracto
Fruta	Omelette	Orgánico
Pasta	Producto	Vegetal
Consomé	Puré	Entrecot
Hamburguesa	Pastrami	Carbohidrato
Libación	Licor	Botella
Agricultura	Ocupación	Permiso
Profesión	Servicios	Experiencia
Fenómeno	Honorarios	Feria
Monarquía	Microónda	Refrigerador
Gabinete	Cristal	Tubería
Fusibles	Plato	Copa
Diccionario	Sinónimo	Actuál
Dificultad	Efectivo	Barbacóa
Preparación	Insolación	Solar
Botella	Ungüento (the ü makes a "w" sound)	

Appendix IV.
Blue Words and Expressions.

This list isn't for everyone, but, for those who are interested, here it is. I was very reluctant to include this section in this book and for various reasons. I do not recommend that you ever use any of these terms for any reason.

However, it seems that almost always, one is inundated with questions by beginning students wanting to know the Blue words and expressions in Spanish, as well as how they are used.

Consequently, after much debate among friends, family, colleagues, and students, it was determined that it should be included:

•   For those to whom it is interesting, and

•   For no other reason than that, if one hears such words being directed at him/herself, it might be important to know what these words mean. It's much easier to avoid a confrontation if one knows that one is being confronted aggressively, even if only in the use of language.

So, here is your list of naughty words ("*palabrotas*") in Spanish, or "green expressions", "*modismos verdes*". It's not exhaustive, by any means, but it covers the majority of the bases.

Be warned. PLEASE, do not use these terms in polite company or in the presence of women (even if you are a woman). If you insist on using them yourself, do not do so unless:

- You are in the company of people who have indicated that they are not offended by such language and you don't care what people may think of you, and/or

- You are otherwise certain that there will be no offense, regardless of your gender, and/or

- You have heard others in your conversation use such language first.

<u>You can get into big trouble using these in the wrong situation, time, place or manner.</u>

That said, if you wish to continue forward into this Appendix IV, the list of Blue Words or "*palabrotas*" begins on the next page.

Please!

IF YOU ARE OFFENDED by off-color and/or vulgar language, words or expressions,

Please DO NOT REVIEW this APPENDIX IV.

THE BLUE VOCABULARY:

Spanish	Sounds Like	English
Coño	*Cone*-yo	Pussy

This is the number one most important word in the Spanish lexicon of "*palabrotas*".

Literally, it would translate as English "pussy". However this word is used in speech in a variety of ways and is more related to the "f" word in English in its usage.

For example: "*Quien coño es Usted?*" might literally mean "who the 'pussy' are you?", but it should be interpreted as meaning "who the fuck are you?"

You will also find it used quite often as an expletive, as in "*Coño!*" (with emphasis on the "o" final), for example, when you have hurt yourself, stubbed your toe, someone cuts in front of you in traffic, someone tells you some exciting news, et cetera. In this context, it's usually accompanied by a hand gesture that is the equivalent of an effort to smack the first and middle fingers together to make them snap.

It can also be similarly used to express astonishment over bad news, over the difficulty of some task, over some perceived maltreatment (e.g., "*¡Coño! Lo han mantenido encerrado en un cuarto durante 20 años.*" ("Damn! They kept him locked in a room for 20 years").

Lastly, it is very commonly used in discussions and/or suggestions about or to women and pertaining to their most intimate parts. It's not used in Mexico or Argentina where they use "*concho*" ("shell") instead.

All in all, this is the most versatile "*palabrota*" in Spanish and the most common.

347

Spanish	Sounds Like	English
Cojones	Co-<u>hoh</u>-neys	Balls, Bollocks

This word is also one of multiple idiomatic uses and the second most important of the "*palabrotas*". "*Me tiene por los cojones*" (May Tee-<u>en</u>-nay Pour Los Co-<u>hoh</u>-neys), means "he has me by the balls". "*De los cojones*", means "from the balls", "*el tiene cojones*" means "he has balls", "*me ha tocado los cojones*" means literally "*he/she touched my balls*", and "*¡cojones!*" means "bollocks!"

"*No me importa dos cojones*" would be interpreted to mean "I don't give a rat's ass." Just plain "*¡cojones!*" could also mean "bullshit" or the equivalent. "*Y un cojón*" means "Like hell it is". "*Hace falta*" as you know means to need something or be lacking in something. "*Hace falta tener cojones*" means "you've got to have balls", and "*Ese tipo no tiene cojones*" means "That guy's a coward".

This is a very versatile word with many, many common uses.

Spanish	Sounds Like	English
Picha (Sp)	*Pee*-chah	Cock
Pinga (Carib)	*Ping*-gah	Cock

"*Picha*" is pretty much universal in use and acceptance, especially in Spain, and is used in terms of the physical appendage. "*Pinga*" is slang for "'penis" in the Caribbean. The proper term for "penis" is "*pene*."

Also, "*capullo*" means the "head of the penis" but is used to call someone an "asshole". "*Frenillo*" is a foreskin, i.e., someone who is "useless."

Spanish	Sounds Like	English
Pendejo (Mex)	Pen-*day*-hoh	Fucker

Commonly used in expressions such as "*Ese pendejo me ha tirado una piedra*" meaning "that fucker just threw a rock at me". More common in Mexico. Seldom heard in Spain.

Spanish	Sounds Like	English
Hijo de Puta	*Ee*-hoh Day *Poo*-tah	Son of a bitch

This expression is used exactly as it is in English with the identical meaning. Can be used to refer to a person specifically or can be used as an exclamatory expression.

Spanish	Sounds Like	English
Follar	Foh-*yar*	To Fuck

This refers to the actual physical act of having intercourse in exactly the same manner as "to fuck" would in English. Since it's a verb, it might be worth noting that it conjugates the same as "*acabar*".

Spanish	Sounds Like	English
Joder	Hoh-*dair*	To Fuck

This word has both a literal and a figurative use, but it is more often used in the figurative sense, as in English.

For example, "*no me jódas*" means "don't fuck with me", or "*estoy jodido*" which means "I'm fucked", or "*¡joder!*" as a term of exclamation as in "fuck!" or "fuck me!". "Go fuck yourself" is not so common in Spanish as in English, but, where one wished to express such a thought, the proper form would be "*¡jódate!*"

The point here is that one can be "*jodido*" without having been "*follado*" (see "*follar*" above). This verb conjugates just like "*tener*" and is most often found used in either infinitive form (*¡joder!*) as an exclamatory, in negative command form (*¡no me jodas!*) or in past participle form (*jodido*).

Spanish	Sounds Like	English
Puta	*Poo*-tah	Whore, Slut

This word is used pretty much as we would use "slut" or "girl of easy virtue" in English. Can also be used to describe prostitutes, although the word "*prostituta*" is in common use.

Spanish	Sounds Like	English
Echar un polvo	Eh-*char* Oon *Pole*-voh	To have a bonk To get laid

For example: "*Me gustaría echar un polva con ella*" means "I sure would like to jump her bones".

Spanish	Sounds Like	English
Que buena está.	Kay <u>Bway</u>-na Es-<u>tah</u>	What a fox!

Perfectly nice ladies out for a walk are very likely to hear this exclamation from admiring Spanish speaking men, especially in Cuba, as they pass by. It's a little suggestive, but it's a compliment nonetheless.

So, ladies, if you hear "*¡que buena estas!*" you'll know that someone just called you a "real fox" and has implied that he/she wouldn't mind taking you to the nearest "no-tell motel" for some fun and games.

And, gents, if you want to make a comment to another male about "what a fox she is!" then, just leave off the "s" and the end of "está".

This next list of words is pretty self-explanatory, and the words and expressions are used in much the same way as in English.

Spanish	Sounds Like	English
Tomar por culo	Toe-*mahr* Pour *Koo*-loh	Stick it up your ass

Used as in "*Díle que puede tomar por culo*", i.e., "tell him to stick it up his ass!"

Spanish	Sounds Like	English
Culo	*Koo*-low	Ass or Asshole

Spanish	Sounds Like	English
Tener hasta los cojones	Teh-*nehr Ahs*-tah Lohs Koh-*hoan*-eys	To have had enough

You'll often hear, "*lo tengo hasta los cojones*", meaning "I have had it!"

Spanish	Sounds Like	English
Hacer la mamada	Ah-*sair* La Mah-*mah*-dah	To give a blowjob
Chupar la pinga (picha)	Choo-*pahr* lah *Peeng*-gah	To suck dick

"*Ella me hizo la mamada en el coche*", would be "she gave me a blow job in the car."

Spanish	Sounds Like	English
Maricón	Mar-ee-*cone*	A gay person Very derogatory

"*Ese tipo es maricon*", i.e., "that guy is a real fag". I really hope that *you* would never use this word.

Spanish	Sounds Like	English
Mamón	Mah-*moan*	Cocksucker

"*Ese mamón me cae gordo*", means "that cocksucker rubs me the wrong way".

Spanish	Sounds Like	English
Cabrón	Kah-*broan*	Literally: A Cuckold
		Figuratively: A Real Prick
"*¡Que cabron!*"		"What a prick!"

Spanish	Sounds Like	English
Marimacho	Mah-ree-*mah*-cho	Dyke (Lesbian)

"*Ella es demasiado marimacho*", could mean "she's too much of a dyke" or "she's too much of a tomboy", depending on context.

Spanish	Sounds Like	English
Tortillera	Tor-tee-*yeh*-rah	Lesbian

"*¡Mira las dos tortilleras ahi!*" means "look at those two lesbians just there." This one is roughly in the same category as "*maricon*", and I would hope that *you* never use it.

Spanish	Sounds Like	English
Mear	May-*ahr*	To take a piss.

"Tengo que mear" means "I've gotta take a piss".

Spanish	Sounds Like	English
Meneársela	Meh-neh-*ahr*-say-lah	To masturbate To play with oneself

"Ese tipo siempre la está meneándose." means "that guy is always wanking himself off."

Spanish	Sounds Like	English
Gilipolla	Hee-lee-*poh*-yah	Dickhead, Dumbshit

"¡Qué gilipolla!" means "what a dickhead!"

Related to this is the term *"giri"* which is applied to foreigners in Spain. It is a subtle way of referring to foreigners as *"gilipollas"* without them knowing what is being said or that it is they who are referred to in a conersation between two locals. It has the same negative connotation as *"gringo"*, which word is seldom used in Spain.

Spanish	Sounds Like	English
Mierda	Mee-*air*-dah	Shit

This last word is not used as an exclamatory word as much or as often as in English. The Spanish speaker uses *"coño"* for that. Instead, it <u>is</u> used in describing things. Go back to the chapter on *Avoiding the Ugly American Syndrome* and read about *La Catalana* to see how this word is used in practice.

Spanish	Sounds Like	English
Cagarse	Kah-<u>gahr</u>-say	To take a shit

"¡Ese niñazo está cagando en la acera!" means "That nasty kid is shitting on the sidewalk!" Or, for example, you might hear *"¡Por poco me cagué (por miedo) cuándo he visto el tiburón"* meaning "I nearly shit myself (out of fear) when I saw the shark!"

Spanish	Sounds Like	English
El SIDA	El *See*-dah	AIDS

(Auto Immune Deficiency Syndrome)

Although this is the official name for the disease, it's also used as an insult, from time to time in selected contexts.

Spanish	Sounds Like	English
Hacer la pelotilla	Ah-<u>sair</u> lah pail-oh-<u>tee</u>-ya	To brown nose, or to kiss ass

"Seguro que ha hecho la pelotilla conseguir las entradas al concerto asi" would mean "he must have really been brown nosing someone to get tickets to the concert".

Spanish	Sounds Like	English
Correrse (Sp.)	Corr-*air*-say	To come,
Venirse (Lat. Am.)	Bvey-*neer*-say	To ejaculate

Used in the sense of "*me vengo*" or "*me corro*" for "I'm coming!" in the sexual sense, i.e., to be about to or in the process of having an orgasm. Be very aware that "*me corro*" also could mean "I am running" in a non-sexual sense. Beware the context in which you use this one.

Spanish	Sounds Like	English
Tenerla dura	Teh-*nair*-la *Doo*-rah	To have a hard on,
Tenerla tiesa	The-*nair*-la Tee-*es*-sa	to have an erection

Spanish	Sounds Like	English
Tirar un peo	Tee-*rahr* oon *Pey*-oh	To fart

"*Me ha tirado un peo en la cara*" means "he farted in my face".

Spanish	Sounds Like	English
Besar	Bay-*sahr*	To kiss
Beso	*Bay*-sew	Kiss
Beso francés	*Bay*-sew frahn-*saisse*	French kiss
Beso Negro	*Bay*-sew *neh*-grow	Black (anal) kiss
Besar con la lengua	Bay-*sahr* cone lah *leng*-wha	To French kiss

"*Están ellos besando con la lengua*", i.e., "they are (lit.) kissing with their tongues (french kissing)".

Spanish	Sounds Like	English
Casado con la viuda de Los cinco hijos	Kah-*sah*-dough cone lah *view*-dah day los *Seenk*-oh *ee*-hohs	To masturbate

"Esta él casado con la viuda de los cinco hijos desde le abandonó su mujer", i.e., "he's married to the widow with the five sons since his wife left him".

Spanish	Sounds Like	English
Tener la visita de Tía Pépa	Teh-nair lah Vee-see-tah Day Tee-yah Peh-pah	To have one's period, (Lit.) To have a visit from Tia Pepa
Tener la bandera roja	Teh-*nair* lah Bahn-*dey*-rah *Roh*-hah	(Lit.) to have the red flag
Tener la mecha puesta	Teh-*nair* lah *Meh*-chah *Pwes*-tah	(Lit.) to be 'on the rag'

"No podemos hacer nada esta semana. Mi mujer tiene una visita de Tía Pépa" means "we can't do anything this week. My wife has a visit from Aunt Pepa (i.e., her period)."

Spanish	Sounds Like	English
No me importa...	No may eem-*pour*- tah	Not give a damn
un pito	oon *pee*-toh	whistle/penis
No me importa... un cojón	No may eem-*pour*-tah oon koh-*hone*	a ball, testicle
No me importa...	No may eem-*pour*-tah	
un huevo	oon *hwave*-oh	an egg, testicle

356

"A mí no me importa un pito lo que hace", i.e., "I don't give a damn what he does".

Now, from Puerto Rico, comes one of my favorites amongst the blue words because it is such a stupid americanization of the language.

Spanish	Sounds Like	English
Foquín	Foh-*king*	Fucking

And, I'm sure you can figure out how to most appropriately use this one.

Spanish	Sounds Like	English
Mearse de risa	May-*ahr*-say dey *Ree*-sah	To piss one's pants from laughing

Spanish	Sounds Like	English
Un bollo	Oon *Boh*-yoh	Pussy
Almeja	Al-*may*-hah	(Lit.) Clam
Conejo	Cone-*ey*-hoh	(Lit.) Rabbit
Conejito	Cone-ey-*hee*-toh	(Lit.) Little Rabbit
Chocho (Mex., Sp.)	*Cho*-cho	(Lit.) Floppy
Papaya (Cuba, P.R.)	Pah-*pah*-ya	(Lit.) Papaya
Tremendo Bollo (Venez.)	Tray-*men*-dough *Boh*-yoh	Great pussy

All of these are simply euphemisms for the same thing.

Spanish	Sounds Like	English
Casa de citas	*Kah*-sah dey *See*-tahs	A bordello, a house where one can have a "date"
Casa de relax (Sp.)	*Kah*-sah dey Re-*lax*	Bordello

These are the most common of the words you're likely to hear in any Spanish speaking environment.

Of course, each Spanish-speaking country has its own lexicon of "*palabrotas*" or blue words, but the ones in this Appendix IV are pretty common to all Spanish-speaking countries.

Use them at your own discretion -- and risk. And, if you do, you'll be known as a "*Viejo verde*", (i.e., "green old man") in Spanish or a "dirty old man" in English. And, yes, ladies, you could be known as a "*vieja verde*", too.*

---

* This is NOT a complimentary term.

About the Author

The author has worked and travelled throughout Latin America for many years, and since 1992, he has lived and worked in Spain.

By his own admission, he is "NOT a Professor of Language in Spanish". Rather, he says, "I'm just a guy who has had a <u>lifelong love affair with the Spanish language</u> and culture and <u>who knows how difficult it is</u> for most people <u>to bridge the gap</u> between the <u>desire to speak</u> Spanish and <u>actually speaking</u> Spanish."

He takes a unique approach that produces concrete, practical results quickly. He demonstrates that he understands how difficult it really is to learn a foreign language and shows a natural gift for making complex aspects of language simple to understand.

Printed in the United States
105319LV00005B/18/A